THE ROUGH GUIDE TO

British Cult Comedy

ROUGH GUIDES

www.roughguides.com

Credits

The Rough Guide to British Cult Comedy

Editors: Paul Simpson, Andrew Lockett
Layout: Jessica Subramanian, Tracy Hopkins, Ruth Tidball
Picture research: Andrew Lockett
Proofreading: David Price
Indexing: Tracy Hopkins, Ruth Tidball
Production: Aimee Hampson

Rough Guides Reference

Series editor: Mark Ellingham
Editors: Peter Buckley, Duncan Clark,
Tracy Hopkins, Sean Mahoney,
Matthew Milton, Joe Staines, Ruth Tidball
Director: Andrew Lockett

Publishing Information

This first edition published October 2006 by
Rough Guides Ltd, 80 Strand, London WC2R 0RL
345 Hudson St, 4th Floor, New York 10014, USA
Email: mail@roughguides.com

Distributed by the Penguin Group:
Penguin Books Ltd, 80 Strand, London WC2R 0RL
Penguin Putnam, Inc., 375 Hudson Street, NY 10014, USA
Penguin Group (Australia), 250 Camberwell Road, Camberwell,
Victoria 3124, Australia
Penguin Books Canada Ltd, 190 Eglinton Avenue East, Toronto,
Ontario, M4P 2YE, Canada
Penguin Group (New Zealand), 67 Apollo Drive, Mairongi Bay,
Auckland 1310, New Zealand

Printed in Italy by LegoPrint S.p.A

Typeset in Bembo and Helvetica Neue to an original design by
Henry Iles

© Julian Hall
288 pages; includes index

A catalogue record for this book is available from the British
Library

ISBN 13: 978-1-84353-618-5
ISBN 10: 1-84353-618-8

1 3 5 7 9 8 6 4 2

THE ROUGH GUIDE TO

British Cult Comedy

by
Julian Hall

Contents

The Canon:

Funny Business:

Atlantic Crossings:

Geography Lessons:

A Comedy Store:

Introduction

Comedian Andrew Maxwell, the triumphant victor of Channel 4's reality show *Kings Of Comedy*, once told me he especially enjoyed performing for people who had never been to a comedy club before. For me, it's hard to believe that, what with the explosion in comedy since the 1980s, anyone over the age of 25 has not yet experienced one of the UK's many comedy nights. But everyone has to have a first time. Hopefully, this book will help many more comedy virgins lose their innocence.

For the uninitiated, especially those in London, there is a serious amount of choice out there, though every comedy night will inevitably be a mixed bag. The trick is not to be deterred by one bad experience and to forget your preconceptions. Camp comic Alan Carr, who happens to be gay and has based his act on this fact, told me he was once introduced to a friend of a friend as a comedian, only to be greeted with: "Oh I hate that Graham Norton!" To which Alan justifiably responded: "Well, come and see me first!"

To miss out on the live circuit is to miss out on the origins of many of the nation's best-loved television comedies such as *The Young Ones*, *The League Of Gentlemen*, *Phoenix Nights*, *Black Books* and *The Fast Show*. So at the core of this book is the Icons chapter, profiling the most influential comedians to have emerged in Britain in the last 25 years, many of whom regularly play live. In true Rough Guides spirit, we have mapped out the major sources of laughter-making geographically, introducing the comedy scene in the major cities and charting the places – David Brent's Slough, Alan Partridge's Norwich, the Royle family's Manchester – that have inspired comics.

By offering various snapshots over the last thirty years, this book aims to inform the budding enthusiast of the comedians and shows that have made each successive generation laugh. But no nation is a comedy island. So this book acknowledges the transatlantic trade in influence, with Christopher Guest's love of British comedy paving the way for his seminal mockumentary movie *This Is Spinal Tap* and Bill Hicks finding that Britain, officially more uptight than the US, welcomed his abrasive comedy.

To give as rounded a picture of comedy as possible, this book explores the craft of writing and presenting stand-up and creating sketches and sitcoms. And, because this is a book about comedy, some funny stories have been thrown in for good measure, the kinds of things that only happen to a comic – or someone watching a comic.

In writing this book, the connections between performers have proved endlessly fascinating. You could probably draw a line from each comedian every which way showing many fewer than six degrees of separation between them. This book will tell you which comic legends started out as impressionists, which foppish film star could have been better known as a live comedian (okay, you squeezed it out of me, it was Hugh Grant) and which comic was rendered utterly helpless as he was laughed off the stage by demonic hecklers.

But the main aim is to increase your enjoyment of comedy, in person or at home. The comedy business is full of underrated comics and there's more to TV comedy than *Little Britain*, funny as that can be. With a thriving live scene and more comics and programmes released on DVD than ever, there's never been a better time to explore new ways of making yourself laugh.

Julian Hall, 2006

Acknowledgements

I would first like to thank Joseph Espiner and Daniel Thomas for their significant contributions to this book, made while they were in full-time employment. Thanks also to my editorial team of Paul Simpson and Andrew Lockett.

I would also like to thank Daniel Bee, Dan Lloyd and Damon Middleton from Avalon for helping to round up a significant amount of information. Thanks also to Danny Julian from Off the Kerb, Paul Sullivan, Fiona Duff, David Burns, Mel Broan, Jacqui Shapiro, Richard Bucknall, Nancy Poole, Dr Oliver Double, Hannah Chambers, Melissa Hall-Smith, Peter Leone, Claire Walker, Fiona Muir, Andrew Foster, Louis Barfe, Toby Hadoke, Iain Christie, Brenda Gleeson, Mel Brown and Lesley Simpson.

Thanks to all the comedians who answered queries and questionnaires. They include: Natalie Haynes, Robin Ince, Stewart Lee, Dave Gorman, Arthur Smith, Nick Revell, Jim Tavare, Russell Howard, Charlie Higson, Simon Nye, Danny Robins, Chris Addison, Simon Munnery, Richard Herring, Alan Carr, Will Smith, Waen Shepherd, Howard Read, Miles Jupp, Mike Gunn, Chris Lynam, Ivor Dembina, Marc Blake, Adam Buxton, Andrew J. Lederer and John Lloyd.

Naturally I would like to thank my family – Janice Hall, Rex Hall, Alice Allison, Richard and Jennifer Allison – and my friends Katie Espiner and David Palmer. Thanks are due, also, to the following people who helped me write this book: Lou Campbell, Deborah Agulnik, Elisabeth Froggatt (who runs The Bookshop in Southwell), Angela Melis, Ann Restak, Danton Hope, Anna Brown, Ria Ulleri, Claire Inness and Geraldine Lambe.

The Comedy Story:
an alternative history

Nominees for the 2001 Perrier Award. Back: Dan
Atopolski, Daniel Kitson, Adam Hills and Jason Byrne.
Front: Alice Cowe, Dean Learner and Garth Marenghi

The Comedy Story:

an alternative history

The human race's need to laugh is as universal as its need to eat. The people whose job it is to make sure we do laugh are constantly looking over their shoulders, searching the past for inspiration or cautionary tales. But, in the 1970s and 80s, a generation of British comedians and actors felt obliged to break with that past to create what we soon knew as "alternative comedy".

The modern British tradition of stand-up can trace recognizable roots back to the days of variety and music hall in the late 1800s, which had itself evolved from back-room pub entertainment. Though variety acts were largely music-based, the appearance of comic patter gradually developed through figurehead performers such as

the Cockney cross-dressing act Dan Leno before the turn of the nineteenth century, and later in the 1920s with the likes of George Formby, Max Miller and Tommy Trinder.

Meanwhile, working men's clubs were growing away from their nineteenth-century philanthropic roots to become entertainment centres and it was on this circuit, along with social clubs, end-of-the pier shows and holiday camps, that variety acts survived the collapse of music hall in the 1960s.

Though the working men's club circuit nurtured such talents as Les Dawson, Frankie Howerd, the legendary Irish comedian Dave Allen and even Lenny Henry, it became synonymous with a series of look- and soundalike comics delivering mother-in-law jokes or gags relying on racial and gender stereotypes. This approach, typified by Bernard Manning, Frank

Dave Allen (1936–2005)

Even though, in posture at least, Dave Allen was more of a sit-down comedian, he became one of the most influential stand-ups in the recent history of British comedy. In the 1970s, a decade not renowned for televising political, satirical or observational humour, the Irish comic's range and ambition made him one of the few stand-ups of his era who wasn't rendered obsolete by the alternative comedy boom.

Born into a literary family, Allen started out in the late 1950s as a Butlins redcoat. After touring Britain's pubs and clubs, he got his big break in Australia with his own TV series. Regular television appearances followed back in Britain and he was given a show on ITV in 1967 before moving, in 1969, to the BBC.

The laid-back stand-up style he adopted from the 1970s onwards combined a few typical formulaic jokes of the "There was this Irishman…" variety with routines that were essentially observational comedy. In between sips of whisky and a drag on his cigarette, Allen mused on the farcical nature of life, taking comic pot shots at modern medicine, Ian Paisley (so righteous, quipped Allen, even God failed to meet the reverend's exacting standards) and automated voices in cars. Such a range, widened further by cheeky sketch satires on religion (one skit, a papal striptease, caused particular offence) and sex, made Allen a comedian of rare longevity. When he died in 2005, Dylan Moran, one of the comics most obviously influenced by him, paid a suitably lyrical tribute: "When he adjusted his waistcoat or shot his cuffs, dragons of unreason gasped and died at his feet. Who was funnier, or more

loveable? He was the uncle to end all uncles, childlike yet oracular and possessed of a ravenous appetite for human folly."

Dave Allen: a comedian of rare longevity and influence

Carson, Lennie Bennett and Jim Davidson, dominated the long-running stand-up TV show *The Comedians* (ITV, 1971–92).

Such comedy was a world away from the wry observation on the everyday offered by Tony Hancock, the political satire offered by *Beyond The Fringe* through to *That Was The Week That Was* (BBC1, 1962–63) and the surrealist flights of fancy embodied by Spike Milligan's *Q* series (BBC2, 1969–82) and *Monty Python's Flying Circus* (BBC1, 1969–74). As these qualities became crucial to new observational and alternative comedy, these shows and comedians would be revered and referenced by alternative comics in the 1980s, while traditional comics were often regarded as pariahs. Ironically, the economic policies of the Conservative government, so reviled by the alternative comedians, shut down many working men's clubs, making it harder for the "mother-in-law school" to prosper. Yet traditional club-style comedy lives on – as the success of Middlesbrough's bluest son, comedian Roy "Chubby" Brown testifies.

Stand-up was honed in the 1970s by comedians operating outside the mainstream, such as Billy Connolly, Jasper Carrott and, a little later, Victoria Wood. Carrott and Connolly worked the folk circuit in their respective homelands (Glasgow and Birmingham), their witty – and in Connolly's case bawdy – patter between musical numbers gradually becoming more popular than the music. Meanwhile, the poetry circuit supported such cult figures as John Cooper Clarke, the drily witty performance poet who was a key influence for many alternative acts, most notably John Hegley, Henry Normal, Hovis Presley and Jenny Eclair.

Protest, poetry, punk and politics were at the core of what became known as alternative comedy. The huge economic and social upheaval of the 1970s and 80s created an angry, ideologically polarized Britain, a mood interpreted through punk. New comics Andy de la Tour (brother of *Rising Damp* actress Frances) and professional rabble-rouser Keith Allen emerged through the punk circuit.

The folk circuit continued to produce comic performers like Tony Allen, the ringleader of the first wave of alternative comedians. But trying to establish a career as an alternative comedian in the 1970s, he told Roger Wilmut, author of *Didn't You Kill My Mother-In-Law?*, wasn't easy: "The only places to play were talent contests in working men's clubs or pubs … it was all mother-in-law jokes and Irish jokes, totally politically against everything I believed in."

Allen was deeply politicized, campaigning for squatters' rights and anti-nuclear groups, marrying his political interests with protest or agit-prop theatre groups, even appearing at Hyde Park's Speakers' Corner, acknowledging an age-old link between political oratory and humour.

Meanwhile, bear-shaped Liverpudlian Marxist Alexei Sayle hit the road with Threepenny Opera, an outfit that provided dynamic, funny, challenging cabaret influenced by Bertolt Brecht. He would later tour the same venues with a bizarre comedy act involving identical bingo cards. As he told Wilmut: "A load of people would win at the same time and I'd get them onstage and humiliate them. It was incredibly dangerous – out of the first five gigs one ended in a riot, several ended in fighting. Nobody understood what the fuck I was attempting – there was no tradition of stand-up comedy in Britain, no one like Richard Pryor or Lenny Bruce."

Stand-up in the US (dealt with in "Atlantic Crossings: the American influence"; see pp.181–214) developed in the 1960s and 70s, significantly ahead of the UK. American pioneers, especially Lenny Bruce, would have a massive influence on British stand-up. However, a visit to the Los Angeles Comedy Store by Peter Rosengard, a 32-year-old life assurance salesman, in the summer of 1978 would allow Sayle to re-educate British audiences.

While on holiday, Rosengard visited the Comedy Store on Sunset Strip and was so impressed that, returning home, he decided Londoners should have an equivalent venue that might breed the kind of fresh talent he had seen in California. In May 1979, thanks to a partnership with nightclub owner Don Ward, London's Comedy Store opened in the first of its three central London locations – the Gargoyle room of the Nell Gwynne strip club on Dean Street, deep in still seedy Soho.

The Comedy Store was to stand-up what The Roxy, down the road in Covent Garden, had been to punk music not long before. For the first time since Peter Cook's Establishment Club, opened in 1961 as a fashionable haunt as much as a home of satire, London had its own comedy club – with auditions for The Comedy Store fittingly advertised in *Private Eye*, the satirical magazine that Cook had helped found.

Sayle was the MC and joined Tony Allen, Keith Allen, Pauline Melville, Andy de la Tour and Jim Barclay as purveyors of non-racist, non-sexist, political and totally anarchic comedy. In some ways, alternative comics were as much defined by the material they wouldn't do as by what they did do, though subjects such as

The Comedy Store still going strong in the 1990s

Alternative comedy and politically correct comedy...

Rather like "indie music", the phrase "alternative comedy" is convenient shorthand for an artistic movement that outstripped its own terminology. "Alternative" was a tag applied to comedians like Tony Allen, Andy de la Tour, Jim Barclay, Pauline Melville and Alexei Sayle by the media, though one that Keith Allen refused to accept. As alternative comedy developed, it became less overtly political – a shift typified by the comedy of Eddie Izzard and Dylan Moran – and often, as in the case of Frank Skinner, acknowledged more traditional influences.

The idea that comedy should be politically correct didn't last long. Indeed, some of the causes were affectionately sent up – a classic example being Pauline Melville's routine on feminism, recounted by Roger Wilmut: "I'm in the Women's Movement you know. I am. I mean I'm not in the most militant branch – I'm just in the branch that pulls faces behind men's backs. Yes, you can laugh, but there's a lot of us."

Sometimes, the dogma behind the humour was more hard-line. Jim Tavare recalls that the prescriptive attitude of acts like Mark Thomas was "a pain in the arse" when it came to making people laugh and even the expression "girlfriend" might provoke hisses from a right-on audience.

Today with the postmodern ironic un-PC remarks of the likes of Jimmy Carr we have almost come full circle. With his over-confident persona, Carr stretched the boundaries of PC and, in 2006, The Gypsy Council persuaded the BBC to apologize for a joke of his they said stereotyped travellers.

The comedian's freedom to be irreverent was threatened initially by the Labour government's proposals to outlaw religious hatred. It took a passionate campaign, spearheaded by Rowan Atkinson, to assure that jokes about religion would not be punished in a court of law. In Britain religion is deemed a choice and consequently fairer game than joking about someone's race or sexuality, though in other countries these matters would be viewed in quite the reverse way.

feminism, gay rights and sexual mores were dealt with more frankly, if, at times, in an ideologically po-faced manner.

Alternative comedians didn't have things all their own way at first, having to share the Comedy Store's stage with variety acts of the Max Miller school, while such established TV acts as Dawson and Bennett appeared. Bennett was gonged off by Sayle, as resident compere, for bragging about his Rolls Royce to a heckler, a sign of the civil war between new and traditional comedy being fought under the club's roof.

Margaret Thatcher was elected prime minister the same month as The Comedy Store opened. Her answer to Britain's sliding economic fortunes carried a large social price tag, led to soaring unemployment and, with Britain playing a significant role in the arms race, reinvigorated the campaign for nuclear disarmament, which all meant there was plenty of political meat for the new comedians to get their teeth into. While many of the original comics (like Tony Allen and Pauline Melville) would move back into acting, the political posturing was not lost on a certain Ben Elton, one of those heading up the next wave of talent.

The television spotlight fell on The Comedy Store in quite a modest way initially, with two half-hour specials called *Boom Boom...Out Go The Lights* (BBC2, 1980), both produced by Paul Jackson, whose previous credits included *The Two Ronnies* and *Cannon And Ball*. Yet TV executives visiting the Store were deeply affected by what they saw, realizing there was a seam of talent that wasn't coming from either the traditional world of working men's clubs or variety or the Oxbridge revues, where most talent scouts spent their time.

Jackson's interest in what he saw led him to produce *The Young Ones* (BBC2, 1982), the

Rik Mayall in his 1980s prime as bassist Colin Grigson of spoof heavy metal band Bad News from *The Comic Strip Presents...*

anarchic sitcom co-written by Ben Elton, fellow Manchester University alumnus Rik Mayall and Lise Mayer, Mayall's then girlfriend. The show starred Mayall and another university pal, Adrian Edmondson, who had played the Store together as mock-vaudevillian double act Twentieth Century Coyote. Nigel Planer, half of The Outer Limits (another Store act), also appeared, while Sayle made frequent cameos. The raucous show, full of physical comedy, loud stunts and screamed dialogue, was a real kick up the backside of the sitcom tradition – a point beautifully made when Vyvyan (Edmondson) laid into that bastion of prime-time comedy *The Good Life* for being "too bloody nice".

At the same time, Peter Richardson, the other half of The Outer Limits, was laying the groundwork for another bastion of new TV comedy, *The Comic Strip Presents...* This series of feature-length shows (there were, in all, 37 shows between 1982 and 2000) was commissioned by Channel 4, a new state-funded channel with an explicit remit to air "minority programmes".

The series sprang from the short-lived club The Comic Strip, set up by Richardson down the road from the Store, and featuring his act with Planer, along with Mayall and Edmondson (this time as physical comedy duo The Dangerous Brothers) and Dawn French and Jennifer Saunders (then in teacher training). *The Comic Strip Presents...* did all it could to snub established social etiquette, Thatcherism and the yuppie culture of the 1980s while acknowledging, as alternative comedy often did, comic performers of a different generation with appearances by Peter Cook, Nicholas Parsons, Beryl Reid and Leslie Phillips.

The momentum of both *The Young Ones* and *The Comic Strip Presents...* pushed the careers of those involved to new heights, particularly Mayall, whose household status had been boosted by his outings as nerdy Brummie poet Kevin Turvey on the sketch show *A Kick Up The Eighties* (BBC1, 1981). As early as 1984, Mayall was touring big venues, with Ben Elton as support and co-writer.

The success of Mayall's tour was no fluke. The live comedy scene was flourishing, albeit mainly in London. By 1984 the capital's venues included Downstairs At The King's Head in Crouch End; Malcolm Hardee's infamous Tunnel Club in Greenwich, The Banana Cabaret in Balham and the first Jongleurs club in Battersea. This circuit nurtured new generations of comics, including Vic Reeves and Bob Mortimer who would enjoy their first foray onto television in 1990. The Comedy Store had become the place everyone wanted to play, the list of its alumni soon sounding like a who's who of British comedy.

Britain's alternative comedy boom was politically and socially well timed but, as media lecturer and analyst Andy Medhurst noted in *Sight & Sound* magazine in November 2000, it also helped fill a vacuum: "In the mid-1980s, the great comic talents of older generations were, in various ways, shutting up shop. By the middle of 1984 Eric Morecambe and Tommy Cooper were dead. Les Dawson had allowed himself to be constrained by hosting *Blankety-Blank* (with its agonizingly 1980s pink and grey set). Ken Dodd was as incomparably magnificent as ever, but mostly shunned television work for the stage. Elsewhere, the second and third divisions of that tradition – Jimmy Tarbuck, Tom O'Connor, Bobby Davro, Cannon and Ball, Ted Rogers – busied themselves wearing pastel jumpers on golf courses, endorsing Mrs Thatcher, or (most criminally) both."

Meanwhile, Bob Monkhouse, Britain's self-styled answer to Bob Hope, was pushing everyone but new alternative talent on his stand-up showcase, although bizarrely his American guests included such cult comic heroes as Steven Wright and Emo Philips. Inspired by his own experiences on US talk shows, genial entertainer Des O'Connor launched his chat show in 1977, giving UK TV debuts to such influential transatlantic talent as Jerry Seinfeld and Kelly Monteith.

Saturday gets Live

Yet the new British comics had their time in the sun. Jonathan Ross's chat show *The Last Resort* helped counter Bob Monkhouse's apparent closed shop. Much more important was *Saturday Live*, another Paul Jackson presentation, designed to ape America's long-running *Saturday Night Live* show. *Saturday Live* (Channel 4, 1985–87) and the later version *Friday Night Live* (Channel 4, 1988) were hugely popular with 18–25 year olds and, in their short lives, enormously influential.

Ben Elton, as MC and ringleader, became nationally famous on *Saturday Live*, his reputation boosted as right-wing newspapers raged against his bashing of "Thatch", as he dubbed the prime minister. Among his charges were French and Saunders, Rik Mayall, Paul Merton, Harry Enfield (his Stavros and Loadsamoney characters launched on the show won huge renown), Mark Thomas and Julian Clary.

The show nodded to comedy heritage with guest appearances from Barry Humphries, Spike Milligan and, now old-school by comparison, Jasper Carrott. After Carrott told a joke about women drivers, Elton rebuked him: "Nice one, Jasper, really taking on the dangerous, controversial issues in your comedy." More apposite was the appearance of Rowan Atkinson with comedy partner Angus Deayton. With his work on

Not The Nine O'Clock News (BBC2, 1979–82), Atkinson could be considered a proto-alternative comic, and with the later series of *Blackadder* (*Blackadder II*, the first with Ben Elton as a writer aired in 1986) he was almost subsumed into the movement even though he had entered the business from Oxbridge.

The same point could be made about Stephen Fry and Hugh Laurie who appeared in all twenty editions of *Saturday Live*. Along with Tony Slattery and Emma Thompson, Fry and Laurie had, as Cambridge Footlights, won the first ever Perrier Award at the Edinburgh Fringe Festival in 1981. The group (minus Slattery who surfaced

David Baddiel (left) and Robert Newman, one half of *The Mary Whitehouse Experience*

From radio to TV

Writing for radio has been one of the first ports of call for budding comedy writers and comedians, especially BBC Radio 4's show *Weekending* (1970–98), while radio, as a medium, has bred new comedy television shows since the 1950s, when Tony Hancock's show moved to BBC1 in 1956.

Comedies transferring from radio to TV in the 1980s and 90s, the heyday of this cross-fertilization, included *Little Britain*, *15 Storeys High*, *The League Of Gentlemen*, *People Like Us*, *Dead Ringers*, *The Day Today* (as *On The Hour*), *Goodness Gracious Me*, *Knowing Me, Knowing You…*, *The Mary Whitehouse Experience*, *Have I Got News For You?*, *They Think It's All Over* and *Whose Line Is It Anyway?*.

Radio's role has changed somewhat of late, with the BBC using its own digital TV channels, especially BBC3, to test out new comedies like *Nighty Night* which, if successful, shift to BBC2 and then to BBC1.

in the Channel 4 improv show *Whose Line Is It Anyway?*) worked with Elton, Robbie Coltrane and Siobhan Redmond on ITV's often overlooked late night sketch show *Al Fresco* (1983).

Footlights pairing Steve Punt and Hugh Dennis, also *Saturday Live* regulars, suffered more from the Oxbridge tag, especially when they teamed up with Robert Newman and David Baddiel, from the same alma mater but with more apparent street cred, to form *The Mary Whitehouse Experience* (BBC2, 1990–92). Once assembled, *The Mary Whitehouse Experience* was a kind of student boy-band comedy outfit (Punt and Dennis the Gary Barlow to Newman and Baddiel's Robbie Williams). But when the show leapt from radio to television, it lost the talents of Mark Thomas, Jo Brand (a *Friday Night Live* star bringing "feminism and cake" to comedy) and the fast-rising star of pure observational comedy, Jack Dee.

Though sometimes puerile and not averse to clipboard comedy (reliance on a kind of *That's Life* format of surveys and so forth), *The Mary Whitehouse Experience* earned both duos their own TV shows. The more glamorous pairing went into comedy hyperspace with *Newman And Baddiel In Pieces* (BBC2, 1993), edgier thanks to characters like Newman's depraved, louche Jarvis, though there was still some knockabout humour, such as the hugely popular "History Today" sketch in which professors traded childish insults. The subsequent tour culminated in the celebrated Wembley Arena gig in December 1993 when the duo, later to split acrimoniously, became the first comics to sell out the venue. The 1990s saw plenty of comics, especially Lee Evans and Eddie Izzard, playing to large theatre audiences. Comedy was now officially, by head count, rock'n'roll. Or so the cliché goes.

1993 and all that

If anything, Vic and Bob were greater student heroes than Newman and Baddiel, with an act peppered with Dadaesque non-sequiturs, loony catch phrases ("You wouldn't let it lie would you?") and so forth in a style that seemed utterly original yet found a contemporary echo in the equally wacky and surreal humour of Harry Hill. The dynamic duo furthered their ironic hip factor as Reeves collaborated with student indie faves The Wonderstuff to produce such singles as "Dizzy" which, as a UK number one in 1991, signalled the commercial marketability of comedians. In 1993, the duo had switched from

Channel 4 (*Vic Reeves' Big Night Out*, 1990–91) to BBC2 with their new show *The Smell Of Reeves And Mortimer* (1993–95), and virtually made the channel their home, later launching the absurd hit game show *Shooting Stars* (BBC2, 1995–97 and 2002–03).

Just as sartorially elegant, if a world away in comedic style, Jack Dee had risen quickly through the clubs from early open spots at The Comedy Store, and by 1992 had his own Channel 4 show. The figurehead for a new wave of non-political observational comics (that also included Jeff Green, a master of relationship etiquette), Dee maintained a distinct deadpan style that owed more to such American wisecrackers as Jackie Mason than to any British comedian.

Dee was said to have partly inspired Lynda La Plante's two-part television drama *Comics* (Channel 4, 1993). A forgotten gem, *Comics* followed the fortunes of a troubled American comic who, while performing in London, witnesses a gangland killing. La Plante has always been a shrewd reader of trends and the series' very existence was a tribute to how relevant and vibrant the comedy scene had become.

Never mind the politics

The shift from political comedy to observational humour came within the context of a kind of grim acquiescence to Conservative rule. The pervasive middle-ground ethos was typified by a shift in Ben Elton's status from loony lefty to loveable lefty. Although Elton argued that he never set himself up as anti-mainstream, perception was everything. Elton had his own BBC series, cosily titled *The Man From Auntie* (BBC1, 1990 and 1994), in prime (but still post-watershed) main-

The Irish influence

This book defines British in a rather elastic fashion, bending to include Irish comedians who have had a massive impact on British comedy. Among the most notable high-quality acts from the Emerald Isle to hit the British circuit are Sean Hughes, Dylan Moran, Ardal O'Hanlon, Tommy Tiernan, Owen O'Neill, Ed Byrne, Jason Byrne and Andrew Maxwell.

Commentators point to the inherent lyricism of the Irish, a Celtic love for words, their natural cheek and charm to explain why Ireland has been so prolific in producing comics. One thing is sure – most of them inevitably end up over here. There are comedy clubs in Ireland, most notably Dublin's The Comedy Cellar which originated from a sketch act involving Ardal O'Hanlon, Kevin Gildea and Barry Murphy. The Cellar was established in 1987 as Ireland's home for alternative comedy and has given birth to a very lively comedy scene in the city. But even its success won't stop the export of Irish comic talent to Britain and beyond.

stream territory and his routines, especially the political ones, lacked their old anarchy.

Among the comics who suddenly found themselves in the ascendancy were poetic and confessional Irishman Sean Hughes, who had crossed over to TV in the decent sitcom *Sean's Show* (Channel 4, 1992). In 1993, Eddie Izzard, surrealist improviser extraordinaire, played an extended critically acclaimed run at the Ambassadors Theatre, the first of many big shows for Izzard who, largely without TV's aid, became a comedy megastar attracting Hollywood's attention. Izzard's talents had been spotted by the Perrier Comedy Award judges, who shortlisted him in 1991. By the early 1990s, Edinburgh had mushroomed into a comedy capital, with stand-up starting to overshadow the Fringe. Izzard was nominated along with Jack Dee, Lily Savage and the eventual winner Frank Skinner.

Emerging from the burgeoning Midlands circuit, Frank Skinner was enormously popular through his cheeky, coarse toilet and bedroom humour, prompting critics to suggest that he was the closest thing to Bernard Manning ever to win the Perrier. A clubbable, laddish figure, Skinner eschewed serious politics but didn't shy away from many other taboos.

In 1992, Skinner and David Baddiel began their fruitful collaboration by working together on American comic Denis Leary's hard-hitting *No Cure For Cancer* show. Skinner and Baddiel's first TV collaboration was *Fantasy Football League* (BBC2, 1994–98), combining lad culture, comedy and football, all three of which were at the top of their game at that time.

The comedy of cringe

The news of Skinner's Perrier win in 1991 was described by Steve Coogan as "probably the most depressing point of my life". Supporting Skinner a year earlier in Edinburgh, Coogan had been cowed by the Brummie's gift for bantering with audiences. Starting out as an impressionist, Coogan feared his gift for mimicry had made him into a "cut price Bobby Davro". But in 1992, he won the Perrier Award with the help of fellow Mancunian comic John Thompson, airing such characters as ne'er-do-well Paul Calf (a precursor of the dissolute Frank Gallagher in *Shameless*) while Thompson performed Bernard Righton, a politically correct comic that was almost a back-handed compliment to Bernard Manning.

Coogan's recovery was accelerated by his involvement with such talents as Armando Iannucci, Chris Morris and double act Stewart Lee (co-creator of *Jerry Springer The Opera*) and Richard Herring on the Radio 4 news programme satire *On The Hour* (1992).

Though parodying news programmes, *On The Hour*, and the subsequent TV version *The Day Today* (BBC2, 1994), spoofed the medium not the messages. With ideological struggles seriously diluted in the 1990s, spin and presentation gave the team – but most especially Morris, a former radio presenter and prankster – the meat for their comedy.

Much of the series' comedy came from the tension between the reporters and anchors with Coogan's pompous but hapless sports presenter Alan Partridge, a throwback to Coogan's impression of sports commentator David Coleman on *Spitting Image*, proving pure comedy gold. Catching the public's imagination, Partridge ushered in an age that comedian and comedy writer Marc Blake has dubbed "the comedy of cringe".

Morris had a knack for making audiences cringe. He exposed the crass stupidity of celebrities on *Brass Eye* (Channel 4, 1997) where they lined up to denounce a fake drug, Cake, crossed the line with taboos (e.g. the *Brass Eye* paedophilia special, 2001) and blurred the division between tragic drama and comedy (e.g. the dark disconcerting *Jam/Jaaaaam* where the comedy touched on torture, sexual blackmail and death). In contrast, Coogan's Partridge years were about bluff, bluster, self-importance and creating a nausea of comedy, his egomania anticipating Ricky Gervais' David Brent, who ruled the small screen in *The Office* (BBC2, 2000–03).

The Office's mockumentary style drew on such shows as *People Like Us* (BBC2, 1999, 2001) and the daddy of mockumentaries *This Is Spinal Tap* (1984). Mockumentaries have no laughter track, the absence of which helped distinguish *The Royle Family* (BBC, 1998–2000), Caroline Aherne and Craig Cash's static, loving portrayal of a Manchester family basking in the glow of their TV. This naturalistic masterpiece used the sound of silence to great comic and dramatic effect.

The rise and fall of the sitcom

Hancock's Half Hour was probably the first true British sitcom, moving from radio to television in the 1950s and signalling a shift away from comedy shows based around sketches or songs to a format where a situation was comically resolved within a programme. The 1960s saw such seminal sitcoms as *Steptoe And Son*, *Till Death Us Do Part* and *The Likely Lads*. *Dad's Army* started in the 1960s and endured throughout the 1970s, considered the golden age of sitcom. For a while, ITV had a stable of decent, popular sitcoms including *Rising Damp*, *On The Buses* and *Man About The House* (plus its even more successful spin-off, *George And Mildred*). But the most enduring sitcoms were made by the BBC and included *Sykes*, *Fawlty Towers*, *The Good Life*, *The Fall And Rise Of Reginald Perrin*, *Butterflies*, *Citizen Smith* and *Porridge*.

In the 1980s, shows like *The Young Ones*, *Filthy Rich And Catflap*, *Blackadder* and *The New Statesman* provided a louder, brasher alternative to such popular favourites as *Last Of The Summer Wine*, *Only Fools And Horses* and *Bread*. In the 1990s the traditional, yet surprisingly dark *One Foot In The Grave* and Simon Nye's laddish send-up *Men Behaving Badly* flew the flag for BBC1, but BBC2 and Channel 4 took over as sitcom champions in the mid-1990s with shows of the calibre of *I'm Alan Partridge*, *The Royle Family*, *Father Ted* and *Spaced*.

Since the late 1990s most of the notable sitcoms – the pick of the crop being Sean Lock's *15 Storeys High* (BBC2, 2003), Peter Kay's *Phoenix Nights* (Channel 4, 2001), Craig Cash's *Early Doors* (BBC2, 2003–04), Armando Iannucci's *The Thick Of It* (BBC2, 2006), *Peep Show* (Channel 4, 2003–06) and *Nighty Night* (BBC2, 2004–05) – have been mockumentaries, with no laughter track. This school has become so quickly and so firmly established that Iannucci had to defend the studio audience laughter accompanying the second series of *I'm Alan Partridge* (BBC2, 1997 and 2002).

Successful, enjoyable sitcoms with a laughter track in the old fourth wall format (the theatrical term describing how the audience forms the fourth wall of the set and is not normally engaged by the performer) have become increasingly rare. The stand-out being, probably, Graham Linehan's *Black Books* (Channel 4, 2000, 2002, 2004), which was much richer, more surreal and ambitious than the likes of *My Family* (BBC2, 2000–).

Although Victoria Wood created a genuinely funny, if mainstream, fourth wall sitcom with *Dinnerladies* (BBC1, 1998–2000), she says she would have preferred a more naturalistic product, believing laughter tracks and brightly lit theatrical sets were old hat. At the British Comedy Awards in 2005, she declared the traditional sitcom dead, saying: "The likes of *The Office* are so good you just can't go back." This view accurately reflected current trends but is the fourth wall sitcom only dead because no one has written a good one for ages?

ITV's comedy programming has dropped away, a victim of the fact that the network doesn't know where to schedule comedy and that, whenever sitcoms are scheduled, they usually only have one series to find an audience and their feet. ITV's passing of *Men Behaving Badly* after two series in 1992 to BBC1 seems, in retrospect, like the passing of a baton. That may change now that Paul Jackson has taken over as ITV's head of entertainment and comedy. The BBC has been more prolific, though not matching the quality of its output in the last three decades. Channel 4 has pioneered another alternative to the traditional sitcom with "dramedies" or "comramas" like *Shameless* (2004–06*)*, *Teachers* (2001–04*)* and *No Angels* (2004–06).

The paucity of decent sitcoms has been variously blamed on the rise of reality TV, wider channel choice and declining viewing figures across the board. Industry figures such as comedy producer John Plowman and writer/producer John Lloyd have lamented Britain's failure to broadly adopt the team-writing system – where eleven or twelve writers pen gags for a show – that services and refreshes such American sitcoms as *Friends* (Channel 4, 1995–2004) and *Frasier* (Channel 4, 1994–2004). Plowman complained: "We can't do that – the economics of the industry don't let us and if we are absolutely honest we haven't got that many writers." That said, team-writing didn't make the only series of *According To Bex* (BBC1, 2005), starring Jessica Stevenson from *Spaced*, sparkle.

The import of US shows onto British TV hasn't helped the UK sitcom. In the 1970s, the only major imported US sitcoms were *M★A★S★H* and *Soap*. In the 1990s, American programming became an essential part of Friday night viewing for many Britons, with Channel 4 scooping up *Friends*, *Frasier* and *Will And Grace*, and recently enjoying cult success with *My Name Is Earl*. BBC2 squandered the most popular US sitcom ever, *Seinfeld*, through erratic scheduling, but did persevere with *The Larry Sanders Show* (BBC2, 1993–99).

While fourth wall sitcom lives on – the most popular post-*Seinfeld* US sitcom is the traditional, but well-crafted, *Everybody Loves Raymond* – such naturalistic American shows as *Curb Your Enthusiasm* (on Channel 4's digital channels) and *Arrested Development* (BBC2, 2004–) have flourished in the UK.

In its own way, *Curb Your Enthusiasm* is as formulaic as a fourth wall sitcom in its plotline. In essence the naturalistic sitcoms and the traditional fourth wallers both feature characters hampered by their own personality traits, causing chaos and resolving issues after various challenges and mishaps. The launch of Graham Linehan's new sitcom, *The IT Crowd* (Channel 4, 2006), a funny fourth wall, laughter track sitcom that involved the talents of Chris Morris and Ash Atalla, producer of *The Office*, contradicted Wood's prediction that naturalism would monopolize the genre.

It is no coincidence that BBC2 and Channel 4 are driving sitcom development. Neither are as enslaved by ratings as BBC1 and ITV have become. *Fawlty Towers*, often dubbed the best sitcom ever, didn't become one of the twenty most watched shows in the UK until 1985, nine years after it had premiered on the BBC.

The golden age of sketch comedy

The sitcom may be suffering from a mysterious, still undiagnosed, malaise, but the sketch show is in better health than ever, with the last fifteen years representing a golden age for this kind of comedy.

Larry David, *Seinfield* creator and the centre of attention in *Curb Your Enthusiasm*

Carry On Dick

The Dick Emery Show's writing team featured an astonishing array of talent, including David Nobbs, (creator of *Reginald Perrin*), John Esmonde and Bob Larbey (the *Good Life* team), Dick Clement (who wrote *The Likely Lads* and *Porridge* with Ian Le Frenais), Keith Waterhouse, Mel Brooks – yes that Mel Brooks – and, oddest of all, playwright Harold Pinter.

The Fast Show's Paul Whitehouse out of character, sort of...

Sketches grew out of the same music hall and variety traditions as stand-up but, owing a debt to more upper-middle-class pastimes (parlour room skits, charades and university revues), the sketch genre can offer tremendous variety of content and style. There aren't many genres that can embrace the hit-and-miss melange of Spike Milligan's *Q* series, which astonished even the Pythons by having the guts to stop a sketch before the punchline, and a show as mainstream as *The Dick Emery Show* (BBC1, 1963–81).

Morecambe and Wise's sketches were like watching countless playlets inspired by Neil Simon's *The Odd Couple* whereas *The Two Ronnies* (BBC1, 1971–87) roamed wider, offering a galaxy of characters completely unlike their own personas. Dave Allen's sketches, often involving the pope, slapstick and sex, were less sophisticated than his sit-down comedy. Sketch shows could be almost exclusively knockabout and grotesque – *Kenny Everett's Television Show* (BBC1, 1981–87) – or weighted to reflect current affairs such as *Not The Nine O'Clock News* and *Spitting Image* (ITV, 1984–96), or they could fall, happily, somewhere between these two extremes.

The alternative era's most enduring gifts to sketch comedy were *French And Saunders* (BBC1, 1987–2004), *A Bit Of Fry And Laurie* (BBC2, 1986–95), which was steeped in the Oxbridge tradition of its practitioners, and *Harry Enfield's Television Programme* (BBC2, 1990–92), which introduced a host of sharply observed, unsavoury characters like the Slobs and Kevin and Perry. Enfield's core collaborators Paul Whitehouse and Charlie Higson then created *The Fast Show* (BBC2, 1994–2000), one of the most innovative and influential sketch shows of the last 25 years.

One secret of *The Fast Show*'s success was having a writing team large enough to supply the volume of sketches required but coherent enough to ensure the show kept its identity. The same tactic worked well for *Smack The Pony* (Channel 4, 1999–2003), and some critics have said that *Little Britain* (BBC2, 2003–) would be even funnier if David Walliams and Matt Lucas had not overstretched themselves and hired too few writers. Yet *Little Britain* quickly achieved mass appeal, with a *Fast Show*-style saturation of catch phrases and caricatures reminiscent of Dick Emery. Other recent successful sketch shows include *The Catherine Tate Show* (BBC2, 2004–) and *Green Wing* (Channel 4, 2004–06), which like *The League Of Gentlemen* is a sketch/sitcom crossover.

The sketch show may be better suited than the traditional sitcom to a modern channel-surfing age where TV viewing is driven by a kind of attention deficit disorder. With *Little Britain's* first series becoming Britain's best-selling DVD ever – and *The League Of Gentlemen* spinning off into a reasonably successful movie – the sketch format seems more popular than at any time since the 1970s.

Meanwhile back on stage…

If you measured the health of stand-up comedy purely by the number of people doing it, you might be forgiven for thinking that it is in good health. If anything there are too many stand-up comedians and the lack of variety on the bills of comedy clubs across Britain is bad for double acts, character acts and stand-ups alike.

The double act has been a comedy staple since the heyday of Laurel and Hardy. In the 1980s and 90s there was a feast of cult comedy

double acts in the UK including The Oblivion Boys, Chris and George, The Rubber Bishops (from which Bill Bailey went solo), Punt and Dennis, Newman and Baddiel, Vic and Bob, and the oft-forgotten Hale and Pace who appeared on *Saturday Live* and were part of the sketch troupe Fundation at the Woolwich Tramshed before Rik Mayall and Adrian Edmondson usurped them. Now we have Ant and Dec, essentially Vic and Bob redesigned by a marketing department, hosting the kind of primetime game shows that are elbowing comedy out of the TV schedules.

Despite the recent success of The Mighty Boosh, the double act may, finally, be showing signs of age, feeling a bit too old-fashioned to appeal to newcomers. Besides, if you're starting out, splitting a small club fee isn't always going to pay the rent.

Character acts have fared somewhat better. Simon Munnery still reprises Alan Parker Urban Warrior in his shows while Al Murray The Pub Landlord has endured on stage and on digital TV. Over the past few years, character acts have won lots of exposure at the Edinburgh Fringe Festival although that has not necessarily translated into regular club slots or TV airtime.

The Perrier Awards judges have, in recent years, honoured New Romantic parody act Gary Le Strange (Le Strange's creator now has his own club night at the Albany Pub in London), character comic Will Adamsdale as cheesy life coach Chris John Jackson (who won the main award in 2004) and Justin Edwards' alcoholic children's entertainer Jeremy Lion (nominated in 2005).

One of the Albany's more intriguing comedy nights is The Book Club, hosted by Robin Ince who gained notoriety as Ricky Gervais' support act. The Book Club was set up in 2004 as a deliberate departure from the boyish boisterousness of some circuit clubs, especially Jongleurs, where the comedy portion of a comedy night can seem the least important item on the menu, an approach typified by the clubs' oft-quoted strap line: "Eat, drink, laugh and dance".

Among the acts to appear at The Book Club are Goodies-style sketch troupe The Trap, character act DJ Danny and one half of The Mighty Boosh, Noel Fielding. The relative success of the fey and fantastical comedy adventures of The Mighty Boosh proves there is an appetite for live comedy that isn't stand-up. The rise of Dave Gorman has reinforced the point. Gorman started as a bread and butter stand-up but, through such fact-based comedy as *Are You Dave Gorman?*, became a "documentary comedian" using facts, not gags, to provoke laughter.

Quirky acts find it harder to prosper now than in the circuit's early days when fringe theatre was more of an influence. Marc Blake, who tours the circuits either as himself or as character act Herman the German, recalls sharing bills in the past with such novelty acts as sound mimic Chris Luby, who could conjure up various aircraft noises, and Keith Allen, who wore a miner's helmet and smeared himself in baby oil to play the character Jerry Arkwright, a Northern industrial gay.

Munnery, who wears a bucket on his head when in character, runs a club night in London that tries to keep such inspired lunacy alive, featuring such acts as veteran alternative clown Andrew Bailey and prop comedian Martin Soan, who came to prominence with "The Greatest Show On Legs", a nude balloon act with Malcolm Hardee.

Mixing poetry and comedy is much rarer now. John Hegley has carried the banner for this art form since the 1980s. In their early days, Jenny Eclair, Phil Jupitus, Mark Lamarr, Mark Hurst (as Mark Miwurdz) and Craig Charles all performed comedic poetry, but the tradition has waned since.

Musical comedians are still popular (e.g. Bill Bailey, Boothby Graffoe, Rich Hall as Otis Lee Crenshaw) but then the worlds of music and comedy have always been close; it's just a pity that only a few of the up and coming acts are exploiting their musical talents.

Making stand-up pay

One man, or woman – though most times it's a man – and a microphone remains the most enduring manifestation of live comedy. This free-wheeling, flexible lifestyle can provide a springboard into television, film and punditry. In the early 1980s a career in comedy wasn't seen as a viable option, but today trained actors sometimes see stand-up as a short cut into TV. The exposure of stand-up was boosted in 1995 with the UK launch of the Paramount Comedy Channel, which widened the range of club acts featured on the small screen and gave TV debuts to such talent as Sacha Baron Cohen (Ali G), Matt Lucas, David Walliams, Dom Joly, Ben Armstrong, Lee Miller and Leigh Francis (of *Bo Selecta!* fame).

The careerism within comedy is most conspicuous at the Edinburgh Fringe Festival, where TV producers invade the Scottish capital in the last weeks of August to suss out acts. This phenomenon has increased the Festival's lure – and the cost of putting on a show – but the strain of writing an hour's worth of new material each year has stretched the talents of many comics, provoking the Perrier judges to bemoan falling standards in 2005.

One of the most identifiable recent trends in stand-up is the emergence of the "poshboy comic", a loose group that includes Will Smith, Miles Jupp, Chris Addison, Michael McIntyre

Daniel Kitson (back, second from left) joins other 2001 Perrier Award nominees for a photocall

and, by far the most successful of the group, Jimmy Carr. One of Carr's Edinburgh Shows was fittingly entitled "Bare-faced Ambition" and he has become the ubiquitous face of Channel 4, hosting so many game shows and top 100 shows as to prompt ridicule – sometimes in jest, but often not – from fellow comics.

Leading British stand-up – and 2002 Perrier Award-winner – Daniel Kitson has taken the opposite approach to Carr. Apart from a bit part in *Phoenix Nights*, Kitson has made it plain he has no desire to pursue stardom through movie, television and advertising roles. Instead of becoming

subsumed by popular culture, Kitson prefers to tour the country amusingly pointing out that culture's inherent problems.

Neither Kitson nor Carr is likely to suffer the same fate as Ben Elton. He may be one of the godfathers of modern British comedy, but in recent years Elton's collaborations with Andrew Lloyd Webber and musical immortalizations of legendary pop-rockers Queen and Rod Stewart have disillusioned many and left him looking about as cool as, well, Andrew Lloyd Webber. Yet Elton's well-received 2005–06 tour was a reminder that he remains an iconic stand-up comedian.

One important measure of the relevance of the comedy circuit is the level of political comedy. Jeremy Hardy, Mark Thomas and Mark Steel have doggedly married gags with politics since Elton was in his 1980s heyday but their comic indignation has lost some of its conscience-pricking power if only because their comedy feels so tried and trusted. Newer comics such as Andy Parsons, Marcus Brigstocke, John Zaltzman and John Oliver have had to battle political apathy and, before the Iraq war, a dearth of issues that excited audiences.

Robert Newman may just be the most daring political comedian of the moment. He reinvented himself as a political comic in the mid-1990s, ironically at the very moment when the shift away from political comedy to observational humour was complete. Newman's comic range has been fascinatingly tested by his desire to discuss such issues as eighteenth-century models for the War on Terror. Critics suggest he has forgotten to be funny, overwhelmed by the factual material he wants to convey. Few comedians have tried to blend facts and jokes as ambitiously as Newman – it's easier to dispense tired one-liners about George W. Bush – and political comedy is all the poorer for it.

"The only thing to look forward to … the past"

Like *The Likely Lads*, comedy's future is all about the past. The scarcity of certain types of comedians will remedy itself, as new trends are sparked off by successful acts and backlashes against the status quo set in. Comedy is – and always will be – a world where styles drift in and out of fashion. So in the last few years Peter Kay and Dave Spikey have successfully redefined the comedy of the traditional club comic, rising star Alan Carr has emerged as the natural heir to Frankie Howerd, and Jimmy Carr and Ricky Gervais have made politically incorrect jokes in the guise of postmodern irony. Meanwhile, on the live circuit, such disparate acts as Ben Elton, Ken Dodd and Roy "Chubby" Brown have all attracted large audiences.

The last word goes to Peter Kay's collaborator on *Phoenix Nights*, Dave Spikey, who told comedy website www.chortle.co.uk: "The mainstream and the alternative – definitions I hate – have come together more. There's more common ground now. There's a place for every sort of comedy. Funny is funny."

Podcasts

Podcasting allows comedians to make their shows readily available on the Internet as free downloadable audio files. The new medium has quickly become a popular outlet for comedy, with amateur comedians joining the famous names and broadcasting their own comedy routines. Given that podcast success is rated by the number of downloads and not sales, it looks like the Internet could produce some new underground hits and perhaps the "next big thing".

The ubiquity of Ricky Gervais, at times testing comedy worship to its limit, is particularly noticeable when it comes to podcasts. The rotund comic was given the Guiness World Record in 2006 for the most downloaded podcast for his weekly shows with co-writer Stephen Merchant and XFM producer Karl Pilkington. David Baddiel and Frank Skinner also released a special series of podcasts, reminiscent of their *Fantasy Football League* TV series, for the 2006 World Cup.

The Icons: the faces of comedy

Simon Munnery dressed to impress

The Icons:
the faces of
comedy

Comedy is an art best savoured live. That's why this chapter tells you all about those who have made them-selves crucial to the genre: the icons who, rather than telling interchangeable jokes, have forced us to see the world through their eyes – and made us laugh in the process.

The idea of artificially crowning one particular performer as the best in a business as subjective as comedy is essentially ludicrous. So what you have here is a list of fifty iconic comedians, arranged alphabetically, in a selection designed partly to reflect the phases in the progression of live comedy since the mid-1970s – alternative, post-alternative and so forth – and partly just to honour talent and influence. As always with such selections, the inclusions and omis-sions may provoke controversy but any list like this that failed to spark such debate would be deeply suspicious.

So Eddie Izzard, as stellar as he is, is cult, partly because his fame has been achieved with limited TV exposure, while Jimmy Carr, more recent, is omitted, partly because of his limitless TV exposure. Lee Evans, another stadium star, is included because he is practically the sole living representative of the great tradition of physical comedy. Elsewhere personalities such as Boothby Graffoe, Tim Vine and Nick Wilty are great examples of good, established circuit acts with dedicated followings. The comedians making waves now – such as Alan Carr, Andrew Maxwell and Mark Watson – suggest the future of live comedy is in good hands.

Under each entry, you are pointed to recommended DVDs, videos, books, CDs or MP3s that give you a flavour of the best of each act and any relevant websites.

This chapter should be read in tandem with The Canon (see pp.109–160), which tells you all about the most influential British comedy programmes on TV – from sitcoms like *Phoenix Nights* to sketch shows like *Absolutely* and satire like Chris Morris's *Brass Eye*.

Keith Allen

1953–

You can be sure that Keith Allen will pop up somewhere, sometime, prompting vague recognition and begging the question: who exactly is he? Certainly his appearance in the video for New Order's seminal World Cup football anthem "World In Motion" in 1990 along with John Barnes et al was, initially, suitably puzzling. But Allen actually co-wrote the song and would later contribute the affectionately satirical football anthem "Vindaloo" under the guise of Fat Les along with Blur's Alex James.

Allen trained as an actor at the Welsh College of Music and Drama and in an on/off acting career has amassed quite a collection of movie cameos, most notably as the flatmate in *Shallow Grave* whose death sparks off a chain of indulgence, betrayal and brutality. As a former borstal boy, brutality has played a significant role in Allen's own life, shaping his persona during his brief and fiery stint as one of the new wave of live comedians in the late 1970s and early 1980s.

Allen's stint at The Comedy Store was remembered by contemporaries for its intensity and confrontations with the audience. He was once knocked unconscious by an off-duty soldier who was incensed by a joke he made about Northern Ireland, while on another night he let off a fire extinguisher in someone's face and, at yet another gig, threw darts at his audience.

Punters who persevered would see something funny and dark. Having only a vague idea of what he might talk about, Allen went on stage as himself with material that usually riled or shocked the audience. In one routine, he admitted he was finding it difficult to do his act because his father had just died. He then added that he was really tired – because he and the rest of his family had been celebrating his father's passing at a disco, they hated him so much.

Allen's uncompromising style – and his refusal to broaden or change his persona – soon isolated him. His antipathy towards The Comedy Store deepened as he perceived audiences demanding more polished acts, complaining the club had become a venue for middle-class careerist comics. But he carried on appearing elsewhere, including spots as Jerry Arkwright, northern industrial gay, at Malcolm Hardee's notorious Tunnel Club.

As a comic actor, the highlight of his career on television was probably writing, producing and starring in an episode of *The Comic Strip Presents* called *The Bullshitters*, a spoof of *The Professionals*, which was one of the best shows in the series.

 The Complete Comic Strip Presents (2005). A must-have DVD for anyone interested in alternative comedy, this also gives you the chance to see Keith Allen's comic acting abilities. Sadly, through Allen's own doing, one of his most memorable performances, in *The Bullshitters*, is not included.

Bill Bailey

1964–

In the wrong hands any musical instrument can be the kiss of death for a comedian. Self-indulgent, act-padding ditties have made us wary of musical diversions in a stand-up show. With Bill Bailey, you know that both instrument and audience are in safe hands.

Bailey is such an accomplished musical comedian he could release his own greatest hits compilation. The album would go back a couple of decades or so to his days as half of the Rubber Bishops double act, when he began striking chords and getting laughs at the same time by, for example, reworking Dire Straits' "Romeo And Juliet" to feature a drunken, kebab-wielding lothario. More recently, Bailey has penned a drum'n'bass George Bush parody mixing up samples of the president's speeches, a Jacques Brel parody (containing the immortal line "Carving your name into my head with a compass was not enough for you, Debbie"), and a Kraftwerk version of "The Okey Cokey".

The musical tinkering of this long-haired and bearded comedian – whose look, he admits, is still "1982, *Stars In Their Eyes*, Meatloaf, West Country heat runner-up" – really hits the high notes. Though his stand-up patter is good in parts, it can be unadventurous, especially compared to his musical tangents.

Yet Bailey is a consistent performer, a veteran of successive, successful tours here and abroad, and he brings a distinctive pres-

Corporate comedy

Corporate gigs are one of comedy's best-kept secrets. The entertainment guides in towns and cities across Britain won't tell you that, for a hefty price, your favourite comic is down the road at the local accounting firm doing their Christmas party. Bill Bailey, socialist comic Jeremy Hardy and Jimmy Carr are just three of the comedians in this line of work. But they don't boast about it.

Comedians have been known to come to blows over issues of artistic integrity. Those who choose to "sell out" can earn anything from under £1000 for a lesser-known circuit comic to upwards of £25,000 for the Skinners and Baddiels of this world. Jimmy Carr has publicly insisted that the lure of a corporate gig isn't just financial: "If you get booked for the right thing they can be great. It's like the whole audience are one gang, so if you hit it right, it's a brilliant gig."

Mike Gunn, a stand-up who made his name on the circuit as an undertaker, but now appears as himself, has less rosy memories:

"I was doing a corporate gig about six years ago for accountants at a hotel near the Barbican. Corporates pay well but the odds are stacked against you from the beginning – there's no PA, no mic, the room is gigantic and there's a big space in front of the stage.

"I was doing my act in character as a funeral director. I arrived as they were having dinner. I could see that there were about 200 people in the room all over 60, far too close to death to enjoy my act. After 18 minutes of the 30 I was supposed to do, I couldn't take the silence any longer and decided to cut and run.

"I'd noticed a door at the side and slipped through that. I found myself in the kitchen and ran into an old guy. I noticed some padlocked doors and asked him if there was any other way out. He said no. Then I saw a dumb waiter with doors about three feet high. The old guy said it led to the ballroom downstairs. I just didn't want to go through the main room again so I got him to agree to lower me down. When I arrived at the floor below, I pushed the doors open to find myself in the ballroom – along with all the people who I'd just died in front of, dancing the night away."

ence to TV comedy, whether he's ably supporting Dylan Moran in Channel 4's *Black Books* or team captain on BBC2's *Never Mind The Buzzcocks*.

Comedy's gain has been a loss to the telesales business. He once quit stand-up to work in telesales because he was so depressed by his intimate knowledge of motorway service stations and tiny Edinburgh audiences. He says: "I went out on stage and there was just one person in the audience – Dominic Holland, another comedian. He said, 'Don't worry, lads, just enjoy yourselves.'" Fortunately, Bailey's telesales career ended when he refused to wear a tie on the not illogical grounds that the customers couldn't see him.

 Bewilderness/Cosmic Jam (2001). Two shows on one DVD gives a long look at Bailey and his musical and verbal talents. *Bewilderness* includes Bailey's celebrated Stephen Hawking sketch and a routine in which the *Moonlight Sonata* morphs into a Cockney knees-up.

 www.bill-bailey.co.uk

Adam Bloom

1970–

Graduating from class clown, Adam Bloom started writing his own jokes when he was 19 and, after watching Harry Hill, decided to take the plunge into comedy.

Many metaphors have been used in a mostly forlorn effort to convey Bloom's furtive, erratic energy on stage. *The Daily Telegraph* came closest, likening him to "a shaven-headed squirrel on speed". His pent-up energy raises audience expectations and his imaginative jokes don't disappoint. He's not afraid to be un-PC either, once asking, "Is it fair to say that there'd be less litter in Britain if blind people were given pointed sticks?"

Bloom's observations stem from a mind that sees past the immediate, so inevitably topical jokes are not in his gag bag: "I'm never topical. I'm not interested in the world around me. I'm a bit of a dreamer. I'm the person sitting on the train looking out the window rather than reading the paper," he told the *Edinburgh*

Evening News. "I'll notice the rain running down the window and have a thought about that more than something in the news … I could have the best Bin Laden joke in the world and I wouldn't use it."

Bloom has made an impact on television without becoming over-exposed. *Adam Bloom: Beyond A Joke* (Channel 4, 1999) was an interesting take on the kudos of being a comedian. The gist of the show was Bloom meeting a woman fan after a show and starting a relationship with her. During their relationship she objects to his material about ex-girlfriends and he soon realizes she is only interested in him when he is being funny. Comic Howard Read has a favourite Bloom story which inverts that theme: "His girlfriend had been complaining all he ever talked about was comedy and it

Adam Bloom: "a shaven-headed squirrel on speed"

After the show

Never underestimate a comedian's need for validation, as industry PR Jacqui Roberts recalls: "Adam Bloom did a cracking show one night in Edinburgh. After the show, we were standing around chatting about how brilliant the show was. Adam asked another comedian standing with us what he thought of the show. The comedian replied: 'Actually Adam, I didn't see the show tonight.' To which Adam replied, 'Yes, but if you had seen the show, what do you think you would have thought?'" Rhod Gilbert offers a twist on the same theme: "I was with a notorious open spot one night who was telling me (and a disinterested friend of his) for the umpteenth time that he had finally discovered his genius. He told me that the previous Thursday he had taken the roof off a London gig. I nodded but this was not enough. He prodded his friend awake and said: 'Tell Rhod how well I did last Thursday at the King's Head'. His friend casually replied: 'I don't know, I wasn't there'. The comic then came out with the immortal line 'I know, but I told you about it!' That sums up comedians."

was putting a strain on their relationship. She challenged him to talk about something else for twenty minutes and, quick as a flash, Adam said 'Will I get a light at 18?'." His Radio 4 series *The Problem Of Adam Bloom* was re-commissioned in 2004, much to his delight: "I love stand-up, but there's something really magical about radio. Unfortunately radio doesn't pay a great deal, so you don't get the big names. Once people have made it they tend to disappear to do TV. It's a shame."

 Stand Up Great Britain (Laughing Stock, 2000). Also available as an MP3 from www.chortle.co.uk, this compilation features, among others, the wit and wisdom of Bloom.

 www.adam-bloom.com

Arnold Brown

1936–

Proud to be the "oldest alternative comedian in the world" – and the first to reach pensionable age – Arnold Brown could have been an accountant if it wasn't for his desire to be "the Finchley Road version of Lenny Bruce". Born Arnold Lizerbram in Glasgow, Brown came to London in 1963. He worked as an advertising copywriter and then at an accountants for fifteen years before he was rescued by writing gags for *Weekending* and appearing at The Comedy Store. He was on the Store's opening night bill in May 1979, though a heckler killed his first punchline.

He derived much of his material from his modest Glaswegian Jewish background, once memorably quipping: "I remember the difficulty in Glasgow of my father being a teetotaller and the shame on Saturday nights of him being constantly thrown into pubs." Brown's gags often required a reasonable amount of concentration and it was at The Comic Strip, founded by Peter Richardson, that Brown found his feet even though he didn't join in the TV spin-off series.

He deservedly won the Perrier Award in 1987 with his *Brown Blues* show, and he has had his own Radio 4 series (*Arnold Brown And Company*), his own programme on STV, and cameo appearances in such British movies as *Comfort And Joy* and *Personal Services*. Perhaps his best moments were opening for Frank Sinatra at Ibrox football stadium in 1991 and supporting legendary American comic Steven Wright in 1993.

Brown does play stadiums but he hasn't become a stadium act and is still a regular on the London club circuit. His appearance and his act seem little changed, his trademark laconic humour as strong as ever. In response to Mel Gibson's controversial film *The Passion*, Brown apologized on behalf of all Jews for Jesus' crucifixion saying, with a glint in his eye: "We promise not to do it again."

 Many items relating to Arnold Brown are expensive and difficult to find (including his part-fantasy autobiography *Are You Looking At Me, Jimmy?* and his video *Live At The Hackney Empire*) so you're probably best to opt for Laughing Stock's audio recording *And Why Not?* (1991), featuring many of his classic routines from the early 1980s.

 There is a very slender biography on www.jeremyhicks.com/arnoldbrown/biog.htm

Brendon Burns

1971–

A fair few tales of comic derring-do and downright derring-don't have involved the mouthy "bad boy" of comedy, Brendon Burns, over the last ten years, both on and off stage. The Australian comic, now living in Britain, can't be faulted for effort, passion and cheek. If he is not always as outrageous as he is hyped to be, it's not for lack of trying.

At the 2005 Glastonbury Festival, for example, he handed out magic mushrooms to the audience and, after taking some himself, proceeded to climb up some scaffolding in the tent he was perform-

Bad boy of comedy Brendon Burns

ing in and launch himself into the audience. Or there is the scene cut from the BBC's *Live Floor Show* programme in 2003 where he kissed a goat and simulated sex with it. The goat was smuggled into his dressing room by the crew in recognition of a Burns routine about a man caught fornicating with a goat in front of a passing trainload of passengers.

While he swears liberally and does his best to shock (for example, he says of Charles Kennedy: "Basically, Charles Kennedy would have to be caught with his dick in a kid's eye, and even then I'd think, well, I don't know, I'd probably still vote for him") he has moments of eloquence and lays the liberal sentiments and resolutions for self-improvement on thick after such lapses in taste. This dichotomy prompted Burns to write an Edinburgh trilogy of shows about the conflict between his stage alter ego and his real personality. It's a brave but indulgent exercise that Burns can afford because of his sizeable, loyal following.

He may have only had a brush with the small screen but Burns is a consummate live performer in the Bill Hicks, Sam Kinison, George Carlin, Jerry Sadowitz, Ian Cognito tradition, at ease suggesting acts of sexual depravity or speculating about international conspiracy and collective stupidity.

 Four MP3 downloads of Burns' works are available from the MP3 section of www.chortle.co.uk, including *Not For Everyone*. Burns ranges over several social and political issues in his inimitable boisterous style. His asides are often better than his endings. You'll either love or loathe the energy of this performance.

www.offthekerb.co.uk

Ed Byrne

1972–

It is hard to pinpoint exactly why Ed Byrne hasn't become a much bigger name. He is accomplished, charismatic and ambitious. He may not have pushed the barriers of stand-up (as he says: "If you want to tell people what you think, become a journalist, a politician or a spoken-word artiste") but he epitomizes good craftsmanship.

Byrne burst onto the London comedy scene in the mid-1990s after setting up and compering his own comedy club in Glasgow. Originally from the suburbs of Dublin, Byrne studied horticulture at Glasgow's Strathclyde University but spent more time embroiled in student politics and in bedding, he claims, a hundred women. "I'm young, free and single and I just want to mingle," was how he once responded to press interest in his love life.

The battle of the sexes is one of Byrne's great themes. He even says one ex-girlfriend nearly drove him away from stand-up because their relationship was so disruptive and tempestuous. His revenge was to talk about her in his act. When Byrne told her what he was saying, she focused on his admission that she was beautiful, reinforcing his initial character assassination and making the routine even funnier.

Starting out, he admits that he benefited from bonding with other such rising comics as Brendon Burns, Adam Bloom and Ross Noble: "We'd drink late into the night having discussions about comedy which we could only have with each other because you think anyone who's been doing comedy not quite as long as you knows nothing and anyone who's been doing it for longer is too jaded to want to talk to you about it." he told *StandupCom* magazine.

A superior line in jokes about booze, fags and birds (including one about a new girl in an office who thinks she has messed up the fax machine because the paper hasn't disappeared) allowed Byrne to rise quickly in the 1990s. Nominated for the Perrier in 1998, he was soon playing to 2000-plus-seater stadiums. Then he had some ill-luck, appearing in two sitcoms – *Sam's Game* (with Davina McCall) and RTE's *The Cassidys* – that were critically panned and swiftly cancelled. He then vowed never to appear in a sitcom unless he had written it.

Certainly the Irishman, whose appearance has graduated from long-haired Harry Potter to a suaver version of Jimmy White, seems to have plateaued in terms of fame but his edge has sharpened as he has got older and his gigs achieve a consistently high standard.

Ed Byrne recorded his very first DVD, a retrospective of his career in the last decade, at The City Varieties Theatre in Leeds in March 2006.

 Stand Up Great Britain (Laughing Stock, 2000). Also available as an MP3 on www.chortle.co.uk, this compilation features Byrne's observations on his own lack of fighting prowess, a theme he often refers to with splendid results.

 www.edbyrne.com

Alan Carr

1976–

Think Kenneth Williams with Eric Morecambe's glasses and you get near to the image and charm of camp comic Alan Carr. Then you

Howerd's way

If it wasn't for Frankie Howerd (1917–1992), *Little Britain* might not exist. The sketch show's Matt Lucas and David Walliams first bonded, comedically, by comparing Frankie Howerd impersonations.

Howerd had a face, one reporter shrewdly noted, like a "landslide of sadness". He put the face – and the stammer that was the only visible evidence of the stage fright that plagued him – to good use. If you were going to deliver lines like "You can't die here, this is the living room!", as he did in the sitcom *Up Pompeii*, you needed all the gravitas a sad face could give you.

As Lurcio, the sniggering slave in *Up Pompeii* (BBC1, 1970), a *Carry On*-style romp set in Roman times, Howerd was not the first comic to break the fourth wall and address the audience directly but he made it look so easy. That show, more than anything else in his career, defined Howerd, as he drew on absurd catch phrases ("Titter ye not"), knowing looks, a wig that

resembled a dead stoat and a mastery of innuendo to create a distinctive comic persona.

There was more to Howerd than one *Carry On* sitcom clone. He had fought back after a nervous breakdown in the early 1960s – caused, partly, by the strain of denying his obvious homosexuality and partly by a sense that his comedy was going out of fashion – to wow a fairly cynical crowd at Peter Cook's The Establishment club. His opening line – "If you expect Lenny Bruce, you may as well piss off now!" – has entered comedy history.

After *Up Pompeii*, Howerd fell back into a kind of showbiz exile, making his unlikeliest comeback of all as a cult stand-up comedian on the university circuit in the late 1980s, popular enough to have his own range of Frankie Says! merchandise. He was, as the diarist Kenneth Tynan put it – and many new wave comedians came to recognize – the "subtlest clod".

Alan Carr, driving in comedy's fast lane

have to add his similarity to Frankie Howerd to get a fuller picture of this cheeky, geeky, gossipy and irreverent comedian.

He insists he fell into the business by accident. He told the Chortle website: "I didn't really want to be a comedian, it's just that I was working in a call centre in a really terrible job, in a big credit card company, on the lost-and-stolen line. So after work I would just tell people about the weirdoes ringing up and how they'd lost their cards, and they'd say how funny it was and that I should go on stage and tell it. So I did, and they started laughing. Then I won the BBC New Comedian of the Year Award. But I never really thought I'd make a career out of it. It just sort of happened. I don't really like comedy. I wouldn't go on a night out to a comedy club or anything."

Carr may not yet have the exposure of his near namesake, Jimmy, but his star is in the ascendant. Since his last Edinburgh show in

2003 Carr has been signed up by one of the two big comedy agencies, been regular warm-up for Jonathan Ross and gained further attention co-hosting Channel 4's *The Friday Night Project*. In 2005, his show won universal critical acclaim and was a puzzling omission from a Perrier Award shortlist that focused on newcomers. He suggested that his style was too traditional for the panel but, given the appearance of Jason Manford, very reminiscent of the mainstream comedy of Peter Kay, this seems unlikely.

Carr's influences are certainly of the old school – his comic heroes include Frankie Howerd and Peter Sellers, but also, among current circuit acts, Lee Mack, Daniel Kitson and Ross Noble – but his material is very up-to-date. His punchlines reflect the topical events or phenomena of the day. In his 2003 show, he discussed how the Iraq war affected his TV career – "I can't help thinking that if Basra had fallen earlier I'd be a big star by now" – and addressed date rape: "How bad can a date be when you spike your own drink with Rohypnol?" His put-downs are of the highest order: "I had my scally neighbour Karen banging on my door with the Matalan catalogue the other day. I thought I'm not going to read it to her again".

Originally from Northampton but now based in Manchester, Carr began to get noticed around 2001 when he won the BBC New Comedian Of The Year Award. He appeared regularly at The Comedy Store and at their Manchester venue and had his own monthly residency there with *Alan Carr's Ice Cream Sunday*. The show's novelty attractions included an appearance by former Tory MP Neil Hamilton and his wife Christine.

If his career keeps progressing at its present rate, he might become so famous that people stop emailing his website in the belief that he is Alan Carr, the stop-smoking guru.

 www.alancarr.net

Julian Clary

1959–

Probably Julian Clary's finest hour was "fisting Norman Lamont", the fictional, much publicized, joke he made at the otherwise rather dull British Comedy Awards in 1993. He made the gag, he claims in his autobiography *A Young Man's Passage*, under the influence of a cocktail of valium and the date-rape drug Rohypnol.

Although building on the comic legacy left by Frankie Howerd, John Inman and Larry Grayson, Clary has rolled back the frontiers for gay comedy and left no stone unturned – and no innuendo undelivered – in the process. Don't be deterred by the relentlessly back passage-related punning titles of his merchandise, his comedy is actually much more versatile than that.

In April 2005, he started to front the National Lottery's *Come And Have A Go* game show, a prime-time job that would have seemed a preposterous dream to the young Clary, whose first job in showbiz, after his drama degree, was as a singing telegram.

His first foray onto the cabaret circuit was as Gillian Pie-Face and then The Joan Collins Fan Club, both starring animal side-kick Fanny the Wonderdog. After Joan Collins threatened legal action, the fan club name passed into cabaret legend and Clary's name stood alone.

Clary paved the way for Graham Norton but did so with immense flamboyance, often bedecked in feathers, sequins and layers of make-up in a gaudy look that, for a while, was part of his act. His most arresting outfit was appropriately his PVC policeman's uniform, all the more fitting as his father was a policeman.

Master of innuendo Julian Clary

He even has a routine about the time he "joined" the police that nicely demonstrates his trademark camp nonchalance: "The other morning they wanted to send me on a dawn raid. I said, 'I'm sorry, but you won't see me before half past ten in the morning. I don't have my porridge till nine, and I'm not leaving the house without something hot inside me, not for anybody'."

Clary's ability to tease an audience without making them feel totally uncomfortable has made him a natural for TV. He enjoyed his best success with *Sticky Moments* and *Sticky Moments On Tour*, a game show satire co-written with Paul Merton and containing all manner of innuendo. For example, this threw up such exchanges as: "What M melts in your mouth and not in your hand?", *"M and Ms?"*, "No, Mel Gibson, sorry!'"

Though his TV work dropped away for a while after the Norman Lamont gag, he eventually made it back into the mainstream and is now much better known than the former chancellor of the exchequer.

 Comic Aid: A Benefit For The Asian Tsunami Appeal (2005). Clary shares this three-hour show with a host of comedians but, as is often the case on multiple bills, makes a good impression, not least with his extravagant outfits which always threaten to upstage him.

 My Glittering Passage (1993). For a more relentless look at Clary's talents try getting hold of a copy of this show.

 A Young Man's Passage (Ebury Press, 2005). Clary had some years earlier penned a semi-autobiographical work with Paul Merton but this more recent effort gives a fuller, and occasionally more graphic, account of the life and loves of the camp star.

 www.julianclary.net is a decent fan site.

Ian Cognito

Although Arnold Brown was inspired by Lenny Bruce, Ian Cognito is more often compared to him. The authoritative comedy website www.chortle.co.uk estimates that Cognito has been banned from more than a dozen clubs because of his "irascible behaviour". One comedy-goer notes, on Chortle, that seeing Cognito is "an odd experience – actually being physically afraid of a comedian. I'd like to say that underneath all the anger and bitterness is something cleverer – but I'm not sure there is. Not that it matters."

Despite never appearing on television, Cognito has amassed a large fan base over the last seventeen years and won the respect of many fellow comedians for breaking taboos, influencing such newer comedians as Brendon Burns. One example of how far he can push the audience's tolerance is a routine where he rants against domestic violence and then suggests what Posh Spice needs is a good slap.

In content, Cognito's act resembles Jerry Sadowitz's, owing the same debt to the combative tradition of reactionary comedian Sam Kinison who liked to offend everyone. John Major was an easy target as an ineffectual Conservative prime minister but Cognito's attack was subtler and more biting than most: "They say you can tell when a Tory is lying when his lips are moving and then we go and get a prime minister with no top lip." Cognito's act has a musical dimension. He can sound like a rougher-edged version of Spandau Ballet's Tony Hadley and his back catalogue includes a song about courting Princess Diana.

Sometimes Cognito's bluntness leaves a gig teetering on the brink, but he usually has the skill to bring his act and the audience back on track. And he can change tack, as another audience member recalls: "I saw him do a gig some years back to an audience of twelve at a failed comedy venue and he ditched his usual act to do an hour of great low-key sit-down story telling, like a favourite uncle entertaining a dinner party."

A Comedian's Tale. This book, downloadable from the website below, offers a useful insight into the world of a gigging stand-up comic on the London circuit and beyond. The agony and the ecstasy is all here, along with some belting anecdotes.

www.iancognito.com

Anglo-Iranian comedian Omid Djalili

Omid Djalili

1965–

For ten years between 1995 and 2005 Anglo-Iranian comic Omid Djalili toured his "just off the boat" Middle Eastern character around the comedy circuit to great success. "Keep the laughter coming, it helps with my asylum application," he would tell his audiences, who would be thrown as half-way through his act he would cease to be a carpet-selling Arab and reveal the kind of pukka accent you might expect from a man who was brought up in Kensington.

Djalili was born in London in 1965. His father was a foreign correspondent on an Iranian newspaper and his mother worked in fashion. In 1979, after the Iranian revolution, the family were granted refugee status, being particularly vulnerable because of their Bahá'í faith, which has been persecuted in Iran. After training as an actor, Djalili went into stand-up when he decided he wasn't going to get the parts he wanted. His wife Annabel was a friend of the stand-up comedian Alan Davies and introduced her husband to the scene with a visit to The Comedy Store in 1994.

At first, he admits, his act was "just a few silly accents and funny walks and funny faces". Having already done Edinburgh as an actor, the portly comic then embarked on a string of stand-up shows including *The Arab And The Jew* in 1996 with Ivor Dembina, which was a response to the assassination of Yitzak Rabin, and *Behind Enemy Lines* in 2002, a response to 9/11.

Though initially worried by how the post-9/11 world would handle his humour – and, indeed, the very idea of an Iranian comedian – Djalili soon found he could reintroduce jokes, reviving his routine about Muslim fundamentalists flying to the World Cup singing: "And we'll really shake them up/When we blow ourselves up." In 2005, he signalled a change of direction with his Edinburgh show *No Agenda*, dropping the Middle Eastern character and playing it straight.

Djalili may not be a household name in Britain but he has, to some extent, cracked America. As well as appearing in Whoopi Goldberg's sitcom, he has had significant roles in such Hollywood movies as *The Mummy*, *Spy Game* and *Sky Captain And The World Of Tomorrow*. He has yet to have his own sitcom in the UK but there's every chance it will happen.

Come what may, he has a philosophical view of fame: "I'm a family man, I don't want to be that famous, I don't want to be unable walk down the street. I'm sure if Ricky Gervais had kids he'd find it a real pain in the arse to take his kids to McDonald's."

 Stand Up Great Britain (Laughing Stock, 2000). One of many comics on this collection, Djalili makes a good impression with his lively material on Iran's appearance in the 1998 World Cup and insights into the lives of Iranians living in London.

www.omid-djalili.com/home

Jenny Eclair
1960–

It's fair to say that Jenny Eclair was the glamorous fishwife of the 1990s comedy circuit. Her brash style and prima donna persona divided audiences between those who liked their material direct and their topics coarse and those who couldn't handle her in-your-face monologues about smear tests and the like.

Jenny Eclair, the glamorous fishwife of comedy

After leaving Manchester Polytechnic, Eclair started on the poetry circuit, following in the footsteps of the legendary Salford punk poet John Cooper Clarke. She moved down to London in 1982 to become "the world's worst waitress" and transferred from the poetry circuit into the cabaret circuit.

It was for cheeky lines like "I came on the train today, though I think I managed to pass it off as an asthma attack" that Eclair was known, loved and reviled. Her career really took off in the 1990s. A run of four Edinburgh shows between 1992 and 1995 culminated in her 1995 Perrier Award success (for which the opening joke was: "I've had my nipples pierced. Why? Because I was sick of losing my car keys. The only trouble is that I have got this really elongated nipple from shoving the keys in the ignition."). Eclair is still one of only two women to have won the award. Subsequently she was involved with a few West End outings, notably *The Vagina Monologues* and *Steaming*, Nell Dunn's comedy about female friendship in a London bathhouse, and has hosted two Channel 5 chat shows.

In 2000, she released her first novel *Camberwell Beauty*, inspired by the area of London she has lived in for nearly a quarter of a century. She has since written a second novel, *Having A Lovely Time*. Even from her early days on the circuit, her brazen attitude to life's complexities attracted magazines to commission her to write for them, something she found highly rewarding, as she told author Roger Wilmut: "That's such a thrill. I was always labelled an illiterate Goth at school – lots of imagination but no spelling or grammar."

As with most successful comedians of her generation, Eclair has survived in the mainstream with regular guest TV slots on such shows as *Richard And Judy*. But she has never quite become as big a household name as fellow female comedians Ruby Wax and French and Saunders, even though, for many, she is just as prolific and funny.

Top Bitch: Live At Her Majesty's Theatre (1995). Nothing can beat the full force of Eclair's stage persona and this is vintage Jenny from her Perrier-winning year.

Eclair is poorly served in cyberspace. However, on www.camberwellbeauty.co.uk you'll find a promo for her novel *Camberwell Beauty*, with some extra info and interviews.

Women and comedy

Stand-up is male-dominated, that's a simple fact. Debates regularly take place about why. Favourite answers include the aggressive nature of stand-up, the suggestion that female wit is subtler, and the idea that men feel threatened by funny women. These theories have major exceptions and reinforce the very stereotypes female comics want to get away from. Yet anecdotal evidence suggests a kernel of truth that stand-up is, in some ways, a boys' club with a boisterous approach that alienates women who, in turn, often tell a different kind of joke.

Jo Brand and Jenny Eclair are the major exceptions to this rule. Their full-on approach won them fans and plaudits. Brand used the skills she learnt as a psychiatric nurse to tame audiences and was unabashed in "bashing" men for bashing women. Her strident, initially deadpan style was refreshing but she has fallen victim to a perception, largely accurate, that she has been peddling the same jokes about men and cakes for too long. The caustic Eclair was ploughing a similarly one-dimensional furrow with her penchant for lurid discussions of sex, but the energy and brashness of her performances make the memory of her live act somewhat fresher. Another female comedy icon, Hattie Hayridge is a lot quieter but her jokes are both much tighter and more wide-ranging. Yet her subtler approach has meant that her clever material is sometimes swallowed up by rowdy venues or bad billing.

Between the art forms of stand-up and television comedy stands the female comic icon of Victoria Wood who has mastered both, albeit with her live stand-up career a reasonably distant memory. Joining her on the roll call of funny women on television are French and Saunders (again with a brief live pedigree behind them), Tracey Ullman, Kathy Burke (the greatest female stand-up that never was?), Sally Phillips and the *Smack The Pony* team, Catherine Tate, Julia Davis and so forth.

From that list, it seems reasonable to speculate that the

Ben Elton

1959–

More than a quarter of a century has passed since the prolific, left-wing motormouth Ben Elton burst onto the comedy circuit so it is no great surprise that his work has been re-evaluated. The fact that he co-wrote such mainstream shows as the Queen musical *We Will Rock You* and the Rod Stewart musical *Tonight's The Night* hasn't helped his street cred with those current comedians who revered him in the early days. The disappointment about his recent work is similar to the disappointment some Labour voters feel with Tony Blair. What the two figures have in common is a definite legacy in both their fields.

From an academic family, Elton always knew he wanted to write and perform comedy when he finished his studies. He had a poor start at The Comedy Store but, after moving away from aped sketch format is best suited to female wit and that once the line between the live circuit and television is crossed, only a few stick with the live circuit. A number of factors dictate this choice – again Brand and Eclair are good exceptions to the rule – but the likes of Jack Dee, Lee Hurst, Lee Evans, Mark Thomas and latterly Ben Elton have all kept gigging despite success on the big and small screen.

Sometimes a parallel live career can simply be overlooked by the public. This was the case with the late Linda Smith who died at the tragically early age of 48 in 2006. A household name on Radio 4, thanks to her appearances on *The News Quiz* and serializations of her stand-up work, Smith continued to tour but her radio status overshadowed her live career. This may, though, have as much to say about the media attention awarded to stand-up as it does about gender balance.

A snapshot of the comedy circuit at the time of writing shows a diverse range of female stand-ups who have done well for themselves and by doing so inevitably – if to varying degrees – have helped to demolish the myth that women aren't funny.

From what now must be considered as an older generation, Gina Yashere, who hails from London via Nigeria, represents a solid, good-value comedian who, while not always receiving rave reviews from critics, is popular with audiences. Australian thirtysomething Kitty Flanagan, who has made the UK circuit her performing home, is an excellent jokesmith and assured performer. An honourable mention should also go to Jo Caulfield, a circuit stalwart and writer for Graham Norton.

The younger generation includes such acts as the elfin Lucy Porter, the verbose and cerebral Natalie Haynes, the controversial Muslim comic Shazia Mirza and another Australian import, Sarah Kendall. Most of the above have been tipped, at various times, to be the first woman to win the Perrier Award since Jenny Eclair in 1995. The winner of that honour actually turned out to be Laura Solon, not a stand-up but a character sketch artist.

It's hard to say anything definitive about the outlook for women stand-ups. More women are trying – and succeeding – in stand-up yet, in 2005, the annual Funny Women competition was won by a comedian who used to be a man.

material to become the cockney social commentator, Elton became The Comedy Store compere in 1982. That same year he scored a writing hit as a co-author of *The Young Ones*.

Elton very quickly became the king of alternative comedy, his status sealed when he became compere of *Saturday Live* (1985) and then *Friday Night Live* (1988). By then, he had done several major tours and written *Filthy Rich And Catflap*, *Happy Families* and *Blackadder II and III*. Though it wasn't remarked upon at the time, *Ben Elton: The Man From Auntie* (BBC1, 1990) marked the point at which his crown began to slip. The show confirmed that the new wave of comedy had become the new mainstream as far as stand-up was concerned. The routines were still fiery but not as hard-hitting as before. They still took in favourite targets like politics and willies, and sometimes a mix of the two as in this routine about the unwanted erection:

"Topless beach? Fuck me I'm surrounded by tits – boing! I'm a lefty, I'm trying to hang on to my politics, I'm thinking I will not ogle, I will not look … but the dick is not a hypocrite!"

His influence has waned from the mid-1990s. To be cool, he said once, was to hold everything in contempt, and that is how he has come to be regarded. The comic majesty of the last *Blackadder* series, set in World War I, only made *The Thin Blue Line* – his attempt to do an ensemble sitcom like *Dad's Army* – even more of a disappointment. Yet, at his peak he was a one-man ambassador for comedy with ideas and gags that were pure comedy gold.

Elton has been a prolific and successful author too, his most famous novels being *Popcorn* (1996), which was turned into a stage play, and *Inconceivable* (2000), which he made into the movie *Maybe Baby* (2000). Elton returned to touring in 2006, a decade after his last live outing, and reminded people that he hadn't lost his gifts as a stand-up.

 The best introductory video is *A Farties Guide To The Man From Auntie* (1996), on which all of Elton's favourite themes are represented.

 Ben Elton Live (1989, Laughing Stock). This CD is the earliest – and arguably the best – recording still available. Elton gets his teeth into "The scum British press" and other favourite targets such as "The Thatch" in a great routine where she suggests his sofa should be privatized to make a profit.

Harry Enfield

1961–

Most stand-ups move into television at some point. With Harry Enfield, this happened almost overnight. His first major television break was as a live character stand-up with Stavros and Loadsamoney on *Friday Night Live*. Both characters were co-created by his friends Charlie Higson and Paul Whitehouse, and Enfield would continue to work closely with Whitehouse as his sketch shows came to dominate British television comedy in the late 1980s and early 1990s.

Stavros and Loadsamoney showed Enfield's gift for exaggerated, broad-brush characterization of recognizable social types, labelled with a handy, easy-to-remember catch phrase ("Hello, matey peeps" in the case of Stavros the Greek kebab shop owner and "look at my wad" in the case of cash-rich decorating wide-boy Loadsamoney).

Enfield took flak for both characters. Stavros, derived from a real-life character and sketched when Enfield was working on *Spitting Image*, was accused of being a racial stereotype. The shameless Loadsamoney with his Neanderthal attitude – such as leading football chants at a Pavarotti concert – was an obvious parody that the tabloids enjoyed taking at face value. Loadsamoney became so powerful a Thatcherite anti-hero that Enfield dropped him from his repertoire.

By accident and design, Enfield was set apart from alternative comedy, representing a second wave of comics who were prepared to lash out at everything. On the live circuit, this was done with a bludgeon by Jerry Sadowitz. Enfield was arguably not much more subtle in televisual terms. Wayne and Waynetta Slob (memorably portrayed by Kathy Burke) were a grotesque parody of lower working-class life with their household a hygienic no-go area filled with remnants of pizza and overflowing ashtrays. The argumentative, shell-suited, violent Scousers, gifted to him by characters on *Brookside*, were unsurprisingly detested on Merseyside. At the other end of the social scale, Tim Nice-But-Dim and Tory Boy seemed pleasant enough parodies but, on closer acquaintance, their stupidity and pomposity became quite grotesque. His last great gifts to the nation were eternally sulky teenagers Kevin and Perry.

For ten years – except for the blip of *Men Behaving Badly*, where he lasted just one series – Enfield ruled supreme in television comedy, often with the aid of such writers as Paul Whitehouse, Graham

Harry Enfield's Thatcherite anti-hero Loadsamoney

Linehan and Arthur Mathews. But when Whitehouse and Higson set out on their own to make *The Fast Show*, Enfield's comedy began to look slightly rusty. Later ventures, including his unsuccessful Sky One series *Harry Enfield's Brand Spanking New Show* and *Celeb* (the *Private Eye* cartoon spin off), have fared poorly, perhaps nudging Enfield even further into acting, the traditional refuge of the semi-retired comedian. Nothing, though, can take the shine off Enfield's comic legacy.

 Although a DVD of *Harry Enfield's Brand Spanking New Video* (2000) is available, you might be better to buy the video of *Harry Enfield's Television Programme* (1990), which contains such Enfield/Whitehouse classics as the pre-war Arsenal team playing the modern-day Liverpool team with hilarious results.

www.geocities.com/harryenf/ is a good unofficial fan site and his management site is on www.pbjmgt.co.uk/clients/harry_enfield

Lee Evans

1964–

For those who dislike the wired antics of Lee Evans he is as irritating as having someone scrape their hand across a balloon. But love him or loathe him, Evans's talent is plain for all to see.

His physical craft echoes the silent greats – Charlie Chaplin, Harold Lloyd and Buster Keaton – though he is most often compared to Norman Wisdom. The elasticity of his body along with his vocal dexterity animate routines that would sound flat if delivered with an ounce less energy, artistry or conviction. In his hands, picnicking by the motorway or shopping at Ikea – though it sounds like an old gag now – become hilarious. The stress of the shopping trip is brilliantly conveyed by Evans contorting his head to show how full the car is on the drive home. Such routines are regularly requested at Evans's live appearances, almost as if they were a rock star's greatest hits.

The son of an old-time variety entertainer, with an acrobat as an elder brother, Evans's act grew out of parodying the rough ride he got as a young stand-up: "I started doing physical comedy, because I was like a moving target. You know what British audiences are like – 'he's shit, kill him!' My upbringing taught me to keep moving." He was a boxer earlier in his career and discovered that ducking and weaving could be as useful in a comedy club as in the ring.

Evans was a huge hit at the 1988 Edinburgh Festival and in 1993 won the Perrier Award there. In 1995 Evans had his first major role in a feature film, starring with Jerry Lewis in *Funny Bones*. Thus began a string of Hollywood successes, including *The Fifth Element* (1997), *Mousehunt* (1997) and *There's Something About Mary* (1998).

Silver screen success hasn't blunted the restless clown appetite for live performance. He starred in two large national tours in 2002 and 2005 and appeared in the West End hit *The Producers*. Even with a large volume of stage or onscreen work, Evans remains hungry for more, though it's apparent he's not the usual showbiz egomaniac. He confessed in one interview: "I feel that what I do is not worth that much … It's just of its time and absolutely meaningless."

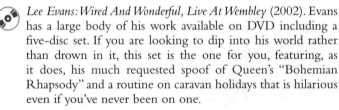 *Lee Evans: Wired And Wonderful, Live At Wembley* (2002). Evans has a large body of his work available on DVD including a five-disc set. If you are looking to dip into his world rather than drown in it, this set is the one for you, featuring, as it does, his much requested spoof of Queen's "Bohemian Rhapsody" and a routine on caravan holidays that is hilarious even if you've never been on one.

www.offthekerb.co.uk

Graham Fellows (John Shuttleworth)

1959–

At 18, Graham Fellows appeared unto the nation as Jilted John, scoring a top-five hit with a single of the same name. His lament that "Gordon is a moron" made for one of the most bizarre singles of the 1970s – no small feat in a decade that also gave us punk and the Wombles. That early flash of glory, back in 1978, still occasionally eclipses Fellows' subsequent two decades of hard work as a cult character comedian. As recently as 2004 a viewer complained when the song was repeated on *Top Of The Pops 2* because of the references to "bitch", "slag" and "slut".

Fellows has carved himself a niche in comedy history for a John more gentle than jilted – his enduring comic creation John Shuttleworth. This northern security guard with delusions of pop stardom cranks out preposterous compositions such as "Pigeons In Flight" ("Pigeons in flight/I want to see you tonight/I want to hold you/If I may be so bold to/And tell you some things that you'd like") with which, in a one-off BBC2 special, he tried to enter the Eurovision Song Contest.

Graham Fellows' Shuttleworth having a ball

The menopausal Shuttleworth, armed with his trademark Yamaha organ, has regaled his fans with everyday odes to biscuits, Bounty bars and so forth since 1985, when he was created by Fellows, then a Manchester drama student, to amuse a friend. From throwaway origins came throwaway songs that have helped win a sizeable fan base, a gig supporting Blur in front of 25,000 people in London and many radio and TV credits, most notably the cult success *500 Bus Stops* (BBC2, 1997).

Fellows has resisted the temptation to shelve Shuttleworth completely, but in the last five years or so has given voice to two new comedy characters, Brian Appleton and Dave Tordoff. Appleton continues the musical theme as a Brummie sound engineer and music lecturer who feels he was the inspiration for many key moments in pop and has numerous pastiche songs to prove it. Tordoff resembles a northern Loadsamoney

Ricky Gervais live

Ricky Gervais was something of a late-comer to live stand-up. This fact is not lost on the 45-year-old comedian. As Darrell Martin, promoter of the Just The Tonic comedy club in Nottingham, explains: "When Ricky was a budding star, appearing on the *11 O'Clock Show*, he saw me doing a gig and we all went off for a drink afterwards. He said he didn't feel he'd earned his comedy spurs, having never done stand-up. I talked him into doing a ten-minute spot in Nottingham – and that is where he did his first ever gig."

In March 2006 Gervais returned to Just The Tonic for a benefit gig, but ironically this time around he failed to wow his audience. Dominic Cavendish of *The Telegraph* described his performance as "underwhelming" and commented: "Seldom can a household name have looked less eager to rise to the challenge of entertaining 2,000 people. What with repeats of *The Office*, the record-breaking success of his podcasts and his [first] *Simpsons* episode [airing this week], Gervais might be able to plead being preoccupied at the moment – but not to the extent of continually eyeing his watch."

However, when Gervais has been able to prepare and perform within a tight structure – as he did with his stand-up tours *Animals* (2003) and *Politics* (2004) – he has looked assured and effective. Like Jimmy Carr, Gervais has built a reputation for political incorrectness (for example in *Politics* he floats the ideas that African countries have independence to blame for their economic woes and that homosexuality was legalized for 16 year olds by a self-interested older generation), but his cheeky persona means he (almost) gets away with it.

character, a rich Yorkshire builder who proudly parades his belongings and adventurous hobbies but without quite so much front as his Essex man predecessor.

When he's not acting as one of his own comic creations, Fellows has had acting roles in *Coronation Street* (ITV), *Comics* (Channel 4), *Coogan's Run* (BBC2) and *Time Gentleman Please* (Sky).

 500 Bus Stops (2005). This follows John as he goes on the lowest-key "rock" tour possible, with his Yamaha tucked under his arm, playing libraries and freezer centres.

 www.shuttleworths.co.uk

Rhod Gilbert

1968–

Rhod Gilbert has rapidly become a must-see on the comedy circuit, even though his career only started in 2002. He had worked as director of a market research consultancy ("I was moments away from a management buy-out situation, before I decided to jack it all in and take up comedy full time," he recalls) but he has scooped several awards, been nominated for the Best Newcomer Perrier and played every major international comedy festival.

Building surreal stories in carefully constructed layers, Gilbert attempts to squeeze every ounce of comedic possibility from his scenarios. He admits Eddie Izzard is a huge influence: "I've never been very interested in political comedy and there was a lot of it about when I grew up; Eddie's surreal flights of fancy really made me sit up and take notice of the genre." His first solo show, *Rhod Gilbert's 1984*, at Edinburgh 2005 (for which he received the Best Newcomer nomination) was a neat showcase for routines he had honed on the national circuit. The year before, Gilbert shared his Edinburgh slot with Mark Watson, another talented comic who, while not officially Welsh, takes on a convincing Welsh persona for his act. The show was called *Stereocomics*, a nod to the successful Welsh band Stereophonics.

The routine that has rapidly become Gilbert's signature piece is his opener where he walks on stage with the handle from a suitcase and proceeds to unravel a tale of what he told the baggage reclaim desk. The slapstick premise is present in other routines, albeit in a more surreal way, for example in a routine about a football match using his grandmother's pancreas. Sometimes, his act is too whimsical to easily carry more raucous audiences with him.

The tone of Gilbert's delivery is that of the world-weary Welsh underdog, put-upon, down-trodden but very much in control of his storytelling. There's no crossover into his own life and he doesn't seem to bring any crosses to bear on stage with him: "I don't even get on stage to get things off my chest. I'm there to tell jokes. I don't care how they arrive in my head."

Though his rich voice is not his only asset, it has helped rather than hindered him. He was recently the voice of the Paramount Comedy channel as announcer between programmes and has been hired as the voice of Wales, promoting Welsh tourism.

 www.rhodgilbert.com

Rhod Gilbert ... say "cheese"

They did give up the day job

Stand-ups recall the work that drove them to comedy, although Dave Gorman, as ever, has his own take on the subject.

Dave Gorman

"I was a student when I first started doing comedy. I suppose I'd worked in a supermarket when I was a kid – as a Saturday boy – and spent one summer break from university in a video shop, but no real jobs. It was an advantage. I know people who started when they were 28, married, with a good job and a kid on the way or whatever. Giving up a good job as some have, that takes balls. I had nothing, so I had nothing much to lose."

Richard Herring

"I worked in Cheddar Caves when I was 18, making sure people didn't break things. I did a couple of archaeological digs. I wrote the West London phone book 1990 in which I changed Stewart Lee's name to Stewart Wee. I did advertising sales and made no sales. I wrote for an encyclopedia about the royal family."

Stewart Lee

"I had a brilliant job doing fact checking for a book by the Royal Horticultural Society, working libraries in Kew, Victoria and the Natural History Museum for 18 months or so. Because I was freelance I could take odd days off when I got gigs out of London. I had to deliver my work to Anthony Huxley, son of Julian, nephew of Aldous, who would tell amazing stories about the people he had met. He was a delightful and inspiring man."

Simon Munnery

"Security guard, road sweeper, dustman, machine operator, computer programmer, data entry clerk – what a summer; busier than Billy Bragg."

Howard Read

"I worked for Help The Aged for a week doing data input. I may have got sacked because I sent packs of energy-saving advice intended for very old people to various friends of mine when the boredom got too much. My longest period of proper employment was in a magazine company's post-room. The hours were even easier than comedy. Eventually I only worked afternoons – entirely pointless for them as all the work in a post-room happens before 10am. My boss basically bank-rolled my stand-up career for the first year and a half I was in London. Eventually my office was closed and I got redundancy, roughly at the same time as I was starting to earn enough to pack it in anyway."

Waen Shepherd

"The only salaried job I ever had was as the editor of an 'amusing' youth-oriented website for British Gas. I've also worked as an animator, a performance poet and toured working men's clubs in a kiddies' panto. And I once had to clean people's shoes with kitchen roll in a Sainsbury's car park."

Arthur Smith

"Road sweeper, teacher of English as a foreign language. I was also in a band gigging in London pubs and clubs although I earned only £19.50 in total in the three years we were together."

Dave Gorman
1971–

Dave Gorman's unique storytelling style has pushed the boundaries of stand-up and created a new category of comic – the documentary comedian – a term for someone who uses exhaustive research, not punchlines, to get the laughs. His style, making funny use of overhead projectors and other visual aids, has inspired many others in his wake.

Gorman started stand-up as a deadpan character in 1990 and hosted his first Edinburgh show in 1995. From 1998 to 2003, Gorman took a string of inventive shows to comedy's annual capital that included: *Reasons To Be Cheerful*, a show deconstructing the lyrics of the Ian Dury song of the same name; *Better World*, where Gorman asked local newspapers what could be done to improve life; *Are You Dave Gorman?*, his Perrier-nominated seminal work where he roams the world looking for namesakes; and *Dave Gorman's Googlewhack Adventure*, inspired by his time spent avoiding writing a book by finding exact Google matches for two different words put together.

Are You Dave Gorman? was made into a book and a BBC television show and was a great example of one joke being sustained over a long period. Gorman collaborated with comedian Danny Wallace on the show; Wallace has since enjoyed a burgeoning career in comedy novel-writing and script-writing, and has penned several features for the national press.

Gorman's googlewhacking began with "Dork Turnspit". This led him to a site featuring innocuous photographs of women with dogs. Gorman met the site's owner and they provided the next Googlewhack and so it went. The original book deal was never honoured but Gorman paid the publishers back with the proceeds from the stage show which enjoyed an acclaimed, three-month run off-Broadway. Ironically, the show then became a bestselling book.

Gorman has earned recognition elsewhere as a writer on the *The Mrs Merton Show* and, continuing on the Mancunian theme, appeared in the movie *24 Hour Party People* (2002), detailing the halcyon days of Tony Wilson's Factory records.

 Dave Gorman's Googlewhack Adventure (2004). Gorman's unique narrative works almost as well on DVD as on tour.

This comes complete with an audience Q&A and out-takes.

Both *Are You Dave Gorman?* (Ebury Press, 2001) and *Dave Gorman's Googlewhack Adventure* (Ebury Press, 2004) transfer to the printed page very well, benefiting in some areas from the extra detail.

www.davegorman.com

Boothby Graffoe

1962–

Boothby Graffoe, a name taken from a small Lincolnshire market town, is the stage pseudonym of James Rogers. He is one of the circuit's most prolific, hard-working characters but, even though he has had at least one Edinburgh show running every year since 2000, he has never quite made the comedy A-list.

Rogers had started out wanting to be an actor and left his home town, Hull, when he was 18 to seek his fortune in London. When the work didn't come his way he grafted on the northern club circuit, basing himself in Nottingham and sometimes working in Butlins.

Graffoe's style borrows from all kinds of influences. He is an accomplished musical comedian. He is rarely seen without his guitar, penning tunes such as "Bungee Girl", a silly but sinister story of arm's-length love ("There are some things that you do that you never do again / one is break the heart of the man, of the man who drives the crane / bungee girl…"). He's equally well versed in the disciplines of

Boothby Graffoe, hard at work in the kitchen

improvisation, stock one-liners ("Who says men can't multitask? I can clean my teeth and pee at the same time – I don't always mean to") and surreal routines often involving cats.

Graffoe's appeal hasn't morphed into massive or significant exposure on television and film but he has won plenty of plaudits. Veteran alternative comedian Arthur Smith says of him: "He writes great gags, improvises as well as anyone, plays the guitar and sings songs that are both beautiful and funny." The late Malcom Hardee was right on the money when he said of Graffoe: "He's a very underrated comic, and should be up there with all the ones who are up there, wherever 'there' is."

Mostly a happy camper, Graffoe can look distracted and morose during performances. Channel 4 viewers caught a dramatic glimpse of his emotional volatility when he stormed out of the reality-TV show *Kings Of Comedy*, raging at the rules. The paradoxical quality of his act was probably best summed up by his first agent who told him: "You're either a genius, or the biggest pile of shit I've seen in my life."

 Wot Italian? (EVA, 2004). Boothby's carefully crafted comedy songs get some beautification courtesy of virtuoso acoustic guitarist Antonio Forcione. Old favourites embellished include "Baseball Playing Spider", his bittersweet tale of arachnid sporting prowess.

 www.boothbygraffoe.com

Malcolm Hardee
1950–2005

The gathering at the funeral of Malcolm Hardee on February 17, 2005 was a who's who of the last 25 years in British comedy. Arthur Smith was the master of ceremonies, comedians like Stewart Lee and Jo Brand contributed, while the throng included Jerry Sadowitz, Jenny Eclair, Harry Hill, Johnny Vegas, Keith Allen and Vic Reeves.

Born in 1950, Hardee spent much of his first thirty years in trouble with the law. Offences that beg to be taken into consideration include stealing the Rolls Royce belonging to former cabinet minister Sir Peter Walker and setting fire to a Sunday school because he

The late, great Malcolm Hardee

Hardee perennials

Marc Blake, who started out as Mr Sponge and now does stand-up as himself and as Herman The German, says Malcolm Hardee's persona was no put-on. "When Malcolm was told by his wife Pip that she was pregnant, his response was to urinate in his wardrobe," recalls the stand-up. Blake later had a fling with Hardee's sister: "Afterwards, I was forever introduced on stage at the Tunnel thus: 'Here he is, he could be good, he could be shit, he's fucked me sister'."

wanted to see "holy smoke". He played harmonica with Neil Innes' Bonzo Dog Doo-Dah Band twice. In 1977, he was released from prison for the last time and made his foray into the pre-alternative comedy scene with *The Greatest Show On Legs*. This cabaret act with Martin Soan, reminiscent of Wilson, Keppel and Betty's sand dance, involved a deft covering of private parts with balloons.

Though the act gained Hardee some recognition, including an outraged leader column in *The Sun*, it was as the founder, promoter and MC of the rough-and-ready Tunnel Club and later Up The Creek that he really made his mark on British comedy. The Tunnel Club was infamous as a comedian's graveyard, where hecklers had free rein but, in their early years, Paul Merton, Harry Enfield, Vic Reeves, Jo Brand and Jerry Sadowitz all emerged from there, relatively unscathed.

The London comedy scene expanded at a furious pace after The Comedy Store opened in 1979. Hardee's clubs were highly influential despite being located in Greenwich and not in the centre of town, providing some ammunition for those who liked to insist that south and southeast London was comedy's heartland.

Hardee's antics at his clubs invariably involved urine. He liked to relieve himself in the drinks of audience members who fell asleep. As you might expect, nudity was never far away. Always a favourite at Edinburgh, where his shows would be first in the brochure because they started with ludicrous variations on the expression "Aaargh", Hardee wrote a review of his own show with friend and comic Arthur Smith which *The Scotsman* published under the name of *Guardian* critic William Cook. He also once drove a tractor through a performance by avant-garde artiste Eric Bogosian which he claimed was disturbing his own show. As Smith said of his old friend: "Everything about him was original apart from his stand-up act."

I Stole Freddy Mercury's Birthday Cake (Fourth Estate, 1996). This highly entertaining autobiography gives chapter and verse on all the capers that made Hardee famous in his early criminal days, and is full of puns and pranks. His first-hand impressions on the commercial direction of comedy, especially in Edinburgh, are an important marker in comedy history.

www.malcolmhardee.co.uk

Hattie Hayridge

1955–

If Eddie Izzard is the king of vague, Hattie Hayridge may just be the queen. This tall, blonde, ethereal, apparently shy and downbeat woman has been dubbed "the Morrissey of British comedy", while *The Times Educational Supplement*, no less, applauded her "mastery of the absurd". One of her discoverers, Malcolm Hardee, warned people not to be taken in by first impressions: "She's not as quiet as she looks – some bloke threw an egg at her one night and she went over and punched him."

Hayridge entered comedy in the mid-1980s as a disaffected office worker who, after some Dutch courage, took her chances at

Hattie Hayridge at the mic

an open spot: "I was in my late twenties, temping as a secretary, and my life was going nowhere. I was at a comedy club, they invited members of the audience to have a go – and I did."

Rather than spend time on the more obvious subjects deliberated on by fellow female comedians (periods, male inadequacy, etc), Hayridge crafts pithy one-liners about absurdities that other people never even notice, once asking: "Those signs outside supermarkets: 'No dogs, except guide dogs' – who are they for?"

Ben Elton recognized her talent, saying: "She has terrific material. Lots of people can rant effectively on stage, but well-thought out, witty lines like hers are a rarity." Yet her comedic gifts have not been fully exploited. Her highest-profile TV role, as Holly the computer in four seasons of *Red Dwarf*, made perfect use of her deadpan delivery. Hayridge has written for Jasper Carrott and Rory Bremner and her lesser-known TV work includes the cult sci-fi series *Lexx*.

In 1997 Penguin published her autobiography *Random Abstract Memory*, a nod to her role as Holly, in which she confirms some of the odd events of her family life ("It's quite true that my dad grew cucumbers for a living") and remembers a very strange audition for Edinburgh.

 Random Abstract Memory (Penguin, 2004). Hayridge's autobiography is a breeze of a read. Or you can download it, read by Hayridge, as an MP3 from www.comedymp3.co.uk /catalogue.php?product=23 or buy it on CD.

John Hegley

1953–

Bespectacled poet laureate of comedy John Hegley, along with Arthur Smith and the late Malcolm Hardee, are best summed up with the phrase, "It wouldn't be Edinburgh without..."

Hegley began writing poetry as a boy, then learned the guitar. He started performing while studying European Literature, The History of Ideas and Sociology at Bradford University. When playing his songs, Hegley found, to his pleasant surprise, that some of the lyrics provoked laughter from other students. After leaving university

Hegley worked as a bus conductor and a nurse in a mental hospital, and wrote plays in a kids' theatre – cumulatively, those jobs were perfect training for a comedy audience.

He helped found comedy music group The Popticians, who performed songs about spectacles and the misery of human existence, and recorded sessions for John Peel on Radio 1. He was also part of a double act with magician and comedian Otiz Cannelloni (then working as John Otis) called The Brown Paper Bag Brothers. Hegley first played The Comedy Store in 1980.

Many years – and almost as many Edinburghs – later, Hegley's work rate has not let up in the slightest. He has toured regularly (sometimes with The Popticians) and, on stage and printed page, become ubiquitous as the comedy scene's bard or, as *The Guardian* put it, "that literary rarity – a successful poet". His crown looks secure partly because of his particular genius and partly because there are all too few comic versifiers on the scene today.

A good example of Hegley's work is his short poem "Glasgow", a tale of two people crossing the bridge across the Clyde which ends: "Is there any hope of a bridge over that divide/Stephen/a rope even/or must we remain as strangers/like the Pope and Glasgow Rangers."

One of Hegley's greatest admirers is Dave Gorman, who says: "John Hegley is still the man I most enjoy watching. He was probably the man most responsible for inspiring me to go into comedy and he remains an incredible comic voice. The best comedy isn't about pandering to the audience's sense of humour, it's about persuading them to your sense of humour."

Most of Hegley's comic poetry is available online. The best value is *The Family Pack* which features the particularly enjoyable *Can I Come Down Now Dad?*, complete with odes about Hegley's home town of Luton.

Hegley's most recent CD, *Family Favourites*, includes much of *The Family Pack*. So if you like the words but want to hear the great man reading them, this is for you. The CD is available from Hegley's website.

 www.johnhegley.co.uk

Harry Hill: "I think these headphones were designed for someone taller."

Harry Hill

1964–

When people discover that Harry Hill (real name Matthew Hall) used to be a doctor it makes a bizarre kind of sense. He may have almost patented the words "offbeat", "wacky" and "surreal" but he has a calm authority and good bedside manner with an audience. He has that air of a career professional who has gone to a works do and revealed his wild side during a cabaret.

Hill synthesizes various elements of comedy history in his act with the influences of Eric Morecambe, Benny Hill, The Two Ronnies and The Goodies all discernible as he issues forth manic non-sequiturs like "Name a bird sir! Partridge? No, already been taken!" or conjures up a world where Kinder eggs threaten dolphins, or all of a sudden breaks into hammy versions of pop songs like Kelis's "Milkshake".

He wowed the critics on his Edinburgh debut in 1992 when his show *Flies* carried off the newly created Perrier Best Newcomer Award, and he was nominated for the main award just two years later. On the club circuit Hill built up what comedy author William Cook described as "a bullet-proof gag-rich" club set with cheeky opening lines like: "Well, I've had a terrible week. I've had that, erm, anthrax, have you had that? Diarrhoea, blood in the urine, the liver was disintegrating … and I found the only thing that really helped … was Lemsip. Just took the edge off."

Over the years Hill has created his own comic entourage which includes goofy characters like his adopted son Alan (played by Al Murray) and animal friends like Stouffer the cat and the ubiquitous badgers which so often grace his numerous TV outings. They include

The management

The two main comedy management powerhouses, Avalon and Off The Kerb, are led, respectively, by the headstrong Jon Thoday and Addison Cresswell, both every bit as boisterous and as outspoken as their acts.

Avalon's acts include Frank Skinner, Stewart Lee, Jenny Eclair, Harry Hill, Al Murray and Simon Munnery, while Off The Kerb represents Alan Carr, Lee Evans, Jack Dee, Mark Lamarr, Jeff Green and Rich Hall. Both agencies exert astonishing control over their charges. Cresswell, who started out in comedy after booking acts as a student social secretary, has never been backward in coming forward and told comedy writer William Cook: "I make it my business to really get involved with them, right down to when they're buying a house. I know everything about them."

Knowing everything about them can be read as knowing what is best for them, which explains why Cresswell once forced Jack Dee to do another comedy gig in New York even though he was sick with nerves after bombing at top club Carolines. It might also explain why Avalon famously asked for £20 million to keep Frank Skinner on the BBC.

Off The Kerb, founded in 1981, and Avalon, established in 1989, have become much more important since the late 1980s, to the point where they now have their own television production companies. As Thoday puts it: "We thought it would be better if we set our own production company up rather than giving a tenth of the profits to a company like Hat Trick."

sketch series on BBC2, ITV and Channel 4 and more recently *Harry Hill's TV Burp*, a clips show. His TV outings have been of variable quality, although he won a Silver Rose at the Montreux TV festival for *The All New Harry Hill Show*. He also has the distinction of being invited onto the Letterman show a record six times.

The undisputed king of kitsch, Hill has continued to innovate and prove himself a welcome antidote to straight lad stand-up. His mind works in such mysterious ways it's hard to know what direction he can possibly take next or what he will invent in terms of characters and conceits. In the wrong comic's hands material like his could easily slip into total irrelevance, but no matter how ephemeral his routines seem, Hill manages to keep a firm eye on quality control.

 Harry Hill: Live (2005). This is actually the Harry Hill In Hooves tour, his latest live excursion. Other recordings have failed to capture the warmth of his performances, but this show was particularly feelgood, with a joyous finale of "In The Mood" played on 25 bulb-horns.

 www.harry-hill.tv

The Perrier Awards

Until 1992, there was only one Perrier Award, given to the best comedy show during the Edinburgh Fringe Festival. Then, in recognition that the fierce competition for the award was leaving many new acts overlooked, a Best Newcomer Award was organized in 1992. The Perrier's role as the comedy Oscars has caused some disquiet but, in 2001, the awards became more controversial when comedian Robert Newman called on comics to boycott them because Perrier was part of Nestlé, a conglomerate controversial for selling powdered baby milk in the Third World. Ironically, one of Newman's supporters was Emma Thompson who, as part of Cambridge Footlights, had won the first ever Perrier in 1991. A rival scheme, the Tap Water Award, was launched in 2001 with the backing of some performers, unions and producers, and has been won by, among others, Robert Newman.

1981 Cambridge Footlights – including Stephen Fry, Hugh Laurie, Tony Slattery and Emma Thompson

1982 Writers Inc.

1983 Los Trios Ringbarkus

1984 The Brass Band

1985 Theatre De Complicité

1986 Ben Keaton

1987 Brown Blues (Arnold Brown and Jungr and Parker)

1988 Jeremy Hardy

1989 Simon Fanshawe

1990 Sean Hughes

1991 Frank Skinner

1992 Steve Coogan, with John Thomson
Best newcomer Harry Hill

1993 Lee Evans
Best newcomer Dominic Holland

1994 Lano and Woodley
Best newcomer Scott Capurro

1995 Jenny Eclair
Best newcomer Tim Vine

1996 Dylan Moran
Best newcomer Milton Jones

1997 The League of Gentlemen
Best newcomer Arj Barker

1998 Tommy Tiernan
Best newcomer The Mighty Boosh

1999 Al Murray
Best newcomer Ben 'n' Arn

2000 Rich Hall
Best newcomer Noble and Silver

2001 Garth Marenghi's Netherhead
Best newcomer Let's Have A Shambles

2002 Daniel Kitson
Best newcomer The Consultants

2003 Demetri Martin
Best newcomer Gary Le Strange

2004 Jackson's Way
Best newcomer Wil Hodgson

2005 Laura Solon
Best newcomer Tim Minchin

Sean Hughes

1965–

Among those comedians who most influenced his move into political comedy, Robert Newman has, in interviews, picked out Sean Hughes. Although Hughes was no radical, Newman credits his confessional style of comedy as inspiring his journey away from teen humour into comedy with a conscience.

Hughes's lyrical style and ability to go deeper than many rivals may stem from his restless childhood. He was moved from school to school and although he was the class clown, he is quoted as saying that his childhood was "unbearable" because of his unsatisfactory relationships with his peers and his parents. No wonder a fair slice of Hughes' material is based on childhood foibles and mishaps.

As with many a comic, a visit to The Comedy Store proved the damascene moment in Hughes's conversion to stand-up and an escape from the usual dead-end jobs. Hughes started on the London circuit in 1987 and, in 1990, when he was just 25, he became the youngest ever winner of the Perrier Award.

There was a childlike charm and gentle reflection about many of Hughes' routines, though he was no soft touch and was perfectly capable of putting down hecklers. His boundless imagination never travelled into surrealism but his delivery was very much stream of consciousness and touched on some sublime absurdities. He once suggested the Nazis could have been defeated by adolescent spies who would baffle interrogators by answering questions thus: "Where were you? "Out." "Who were you with?" "You wouldn't know them." "What were you doing?" "Nothin'." "We can't crack them!"

Of Hughes' various television appearances his sitcom/stand-up hybrid *Sean's Show* (Channel 4, 1992) was a good crossover effort. Yet most critics overlooked the nice set pieces and motifs such as his protracted goodbyes at the end of phone conversations with his mother to dismiss it as a poor clone of the American sitcom *It's The Garry Shandling Show!*

Hughes' other noteworthy credits away from stand-up include being a team captain on *Never Mind The Buzzcocks*, and appearing in *Art* and *As You Like It* in the West End, in *The Last Detective* on television (with Peter Davison), and in the movies *The Commitments* and *The Butcher Boy*. Hughes has written two novels and had three collections of stories and poems published.

 Sean Hughes Live (1995, Laughing Stock). Recorded in Glasgow this is Hughes's "turning 30" album. But it's not all doom and gloom, and routines range freely from ageing to sport. The Olympics comes in for a ribbing, with Hughes's trademark laconic take on the more bizarre examples of sporting endeavour.

www.pbjmgt.co.uk/clients/sean_hughes/ is his management company's website.

Reginald D. Hunter
1969–

Reginald D. Hunter has lived in the UK for nearly a decade now but has lost none of his gentlemanly, southern-American charm. Born in Georgia, Hunter moved to the UK to study at RADA. Hunter's comedy career started almost accidentally when he accepted a bet at a London club to do an open spot.

In some ways, Hunter is an unlikely comedian. His relaxed drawl is neither deadpan nor laddish. His demeanour is gentle, and sometimes his take on race, sex and class can be endearing rather than revealing, but at other times his material packs a sucker punch.

He can deliberately make his audience feel uncomfortable, as when he asked who the audience thought was more likely to beat up their girlfriend – a white man or a black one? Many of his gigs have a confessional feel, in particular his 2003 *White Woman* show where he admits to being fixated with the imagery of white women, a revelation that leads to obvious notions of how they would behave in his company. He has also memorably poked fun at those who maintain they are blind to racial distinction: "Sometimes you see someone's colour before you can tell if they are a man or a woman."

For his show in 2002, *I Said What I Said*, Hunter was attacked by Alex O'Connell, then *The Times*' comedy critic, for being "flagrantly misogynist and enforcing racial stereotypes of black people" to which she added a year later, that he had "a lot of problems in terms of women and race". Others think that Hunter is striving for a more honest approach to race and sex. The point of the *White Woman* show, for example, was to examine his reaction to women, expose fears and move on.

Hunter subverts previous notions about gender and race, without pigeonholing anyone. This explains his reluctance to get behind the shortlived Richard Pryor Award. He branded the award "racist" and accused it of lowering the bar, saying: "If you are a comedian, don't you want to be the best comedian not the best black comedian or the best female comedian, just the best?"

Reginald D. Hunter saying what he says

www.reginalddhunter.co.uk. More famous comics should have sites like this: there's a collection of reviews, a reasonable biography section and a good selection of clips.

Lee Hurst

1963–

Despite leaving *They Think It's All Over* back in 1998 Lee Hurst is still most recognizable to the public at large as a panellist on BBC1's popular comedy sports game. Yet Hurst felt that the show didn't reflect his style of comedy and quit, "unhappy and exhausted", amid rumours he had fallen out with co-star Gary Lineker.

Hurst has since declared that "the trouble with television is the talent goes and the shit stays" but the exposure and financial benefits from the show allowed him to start the Backyard Club in Bethnal Green. Opened in 1998, the club has become one of London's premier comedy venues, getting past a sticky point where punters would turn up in hope, mainly, that Hurst himself would be performing. When the Backyard was threatened with closure in 2003 the bald-headed jester said he might enter the race for London mayor to publicize his cause. He even laid the floor of the club using the skills he had learnt as a builder. (Hurst didn't go into comedy until he was 27.)

Hurst's role as compere hasn't stifled his act. He is on stage for as much time as any of the three comics on the bill. Among the more memorable examples of his keen-eyed material is his take on women sharing frontline duties in the army. Likening conflict to a scrap outside the pub, he has the female army members chorusing: "Leave it sergeant major, he's not worth it!" A perfect Friday or Saturday night-out joke that also suggests the futility of conflict as much as any gender stereotyping.

Now in his forties, Hurst has experienced some eventful gigs in his career. In 2000, at a convention of young farmers in Blackpool, one of the crowd squirted Hurst with a water pistol and a fracas ensued. Some years earlier at the Leicester Comedy Festival, Hurst had to struggle against an allergy bringing on his asthma: "When I went out on stage I was light-headed and the audience was spinning. I finished the show and made it to the dressing room. They were calling for an encore and I was virtually collapsed on the floor, I couldn't go back on." More seriously the comic has had to battle against ankylosing spondylitis, a debilitating spinal condition that only affects one percent of the population.

 Live At The Backyard Comedy Club (1998). Hurst on form, literally in his own Backyard. Though no substitute for seeing him compere live, the DVD gives some flavour of Hurst's enthusiasm and cheeky charm.

 www.leehurst.com

Cult comedy: the coolest live acts

1. Eddie Izzard

Without question the showman of comedy. Lavish stage and stadium sets don't, however, distract from his own inspired moments.

2. Daniel Kitson

Just set him off and watch him go, Kitson has no problem filling ninety minutes with memorable observations and witty repartee with the audience.

3. Andrew Maxwell

Extremely skilled, cocky but engaging Irish comedian makes for an excellent compere who more than holds his own for short club sets and longer Edinburgh sets.

4. Alan Carr

Carr is now known to a wider audience thanks to Channel 4's *Friday Night Project*, but the TV limelight only really shows up half this comic's charm.

5. Robert Newman

Prepare to have your comedy boundaries challenged and to absorb some lesser-known facts about global politics at a rate that would outstrip even exam cramming.

6. Ross Noble

The sweat that covers Noble's shirt at the end of his performances is testimony to the effort he brings to his surrealist comedy.

7. Mark Watson

Using his Welsh persona as part of his shtick, Watson's wizardry involves making a slightly existential outlook come over as charming and inclusive.

8. Jerry Sadowitz

The Sadowitz experience is feeling the full force of his ire. The anger he puts into his punchlines can make them funnier than the gag itself.

9. Brendon Burns

The unpredictable, energetic raucous Aussie is a favourite on his adopted UK circuit, though he's not to everyone's tastes.

10. Tim Vine

Vine's endless collection of quickfire puns are so uncool that he becomes cool again. He may make you groan but he is far more likely to make you laugh out loud.

Eddie Izzard
1962–

Expat comedy

Eddie Izzard's famous gigs in French in the 1990s were a reminder that comedy really does cross borders. In 1994, Izzard played a venue – the Laughing Matters in Paris – that programmes comedy today. Elsewhere in Europe, a club night opened in 2003 at the music venue Scimmie in Milan with a performance by Ross Noble. Meanwhile in Germany – not the comedy-free zone it is lampooned as – The Comedy Store programmes a night in Berlin. Other British comedy nights happen in Brussels, Antwerp and Amsterdam. It's a veritable European Mirth Union.

Arguably Britain's most iconic comedian, retaining more genuine credibility than Ben Elton, though not as flavour of the month as Ricky Gervais is after *The Office*, Eddie Izzard made the transition from one-time street performer in Covent Garden to fringe Hollywood star almost without the aid of the small screen.

Born in Aden, South Yemen in 1962, Izzard had an unsettled childhood. His father worked for BP and Izzard lived in Belfast, South Wales and East Sussex. His mother died when he was 6. The effect of this loss on him and his father he describes as "emotional compression", saying once: "We don't get too elated by things because we've had bad stuff happen and more shit could be just around the corner. But we don't get too depressed either. We quite like pootling around but try to be more windswept and interesting, as Billy Connolly once said." Therein lies the key to his act and the state of mind that produces it.

The undisputed "king of vague", Izzard's trademark flights of improvised and surreal fancy have been compared to a jazz musician jamming. The high notes include routines ruminating on such topics as catering on the Death Star, the fine line between cool and "looking like a dickhead" (where he uses James Dean chewing one match as his baseline for cool and where it would all go wrong if he were to chew two matches) and deep questions such as whether earwigs make chutney. Even his below-par routines can have a mesmeric effect on audiences and he is one of the few comics loved equally by men and women.

Gender issues are crucial to Izzard's shtick. In 1991, Izzard came out as a transvestite, a move which only enhanced the popularity he was quickly building up either onstage or indeed, judging by his comments at the time, offstage: "Women seem to like a boy in a skirt. I am very, very happy about that." He has also described himself as a "lesbian trapped in a man's body".

Despite his early gallop towards fame – he sold out a six-week West End run back in 1993 – Izzard has only really graced the small screen on chat shows. He did make a sitcom for Channel 4, but the project, *Cows*, failed to get past the pilot stage. Izzard has more often succumbed to the lure of the silver screen, most notably appearing in the lavish but vacuous *Velvet Goldmine* opposite Christian Bale and playing a lascivious Charlie Chaplin in Peter Bogdanovich's *Cat's Meow* (2003).

As well as his award-winning live shows, such as *Definite Article* (1995), Izzard was superb in the title role in Sir Peter Hall's production of *Lenny* (1991), the life story of Lenny Bruce, described by one critic as: "An outstanding comedian played by an outstanding comedian."

 Happily, most of Izzard's live shows are available on DVD, with the pick of them being *Definite Article* (1997). The priceless routines include "Pavlov's Cat", a lovely take on how this infamous experiment would have given exasperating results had cats been the subjects rather than dogs.

 www.eddieizzard.com is his official website, while www. auntiemomo.com/cakeordeath/ is a fine fan site.

Milton Jones

1964–

Like Tim Vine, Milton Jones is an out-and-out gagsmith. While Vine's one-liners are silly, Jones's lines are more surreal. Both have won the Perrier Newcomer Award (Vine in 1995, Jones in 1996) and both deserve to be more widely recognized for their comic genius.

While his dishevelled appearance (he dressed in pyjamas for his 2004 Edinburgh show), dazed manner and eclectic clothes suggest a dope, Jones is really very sharp. He likes to juxtapose two titles to create a link the audience can't believe they had never spotted: "Tell me, if you're an earl and you get an OBE do you become an earlobe?"

At other times you can virtually see the craftsmanship that goes into forming a joke without necessarily seeing the sum of its parts in the punchline: "I'd just like to say to the old man who was wearing camouflage gear and using crutches and who took my wallet earlier today – you can hide but you can't run."

During his act, Jones uses lines you expect to hear from any regular stand-up on the circuit but inverts them to make a stock

Gagsmith Milton Jones

joke far more original: "You know when you're in a relationship – what's that like?"

The pitfall with acts like Vine and Jones is that an hour-long slot, the standard duration at Edinburgh, can be hard to sustain year in year out. *The Guardian* critic Brian Logan said as much in his 2004 review of Jones's performance but admitted: "I've no quibble with the quality of his mind-bending quips." In that particular show Jones mixed up proceedings with sketches and a hilarious routine where he bakes a cake with the help of pop songs from the 1980s.

Jones, like Vine, hasn't broken into the more popular outlets for comedy on television, with shoestring comedy show *Planet Mirth* and *The Strangerers*, the first homegrown sitcom on Sky One, again on a sci-fi theme, among his credits. Such televisual obscurity is, for fans of his stand-up, utterly irrelevant. One comedy-goer on Chortle noted: "If only this guy wrote the gags for crackers – Christmas would be a happy occasion."

Phil Kay
1969–

If Johnny Vegas can be described as variable, Phil Kay is positively unpredictable. That unpredictability, of course, is his shtick and, although a framework is in place to channel Kay's rambling thoughts, it can all go very wrong or he can go down a storm. It's a roller-coaster ride with Kay and two people can come out of the same gig with completely opposite views of his performance.

Described by Jerry Sadowitz as "an anorexic Billy Connolly", there are few comedians whose state of mind is quite so accurately reflected by their appearance. Kay's straggly hair and dishevelled demeanour reinforce his image as a rougher-edged precursor to Ross Noble. Both men will pick up any interaction with an audience member, sound or disturbance and riff on it. If the riff is strong enough it can be repeated but often Kay will go completely "freestyle" and lose the plot – as much as there is a plot for Kay's stories.

After his 2002 Edinburgh Show, *Branding The Ass Of A Heckler*, Steve Bennett, who runs the Chortle website, said of one Kay rou-

The Melbourne comedy festival

When Phil Kay wowed the 2006 Melbourne Comedy Festival, partly by the simple gimmick of borrowing the left shoe of every child in the audience, he was far from the first British comedian to make an impact at this event.

The festival was originally conceived by Peter Cook and Barry Humphries as a way of showcasing Southern Australia's native comic talent. But the Melbourne International Comedy Festival is now, alongside the Edinburgh Fringe and Montreal's Just For Laughs, one of the world's largest comedy gatherings.

Over 300,000 people flock to the city every April and May, Australia's autumn, to watch a variety of stand-up, cabaret, street performance and theatrical events. The festival started in 1987 and has, over the years, established its own traditions and accolades.

Popular events include The Gala, an evening of buffet-style comedy from a range of international performers, broadcast across Australia, and The Great Debate, a battle of comic wits that is almost as old as the festival itself. Outstanding performers are given Barry awards, in Humphries' honour. Alongside the traditional elements of a comedy festival, Melbourne also celebrates comic short films, and puts on an event called Class Clowns, in which the next generation of young Australian comics can prove their mettle.

tine: "When he hits a fertile seam, he flies – on this night he conjured up an inspired routine about the *Play School* toys simply from the hissing of the bar's drinks pumps. But surely the room shouldn't have been quite so silent that this low-level noise was a distraction in the first place."

The consensus is that the comic fire which burned so brightly for the decade after Kay first came to prominence in 1989, winning the So You Think You're Funny Award in Edinburgh, has petered out. In the 1990s, his Channel 4 series *Phil Kay Feels*, where each episode has a loose title (such as "Natural", "Lovely" or "Technical") that framed his creative babbling, was enjoyably off the wall. But his shows in the last five years or so have elicited not accolades but vociferous criticism.

Daniel Kitson

1978–

Daniel Kitson puts the rope back into misanthrope and ties up his willing audiences, leading them wherever he wants to go. That direction is usually towards the bittersweet experience of love. Of balancing this sentiment with his demeanour he says: "I don't think that misanthropy and compassion are mutually exclusive. I think it comes from having faith in the humanity of individuals. As a race we're pretty fucked, but individuals are still beautiful. Yes, most people are cunts, but I don't think that's a depressing point of view, it just heightens the quality of the few."

Looking every inch the 1970s student radical with his unkempt beard and lank long hair, Kitson tells jokes with no gimmicks, no message, no agenda. Kitson's intelligence lies in the way jokes are constructed, the asides and the follow-ups, not necessarily the subject matter.

Between 2000 and 2005, Kitson had a run of successful Edinburgh festivals, winning the Perrier in 2002. In 2003, he abandoned the stand-up format and went with a collection of simple stories about a nocturnal girl, a lovelorn boy, a suicidal man, a bus driver and so on. The show achieved mixed reviews and he brandished the least flattering review, tearing into it in a blaze of trademark foul-mouthed fury, at the one festival stand-up spot he did outside of his actual show.

Kitson appeared in Peter Kay's *Phoenix Nights* as Spencer, the glass collector ("I hated it") but has never been tempted back onto TV since. He fears over-exposure, and has shirked the Fringe's larger venues for the same reason.

Sometimes he performs with his notebook, claiming that by referring to it he is cocking a snook at the rules of comedy, "or is it that some comedians are professional and have a modicum of respect for their audiences?" That depends, he concludes, on which way you pronounce potato. Fellow comic Chris Addison calls Kitson "an annoyingly effortless genius with a brilliant facility for language which isn't all that common in a stand-up".

An audio recording of Kitson's stand-up is scheduled for release shortly.

www.danielkitson.com

Mark Lamarr

1967–

"He's a Fifties throwback", as Vic Reeves would lovingly point out when Mark Lamarr was a team captain on the absurd game show *Shooting Stars*. The quiffed comedian started out over a decade earlier, discovered when his teen poem "Too Fast To Live, Too Young To Work" was picked up and published in a Faber anthology. Lamarr had moved to London by then, leaving his native Swindon with alacrity, and the poem earned him his first appearance on stage at The Royal Court Theatre, as part of a young writers festival. Soon afterwards, he was making his way on the comedy circuit.

Lamarr's stand-up style always relied heavily on confrontational episodes (one fellow comic calls him an "eloquent bully") giving him a rare edge and intensity for a post-alternative comedian. Exchanges with hecklers often made up the bulk of his act. At times, Lamarr got his teeth into someone and ended up crucifying himself rather than the heckler. Yet when he was on a roll, he was unstoppable. His inspired put-downs could destroy someone. At one gig in Harlow, Lamarr paid so much attention to one heckler that the punter's girlfriend complained to the comedian afterwards.

His uncompromising style led to inevitable fracas but held him in good stead for the unenviable task of co-presenting slapdash youth magazine programme *The Word*. He memorably walked off the set when rap star Shabba Ranks was expounding his views on crucifying homosexuals.

That Lamarr managed to come out of *The Word* unscathed and looking like a hero is to his credit, yet his tailor-made TV vehicles, such as *Leaving The Twentieth Century*, have failed to impress and his stand-up show was running out of steam by the late 1990s. As a team captain on *Shooting Stars* and question master on *Never Mind The Buzzcocks* Lamarr found a good groove and has enjoyed, in the literal sense, more good grooves on Radio 2 where his show *Shake Rattle And Roll* has acquired cult status.

 Finding *Never Mind The Buzzcocks* or *Shooting Stars* on video, let alone DVD, is harder than you might expect. Though these are the best examples of Lamarr's work, try to find *Mark Lamarr: Uncensored And Live* (1997), his only stand-up video. Some of the routines are beyond unsubtle (especially the gags about alternative poses for the queen on a banknote), but you can see why catching him live was quite an event. The same set is available, secondhand, on cassette.

www.offthekerb.co.uk/artists/a_artists_home.jsp?artist= mark_lamarr is his management site.

Gary Le Strange
1971–

Waen Shepherd's creation of Gary Le Strange, the self-styled Byronic Lord of Pop, is a fantastic musical and fashion mix of Adam Ant, Gary Numan and David Bowie, and gives more than a nod to other New Romantics (especially Visage and Spandau Ballet). His songs tackle such urgent topics as dandies, geometry and shop window dummies, while he sports a hybrid costume of kilt, ruffled blouse, a glammed up Sergeant Pepper jacket and face paint.

Among the tracks he showcased in his 2003 Edinburgh show (which won the Perrier Best Newcomer Award) was "Is My Toaster Sentient?", a great tribute to Numan in which the pop prince asked other such pointed questions as "Is my telephone autistic?". In the following year's show, *Face Academy*, he was in Bowie mode as "a Nazi homosexual injecting morphine in a Berlin brothel".

Between songs, Le Strange reveals the ups and, more frequently, the downs of his musical career and gives his unique view on the art form and on life: "I don't like going to watch other people play music. I always find myself shouting at them. I don't really like loud things either because they make my ears pop."

Creator Waen Shepherd started on the circuit as a stand-up poet, contributing to Simon Munnery's Club Zarathustra. The road to Le Strange began after Shepherd built a collection of characters work-

Waen Shepherd pouting as Gary Le Strange

ing either solo or with Simon Farnaby. One of his early characters was William Whicker, a ranting northerner with a penchant for smashing up Cornish pasties.

Le Strange has clocked up a few radio and TV credits, including a curious, seemingly semi-autobiographical fifteen-minute film called *Origen's Wake*, in which he starred with Mackenzie Crook from *The Office*. He has also co-written and narrated an animation for Channel 4 called *The Wolfman* that was remade into a Sony Playstation ad.

In 2005, Le Strange started his own club night at cult comedy venue The Albany on Great Portland Street, London. The club showcases new music from Le Strange and includes numerous other sketch character acts Shepherd has worked with before.

 Two albums, *Face Academy* and *Polaroid Suitcase*, are available from Le Strange's website (see below). *Polaroid Suitcase* contains "Grey", an ode to the dispirited Prince of Pop, cramming in as many references to 1980s fads and fashions as possible: "Leaning in a darkened underpass/With a robot made of glass/ In a pinstripe suit, a Pierrot hat and a David Niven tash."

www.garylestrange.co.uk

The deadpan Stewart Lee

Stewart Lee

1968–

Fellow comedian Arthur Smith rightly describes Stewart Lee as the "eminence grise of comedy". Waen Shepherd, better known as his alter ego Gary Le Strange, describes Lee as "idiosyncratic, courageous, and brilliantly clever with a killer sense of timing". Many live comedy fans cherish Lee because, unlike so many of his predecessors, he hasn't sold out.

Lee's career started in the 1980s with Oxford University revue group The Seven Raymonds alongside his future partner Richard Herring. Lee and Herring wrote material for Chris Morris's *On The Hour*, while writing and performing their own shows *Lionel Nimrod's Inexplicable World* (Radio 4) and *Fist Of Fun* (Radio 1). *Fist Of Fun* crossed over onto BBC2, with *This Morning With Richard Not Judy* following in 1997. The duo were mooted as the "next Newman and Baddiel" but the rock'n'roll comedy boom had already begun to dissipate before their double act – Lee permanently deadpan, Herring ever-affable – could become a household name.

Lee even contemplated quitting stand-up, claiming boredom, and deliberately junked his act to force himself to work harder to improve it. Yet he has consistently had a hand in successful comedy ventures, such as directing The Mighty Boosh and working with Simon Munnery, before earning a place in the comedy history books by collaborating with composer Richard Thomas on *Jerry Springer The Opera*.

The stage show was a smash but, as the furore over alleged blasphemy mounted, Lee received death threats. Typically, he turned his experiences into a set for his 2005 Edinburgh show, where he recounted how Jesus sacrifices himself to Lee so he can avail himself of the excesses of a drunken evening. The routine has many of the Lee trademarks; a slow build-up of repeated actions and punchlines relating to other routines.

At its most indulgent, Lee's work requires a patient audience. You can see the crafting taking place and a live work in progress will always be hit and miss, especially as Lee deliberately pushes himself and the audience. With Lee, you live dangerously waiting to see if the craftsman will come up with the goods. More often than not he does.

 Stewart Lee: Standup Comedian (2005). This set conveys Lee's best and worst points. The Glasgow audience and Lee keep each other on their toes as he delights some and baffles others with his attempts to make stand-up an art form, not just an attitude. Also check out *Jerry Springer The Opera* (2005).

 www.stewartlee.co.uk and www.leeandherring.com

Andrew Maxwell

1974–

This charming, cocky Irishman is one of the most skilled practitioners of pure stand-up on the circuit. Born into a Protestant family in Dublin, Andrew Maxwell is at the younger end of a long line of successful comics emanating from Ardal O'Hanlon's Comedy Cellar that included Dylan Moran, Barry Murphy, Alex Lyons, Dermot Carmoody, Kevin Gildea and Jo Rooney.

As Maxwell recalls: "All these guys were 28, 29 and I was 18 when I started, they all had university educations and I was a rough. I was dressed in hooded tops and baseball tops. They thought who's this little car thief among us? But they'd put me on and all were really supportive when I came to London where I'd stay at Dylan's place, and Ardal would get me gigs."

Despite such support, Maxwell considered quitting at one point, but he stuck with it and has, in recent years, put together some top-quality sets, most notably his 2004 Edinburgh show, *This Is My Hour*, which married political themes with personal experience to great effect.

In *This Is My Hour*, Maxwell agitates the conservative lobby on both sides of the Atlantic many times, most skilfully when he leaves them in a quandary about teenage mothers: "They are paying for the older generations to come, we're all right because we have slags!" He also has a very stylish way with a heckler, famously reducing one to tears as a warm-up for the Jonathan Ross show.

Though Maxwell has a happy-go-lucky style that rarely errs on the whimsical, there are times when perhaps he relaxes too much, clearly enjoying what he does. More often than not his focused enthusiasm carries an audience with him, such as his routine about the lure of cheap flights to Baghdad.

Maxwell is now a veteran of five Edinburgh Festivals and was hotly tipped to receive a nomination for his 2005 show, though in part this could be seen as making up for not being nominated the previous year. Maxwell did triumph in Channel 4's *Kings Of Comedy* reality show, which pitched Maxwell, Boothby Graffoe, Janey Godley, Scott Capurro and Ava Vidal against old-school comics Stan Boardman and Mick Miller, and was awarded his own TV series.

 www.andrew-maxwell.com

Paul Merton

1957–

If improvised comedy has a figurehead it is Paul Merton. Originally known by his real name, Paul Martin, he became Merton after choosing a stage name based on the London Borough he came from. He made his debut at The Comedy Store in 1982 and became part of the furniture with The Comedy Store Players. Today, Merton is most famous as the "little boy lost" figurehead of cult topical TV game show *Have I Got News For You* where, even allowing for rehearsal time, his quickfire wit on an impressive variety of subjects remains fresh and spontaneous.

He was inspired to become a comic as a boy, watching clowns at the circus and, on only his second or third night at The Comedy Store in 1982, found the dour persona that has served him so well. Things didn't always go well for him on the stand-up circuit, but he could usually rely on his routine about a policeman who has been slipped an ecstasy tablet in the course of his duties (referred to as a "smartie") and starts to hallucinate, with hilarious results.

Hallucinations, as Merton later discovered, are not always hilarious. Afflicted by mental illness in 1990, he started to imagine conversations between friends. He spent six weeks in the Maudesley hospital where he had to convince one of the medical staff he really was a TV personality by showing him a tape of a show. The episode was probably due to overwork: at the time he was performing on Channel 4's *Whose Line Is It Anyway?* and Radio 4's *Just A Minute*, as well as writing *Sticky Moments* with Julian Clary and masterminding his own sketch show, again on Channel 4.

Like many of the best comedians, Merton is no stranger to tragedy and bad luck. In 1986, while performing in Edinburgh, he was mugged so badly he ended up in hospital. In 1987, as his own show started to gain acclaim, he broke his leg during a football match with fellow comedians. His second trip to hospital was more serious, as he suffered a pulmonary embolism, contracted hepatitis A and went into a coma.

The Comedy Store was to prove a source of strength for him when, in 2003, his second wife, Sarah Parkinson died of breast cancer aged 41. Before marrying Parkinson, Merton had been married to comic actress Caroline Quentin and he is now in a relationship with another comedian, Suki Webster, who regularly appears with Merton in The Comedy Store Players.

His Channel 4 sketch show was hit and miss but occasionally as inspired as *Q*, the Spike Milligan series which had so obviously inspired Merton's series. He teamed up with Galton and Simpson on ITV to re-create some of their best vintage comedies, but succeeded only in proving that he is not the new Tony Hancock. His speciality, on *Have I Got News For You?*, is to indulge in surrealist riffs that expose the absurdities of contemporary life. On a story about plane crash victims, he wondered: "I'm always amazed to hear of air crash victims so badly mutilated that they have to be identified by their dental records. What I can't understand is, if they don't know who you are, how do they know who your dentist is?"

Have I Got News For You? The Best Of The Guest Presenters (2003). The episodes of the post-Deayton era have some intriguing guest presenters. Paul Merton even took the chair himself once. His sketch series and *Whose Line Is It Anyway?* are still available on video.

The Mighty Boosh
Noel Fielding (1973–) and Julian Barratt (1968–)

The general consensus about The Mighty Boosh, named indirectly after a hairstyle, is that they push their twee but charming brand of fantastical comedy to its limit but somehow get away with it.

Julian Barratt and Noel Fielding met in 1997 when a friend of Fielding's urged him to see Barratt on the circuit because "he talks absolute shit like you do". Barratt noticed Fielding at a lot of his gigs and suggested he do an open spot. When that went down well, he asked Fielding if he wanted to write "the new *Goodies*". The Goodies can't agree on how much of an influence they are on the duo, but both acts share a fascination with animals. The Boosh's work has featured many talking animals, including a lecherous yeti, boxing kangaroos, a wolfman who sounds like Clint Eastwood and so on.

Fielding has explained that the pair really stumbled on comedy: "When we tried to make a show we didn't really think it out to be just jokes. We didn't know what it could be, so we just started writing all sorts of things – songs, poems – and started doing stuff live where we got a girl on stage and Julian used to sing to her and we used to try and make her cry on stage so we could get her tear and put it into a smoothie. It was because we were naïve and didn't know much about comedy that we were trying stuff like that. And it was kind of working, so we just continued to do stuff like that."

Comedically, The Boosh owe as much to early Reeves and Mortimer and Eddie Izzard, although they have also been likened to a David Lynch movie with a Pink Floyd soundtrack – a comparison that was intended as a compliment.

The first Boosh TV series (on BBC3 and then BBC2 in 2004) cast the curly-haired Barratt and glam-rock-styled Fielding as zookeepers Howard Moon and Vince Noir, the characters they have played in successive Edinburgh shows since they won the Perrier for Best Newcomer in 1998. Barratt/Moon is a world-weary, anguished genius while Fielding/Noir is a cheeky, spacey and seemingly green partner-in-crime who always comes up trumps.

In 1999, The Boosh were nominated for the actual Perrier Award for *Arctic Boosh*, in which they played bored postal workers on a trippy, mystical journey in a frozen wasteland. In 2000, with *AutoBoosh*, they were outward-bound explorers encountering spooky hitchhikers.

Outside The Boosh, both Fielding and Barratt have appeared in Chris Morris's sitcom *Nathan Barley*. Barratt's role as disillusioned journalist Dan Ashcroft was one of the enduring features of the otherwise low-key comedy. Meanwhile, the last series of *The Mighty Boosh*, produced by Steve Coogan and Henry Normal's Baby Cow, was the first television series to be streamed over the Internet.

The Mighty Boosh – their jokes are better than their shirts

The Mighty Boosh Series 1 And 2 (2006) was released just as The Boosh's 2006 tour gathered steam. The dynamic between the two is almost as good on screen as it is live and their comedy benefits from the extra range television provides.

www.themightyboosh.com

Dylan Moran
1971–

At the end of some live shows, Dylan Moran does a joke about "Irish hair", pushing back his jet-black locks to show a high forehead and a "bad hair day" pose. The gag is a rare moment of wackiness from a man better known for his misanthropic musings, who thinks street beggars look like a "slouched" version of him and has nothing but disdain for modern life.

Moran set out on his comedy career when he was 20, inspired by Ardal O'Hanlon's success, and often playing the Comedy Cellar, the Dublin comedy club O'Hanlon had helped found. Before turning to comedy, Moran had, by his own admission, not done much except "develop acne, work on being awkward and write toxically bad poetry". His performing gamble soon paid off. In 1996, when he was just 25, he won the Perrier Award.

Moran's onstage persona is not so far removed from the drunken, charismatic, miserablist Bernard Black he plays in the sitcom *Black Books* (Channel 4, 2002–2004). Moran is more likely to be drinking Guinness or whiskey on stage than red wine (as Black does) but both character and comic seem to be permanently dragging on a cigarette.

As a comedian, Moran subtly breathes new life into popular observations, for example, a woman's ability to drop everything to comfort someone at the first sound of a sigh, as opposed to men who need more dramatic signs. He has been criticized for lacking range on these matters, with *The Guardian* huffing: "If there's one thing less funny than the differences between men and women, it's stand-up comics who reflect on them." Yet Moran's deft touch can turn simple moments into gold, as when he observed: "You know it's a sad day when your child looks at you and asks 'Daddy, are these organic?'"

Despite having many movie credits to his name, including *Shaun Of The Dead* and *A Cock And Bull Story*, and having starred in the BAFTA-award-winning *Black Books*, Moran is, he says, "about as famous as a fourth division footballer in the 1970s".

 Dylan Moran Live (2004). Moran's only DVD so far rambles delightfully through Iraq, children, Irish news, modern technology, the French, alcohol, cookery programmes, the Smurfs and how his parents' generation got free love and the Rolling Stones and his got AIDS and MC Hammer.

 www.dylanmoranrules.com is a good fan site.

Simon Munnery
1966–

Simon Munnery is one of the finest exponents of character comedy. The various guises of his career have echoed the origins of cabaret in their intimate relationship with the audience and their experimental feel. Malcolm Hardee always felt that Munnery's work was fuelled by anger: "He is what people call a comic genius and he is a genius on the Mensa scale. He could have been a nuclear physicist. But he's better as a comic. Better to get his anger out in comedy than in making bombs."

A natural sciences graduate from Cambridge, Munnery usurped the standard Footlights route and came to prominence in the early 1990s as Alan Parker Urban Warrior, a character based on 1970s punk heroes Sham '69 and The Clash, who saw himself as "the most left wing person in the world". One of Parker's most memorable maxims was his cry: "People of Briterrrrrrrrrn! Don't let them trample you into the ground! Trample *yourselves* into the ground! Then blame them."

Munnery had a successful run on Radio 1 with *Alan Parker's 29 Minutes Of Truth*, crossing over onto television with *Saturday Live* (1996 version), an unsuccessful attempt to resurrect the decade-old show which didn't work, even if Munnery did impress alongside co-hosts Harry Hill and Lee Hurst.

The next discernible stage in Munnery's work was *The League*

Simon Munnery: "He could have been a nuclear physicist"

Against Tedium, a project that brought together the comedy talents of Stewart Lee, Johnny Vegas, Kevin Eldon and Sally Phillips. The League's Club Zarathustra had Munnery bedecked in preposterous Napoleonic military gear. Fusing Nietzche, Beckett, Kierkegaard and Kafka, he would deliver such memorable one-liners as: "Many are willing to suffer for their art, few are prepared to learn to draw" and "Supposing conventional wisdom to be a forest … I am a chainsaw … You are squirrels."

The League was critically acclaimed, enjoying both radio and TV outings. In recent years Munnery has suffered personally with cancer and professionally with some of his new work being indifferently received, though his cult following remains strong. His *Annual General Meeting* at Edinburgh in 2002 got mixed reviews, while his *Buckethead* venture, a play about buckets, was criticized as rambling, although it did inspire Bruce Dessau to call Munnery "the missing link between Ionesco and Kenny Everett".

Character comedian Waen Shepherd says that Munnery, by sticking to his guns, hasn't always got the recognition he deserves. "I first saw him in Edinburgh in 1991, playing Wagner out of his arse while inflating a huge plastic penis and grinning manically. That performance taught me anything is possible in the name of comedy, and I've never forgotten that."

Beyond the pail

Simon Munnery will never forget the Big Chill Festival at the Larmer Tree Gardens near Salisbury in 2001. As is his wont, he entered the stage in the cabaret tent for his 1am slot with a bucket on his head and stood in silence for ten seconds. The quiet was interrupted by a shout of "Oi mate" from a punter. After two further shouts of "Oi mate", Munnery finally broke his silence and asked: "What?" The dialogue carried on as follows.

Punter: You should get out a bit more.

Munnery: Why's that?

Punter: You need some sun.

Munnery: Why do you say that?

Punter: You're looking a little pail.

At that point, Munnery and his bucket vibrated in silent giggling.

The pick of the CDs available from the website below is *Alan Parker Urban Warrior: Blast From The Past*. Recorded between 1993 and 1997, these were the best days of Munnery and his character. As well as the punk prophet's usual epigrams, the CD features Stewart Lee on guitar and Al Murray on drums.

www.leagueagainsttedium.co.uk

Al Murray

1968–

Twelve years after his creation, Al Murray's Pub Landlord character continues to serve "pints for the fellas and wine for ladies". Along the way the patriotic publican's bar room bravura has been rewarded with a Royal Variety Performance, an *Audience With* show on ITV and a Perrier Award.

A descendant of William Makepeace Thackeray, Murray studied history at Oxford and became involved in the Oxford Revue with Stewart Lee, Richard Herring and Ben Moor. As well as writing for *Spitting Image* and *Weekending*, Murray started to build his own solo act in which he displayed an unnerving ability to replicate the sounds of machine guns. The patriotic Pub Landlord character took off when he appeared in Harry Hill's Pub Internationale Edinburgh show in 1994. This came as a great relief to Murray, who was tiring of his sound effect act.

Taking a slightly more ironic approach than that other laddish hero Loadsamoney, the Pub Landlord was still a popular icon in sim-

Al Murray as the opinionated Pub Landlord

ilar vein whose bar-room wisdom went down particularly well with punters who came as much for the beer as for the comedy. Though uncomfortable with homosexuality and comparing Switzerland to a house that would never sell because they have the Austrians, Germans, French and Italians as neighbours, the Pub Landlord is less than reverential about "little Englanders" like Robert Kilroy-Silk and has suggested George W. Bush should be the American that NASA sends to Mars.

Murray appeared on *The Harry Hill Show* from 1997 to 2000, making the Perrier Award panel reluctant to give him an award because he was too famous. They relented in 1999, the fourth straight year he had been nominated. After the win, Sky One's *Time Gentleman Please* sitcom soon followed. A patchy affair, the show had its moments but then the cast did include *Absolutely Fabulous* star Julia Sawalha and Phil Daniels, with supporting appearances from Jenny Eclair, Frank Skinner, Hywel Bennett and posh boy comic Will Smith.

 There are four DVDs of Murray's work, probably the most enjoyable being *My Gaff, My Rules* (2003) where Murray's beery banter with the audience rarely misses the target.

 www.thepublandlord.com

Robert Newman
1964–

The former golden boy of student comedy Robert Newman has, after his popular collaboration with David Baddiel, become one of Britain's top political comedians. Arthur Smith says: "You've got to hand it to Robert, he's got an integrity about what he does … he has an almost saintly quality, having chosen not to go further down the road that was open to him of the 'handsome comedian'."

Newman, who is half Greek Cypriot and half British, was adopted by a working-class family in Hertfordshire and wanted to be a novelist. But he met Baddiel at a BBC comedy writers workshop and, after the two had bonded over a cricket sketch, they wrote material together for Radio 4's *Weekending*.

Robert Newman eclipsing his peers

Newman and Baddiel worked together for four years, initially on *The Mary Whitehouse Experience* (on radio and TV), latterly with the more orthodox satirists Steve Punt and Hugh Dennis. In one interview, Newman gave the impression that Punt and Dennis had been foisted upon them: "The radio version of *The Mary Whitehouse Experience* was pretty good. We had Jack Dee, Mark Thomas and Jo Brand. And then we went to television, and the executives said, 'Well, this lot aren't going to make the cut. Get rid of them. But that Punt and Dennis, that's what you want'."

Launched on BBC2 in 1993, *Newman And Baddiel In Pieces*, a darker, more ambitious, collection of monologues and sketches, made the partners cult heroes, especially among students, and culminated with their famous gig at Wembley Arena. So much underwear was being thrown at the stage that Newman was labelled a heart throb, inspiring the cliché about comedy being the new rock'n'roll. But the duo split acrimoniously, just as they reached their commercial peak.

Less brash than his partner, Newman was always more of a dandy, philosophical and self-deprecating, and, though he cites Eddie Murphy as an unlikely, politically incorrect inspiration, was never attracted by a move into new lad comedy, the route Baddiel pursued with Frank Skinner.

Mark Thomas would remain a major influence on Newman's political direction, post-Baddiel. After publishing his first novel, the semi-autobiographical *Dependence Day*, in 1994 and going on a solo tour of the same name, Newman fell out of the limelight. But he re-emerged with a politicized act, appearing at benefit gigs for striking dockers in 1996 and familiarizing himself with a host of pressure groups such as Reclaim The Streets and People's Global Action. His subsequent shows – including arguably his best work, *From Caliban To The Taliban: 500 Years Of Humanitarian Intervention* – are a showcase for all his comedic abilities, featuring impressions of Tony Blair, comedy ditties and his own take on world affairs, such as his claim that Archduke Franz Ferdinand's death could not have caused World War I because "no one can be that popular". It's quite a show for a man who started out in showbiz doing Ronnie Corbett impressions.

 From Caliban To The Taliban: 500 Years Of Humanitarian Intervention (2003). A superb set complete with songs about turtles accompanied by his ukulele and some serious political points about global conspiracy and corporate politics.

 www.robnewman.com

Ross Noble

1976–

The stage set for Ross Noble's 2004 show *Noodlemeister* consisted of entwined coloured foam strands, like giant confectionery, and was a fitting metaphor for Noble's own style and appearance. The 30-year-old comic is a master at conjuring fantastical and apparently improvised stories out of thin air and weaving them together as, all the while, his long curly hair billows like the foam strands.

Noble's material consists of riffs on scenarios as bizarre, yet intriguing, as a ping-pong-playing Jesus or embroidering a street scene involving drunks into a piece of street theatre. His act has evolved, with routines that came out of nowhere in previous shows gradually becoming integrated as comic mainstays. Though different in style and more physically reminiscent of Phil Kay, Noble is often likened to Eddie Izzard as a potential stadium-filler, the kind of gig, Izzard says, every comedian should aspire to.

Noble's career has soared without much television exposure beyond occasional appearances on *Have I Got News For You*. His reputation as a live comic has grown since his first worldwide theatre tour in 1999, with a tour every year since. An Edinburgh favourite,

Ross Noble, a face you may
recognize from Radio 4

Noble has completed acclaimed stints at The Garrick Theatre in the West End and toured Australia where he has a big following.

Not, so far, tempted by sitcoms or acting, Noble has found a comfortable niche on BBC Radio 4, as a guest on the panel show *I'm Sorry I Haven't A Clue* and fronting two series of *Ross Noble Goes Global*, a show that mixed gags with a very unorthodox travel commentary. Talking about his exploits in Belgium, he explored, in his popular surrealist style, the effects of over-indulging in chocolate when visiting an art gallery: "After the first couple of kilos … the Magritte picture appeared to be moving. After a few more, in a chocolate haze, I heard the voice of Tintin telling me to kill the Smurfs."

Unrealtime (2004) and *Sonic Waffle* (2005) are both available on DVD and both recommended. *Unrealtime* features his atmospheric open-air concert in Regent's Park and *Sonic Waffle* includes Noble's performance on Jack Dee's BBC1 showcase *Live At The Apollo*, which sees him on particularly good form.

www.rossnoble.co.uk

Hovis Presley
1960–2005

Hovis Presley, who died of a heart attack when he was only 44, passed up many chances to become a household name outside his native Bolton, but those who saw him thought he was the best thing since sliced bread.

Hovis started life as Richard Henry McFarlane in Bolton in 1960. He started writing poetry and revue sketches in his twenties and taught a comedy course at Bradford University where he had been a student. He began performing his own work in the early 1990s on the Manchester alternative comedy and poetry scene, notably at the popular Buzz Club.

Often compared to John Hegley (another Bradford University alumnus) and John Cooper Clarke, Presley had a legendary gift for turning ordinary phrases into something extraordinary, as when he said: "Take away that woodstain and don't darken my doorway again". His one-liners had a habit of heading in unexpected directions as when he declared: "It's true what they say about women, it's an irregular plural."

His poetry was both heartfelt and humorous and his oft-quoted work "I Rely On You" is included in a list of wedding readings at Salford Registry Office. One verse runs:

> I rely on you
> like a handyman needs pliers
> like an auctioneer needs buyers
> like a laundromat needs driers
> like *The Good Life* needed Richard Briers

Presley's popularity reached a high point in 1997 when his poetry anthology, *Poetic Off Licence*, was updated and his Edinburgh show *Wherever I Lay My Hat, That's My Hat* was tipped for a Perrier Award. But the attention proved too much for him and he abruptly abandoned his run.

For a man who had travelled the world, Presley became oddly reluctant to stray too far from his native Bolton, where he ran his own comedy club. Though he continued to perform live after his Edinburgh experience, he would often refuse gigs if he couldn't get back home that same night.

Such reticence made it no great surprise when he spurned a part in *Peter Kay's Phoenix Nights*, fearing he might become typecast. He was, however, happy to contribute to several radio shows and appeared with John Shuttleworth on BBC Radio 4. His idiosyncratic approach to his career was not a reaction to the pressures of fame. Even as a schoolboy, he had only agreed to perform a sketch after his teachers had agreed to give him five Curly Wurlys, which he used as props.

Presley's classic collection *Poetic Off Licence* (available from the website below) contains the aforementioned classic comic poem "I Rely On You" and many other gems.

www.hovispresley.co.uk

Reeves and Mortimer
Vic Reeves (1959–) Bob Mortimer (1959–)

Love them or hate them – and there's very little room in between – it was hard to avoid Reeves and Mortimer in the early to mid-1990s when *Vic Reeves' Big Night Out* and *The Smell Of Reeves And Mortimer* reigned supreme.

A former pig farmer, Jim Moir moved to London from Darlington and played the music and comedy circuits calling himself Vic Reeves after his favourite 1950s crooners Vic Damone and Jim Reeves.

His anarchic *Big Night Out* evening – a mix of slapstick and sur-real nonsense – started out playing comedy clubs in South London in the mid-1980s. Bob Mortimer, a solicitor, regularly watched the show when it was at The Goldsmiths Tavern in New Cross and went from being Reeves' drinking buddy to his comedy partner.

This weird and wonderful extravaganza attracted influential audience members such as the then controller of BBC2 Alan Yentob and Jonathan Ross, who helped the duo gain TV exposure on his chat show *The Last Resort*. *Vic Reeves' Big Night Out* (Channel 4, 1990) won a BAFTA and captured the imagination of younger, particularly student, audiences. The catch phrases from the show (notably "You sad man" and "What's on the end of the stick, Vic?") abounded in bars and student unions up and down the land, while zany characters such as Wavy Davy, a man who waved, and Les, the odd scientist, were cherished. The duo's next big TV venture, *The Smell Of Reeves And Mortimer* (featuring legendary comedy circuit oddity Charlie Chuck) included new characters such as naff folk duo Mulligan and O'Hare and the prototype for their loopy game show *Shooting Stars* (BBC2, 1995–2003).

Shooting Stars featured such comic talent as Mark Lamarr, Johnny Vegas and Matt Lucas. Though nodding to the mainstream, it main-tained their trademark otherworldliness with ridiculous rounds (guess which song Reeves, as the indecipherable Pub Singer, was crucifying), arbitrary answers to already daft questions ("True or False: Bill Cosby was the first ever black man? False, it was actually Sidney Poitier"), silly catch phrases ("Uvavu!") and slapstick games far wackier than anything in *It's A Knockout*.

In 2005 Reeves and Mortimer appeared on stage for the first

time in fifteen years to promote a DVD of their shows. They have worked steadily on TV in the last decade, though not much of their output has been pure comedy. Their dark comedy *Catterick* (BBC3, 2004) was refreshingly bizarre, but perhaps too odd for its own good, as, despite the presence of a wealth of comic talent (Charlie Higson, Morwenna Banks, Matt Lucas and Reece Shearsmith), the BBC don't want to commission another series.

 The Original Vic Reeves' Big Night Out (2005). The very beginning – and some would argue, the best – of the Vic and Bob phenomenon.

 I Will Cure You (Spectrum, 1999). Vic Reeves' solo album contains some of the songs that were used in *Big Night Out* as well as the number-one single "Dizzy". Elsewhere comedy songs such as "Empty Kennel" and "Oh Mr Hairdresser" are helped by the fact that Reeves can actually sing.

 www.vicandbob.net is a good fan site; their management site is www.pbjmgt.co.uk

Jerry Sadowitz
1961–

"My name's famous, but I'm not", Jerry Sadowitz the curly-locked, bowler-hatted, magical misanthrope of comedy lamented once. It is little wonder that mainstream fame, which he might have hated anyway, has eluded such an uncompromising comedian. Sadowitz led the rearguard action against the leftie, liberal social worker brigade who loved the political correctness of some alternative comedy. The philosophy of this angry Glaswegian Jewish comedian – "I hate fuckin' everythin" – produced jokes of staggering bad taste about cancer, AIDS, the latest disaster and every minority and majority in society.

As comedy academic and ex-performer Oliver Double points out in his book *Stand Up: On Being A Comedian*, Sadowitz was no Bernard Manning figure, being completely even-handed with his hate. But he is still too much for some. His jokes about rape still provoke walk-outs and his jokes about Pakistani shopkeepers send

Jerry Sadowitz – you really don't want to know where the rest of the pack is!

frissons of unease through an audience who thought that such material had been left behind by the comedy revolution. At the 1991 Just for Laughs comedy festival in Montreal, Sadowitz's opening line, "Good evening Moosefuckers", led to him being assaulted by someone in the audience.

Sadowitz is a consummate magician with a range of clever card tricks. Magic has, if anything, become more central to his act. He is so passionate about it that he works part-time at a magic shop in London. Magic helps Sadowitz keep the world at a safe distance: "If I do a trick, or an effect as magicians call it, you see the effect not the method. Isn't that a fair analogy to the universe? The effect is that we are on a planet that appears to be home and that everything is quite natural but we don't actually see the method. There is a magician I think, and he's a very good magician, he's not going to tell us what the method is."

 For pure, unadulterated, in-your-face abuse get hold of *Jerry Sadowitz Live* (1988), recorded at the height of his magical stand-up powers.

 www.jerrysadowitz.com

Alexei Sayle

1952–

Asked at the Edinburgh Book Festival in 2003 if he followed the comedy circuit, Alexei Sayle noted disdainfully that the current generation of comics all seemed to have attended "the University of Comedy". In 2004, he criticized the plethora of "chav" jokes, arguing that the comedy circuit seemed to have gone in the opposite direction to the politically correct, pioneering days his early success had seemed to herald.

Sayle was born in Liverpool and grew up, as he said, "in a household where the greatest mass murderer in history, Joseph Stalin, was revered as a hero". His parents were card-carrying Communists and, because his father worked as a railway guard, travelled widely in Eastern Europe. After attending art school in Chelsea, Sayle tried his luck as a freelance illustrator before becoming part of Threepenny Theatre, a Brechtian troupe started by an old school friend. The troupe morphed into a sketch show featuring famously surreal bingo games as Sayle honed his stand-up act.

When Sayle responded to the ad in *Private Eye* for acts for The Comedy Store, founder Peter Rosengard knew he'd found his compere. Sayle – a self-confessed "fake working-class hard case" – had the material, vociferous delivery and the stature to handle (sometimes literally) raucous members of the audience. His material covered many bases but politics was never far away: "Recently I had to get married, 'cos I got my girlfriend into trouble – I got her involved in the civil war in Angola."

Though his live performing career ended in 1985, he remained in the public eye with his TV sketch and stand-up shows, *Alexei*

Sayle's Stuff (1988), *The All New Alexei Sayle Show* (1994) and *Alexei Sayle's Merry Go Round* (1998). He was also a key supporting player in *The Young Ones* (some felt his madcap cameos stole the show) and *The Comic Strip Presents*. In 1982, he was an unlikely addition to *OTT*, ITV's short-lived late-Saturday-night injection of anarchy, featuring Chris Tarrant, Lenny Henry, Bob Carolgees and Sally James, but bailed out before the series ended.

In recent years, Sayle has given up his career as the hectoring stand-up in the too-tight suit to write novels. In his bestselling short story collection *Barcelona Plates* (2000), he mocks an undeservingly successful comic duo called Nic and Tob whose arrival "had fortunately coincided with the rise of stupidity, the public having tired of being shouted at by fat men about things that weren't their fault as a form of light entertainment".

 Stuff Series One (1988). Alexei Sayle's *Stuff* merged stand-up rants with hyper-surreal sketches. Though dated by references to Margaret Thatcher and other politicians of the age, it remains a solid testimony to the anger and energy of this performer and writer.

 www.msdivine.net/alexeisayle is a good fan site.

Arthur Smith

1954–

Now billed as one of BBC2's *Grumpy Old Men*, Arthur Smith is a comedy perennial whose durability may owe something to the fact that he's never been seriously over-exposed.

Born in Bermondsey, Smith studied creative writing under *The History Man* author Malcolm Bradbury at the University of East Anglia, though Bradbury suggested Smith should "stick to comedy". Smith did just that. His first gig was at The Comedy Store in 1979. He admits to feeling blown away by the material of such performers as Alexei Sayle and that his own, initially garnered from student revues, was fey by comparison.

When Smith literally got his act together, he became one of the circuit's most sought-after MCs. This owed something to the fact that he looked like a bloke who had just stepped out of the audience and something to his pleasantly absurd banter. Indeed, Smith was once challenged by a comedian he had heckled for using an offensive put-down to come up on stage and do better; he did just that – for twenty minutes.

His stint hosting *Paramount City*, a lame attempt to re-create the club atmosphere on TV, wasn't a great success. Producer Janet Street Porter dismissed Smith as "a thoroughly irritating man, neither young, attractive, nor witty". Despite these alleged handicaps, Smith enjoyed success in other areas. He scored a number of theatrical triumphs including *Live Bed Show* (with Caroline Quentin), *An Evening With Gary Lineker* (a funny, heartbreaking, nostalgic play about the 1990 World Cup, written with Chris England) and *Arthur Smith Sings Leonard Cohen* (a tribute to the singer Smith calls "the greatest comedian of the twentieth century, so great he's never actually got a laugh").

The eternally grumpy Arthur Smith

In 2001, Smith was hospitalized with pancreatitis and told that more drink could kill him. Eminently sociable and prone to a drunken antic or two, Smith was forced to give up and, returning to Edinburgh, was spotted clutching a bottle of water and exclaiming: "The drink has changed, but the jokes are still the same." He later developed diabetes and had to become the world's funniest non-smoking, non-drinking comedian.

Smith still contributes to all manner of radio programmes, including *Loose Ends*, and has written for *The Guardian* and *The Stage*. He also continues to take his legendary alternative tours of Edinburgh during the Festival, an event that sees a melange of cabaret acts and has seen several arrests over the years.

Miner embarrassment

Arthur Smith says that comedy and the 1980s miners' strike didn't always sit comfortably:

"During the miners' strike, comedians were on full alert at all times. Sometimes the relationship between these tough blokes from the North and soft Southern comics was awkward. In truth, many striking miners would rather have watched Bernard Manning than Ben Elton. At one benefit I did the raffle. I was given the prizes but looked at them only as the winners were announced. 'And the prize,' I noted 'appears to be a cheap nylon tie and some cuff links. Cuff links? Who the hell wants cuff links?' A voice rang out clearly from the audience: 'They are NUM ties and cuff links.' At the end of the gig, I tried to create a stirring finale. It's curious that such a strident invocation can be ambiguous but my cry of 'Up The Miners!' did not sound right."

Grumpy Old Men (2004). The popular BBC2 series, which also featured John Peel and Will Self, is a good showcase for Arthur Smith's wry, rueful observations on everyday life. The TV version of *An Evening With Gary Lineker*, with Clive Owen and Paul Merton, is still available on video, though some prefer the original script, available from publishers Trench Kiss.

Jim Tavare

1963–

Jim Tavare became famous for his unusual double act: his partner wasn't the traditional straight man comic foil but a double bass called Bassie.

He had taken up the bass at school in Macclesfield, allegedly because it forced his parents to give him a lift home. He trained at RADA between 1985 and 1987 alongside, as is often noted, a young Ralph Fiennes, but left determined to become a comedian. His act went badly, with some clubs running competitions to "Get Jim Tavare off in three minutes". Malcolm Hardee, who watched Tavare in these early years, recalled: "Jim used to die a death week after week after week at the Tunnel until, one week, he turned up and did exactly the same jokes while holding a double bass. He's never died since." The double bass provided company and protection, and helped Tavare with just one joke, but ended up being his act's trademark.

"To begin with", says Tavare, "the bass was literally no more than a prop I could lean on – something to hold onto, like Dave Allen's cigarette. I was really using it as a surreal sight gag, not at all as an instrument."

Bassie was later to prove a typecasting curse, but it helped Tavare's reputation soar. From 1995 to 2001, he appeared in *Jim Tavare Pictures Presents* (six short films for BBC2), *The Comedy Network* (Channel 5), *The Jim Tavare Show* (Channel 5) and the BAFTA-winning *The Sketch Show* (ITV1).

Tavare has appeared at various Royal Variety shows and royal engagements, territory normally associated with more mainstream comics – and fellow Jimmys – Tarbuck and Davidson. Such gigs

Jim Tavare looking dapper

reflected the fact that, although Tavare was a product of the alternative comedy scene, his humour owed an obvious debt to entertainers like Tommy Cooper and Max Wall.

Tavare has translated his act across the Atlantic. An entire episode of *Wings*, the sitcom from the producers of *Cheers*, was written around his act. Tavare has appeared in *Harry Potter And The Prisoner of Azkaban* and, after recently creating a new range of characters, including the Politically Correct Dancers, is now working on new material that doesn't involve Bassie. And probably hoping he won't die a thousand comic deaths again.

www.jimtavare.com

The "diabolical" "genius" that is Johnny Vegas

Johnny Vegas
1971–

There cannot be anyone in comedy who divides audiences like Johnny Vegas can. Punter verdicts range from "a bloody genius" to "diabolical", with little in between. Certainly his onstage drunk persona (and sometimes the line between on and offstage is literally blurred) alienates some of his audience who can't see past the self-pity and certainly don't feel the pathos that he engenders in others. Big, loud, brash, lewd and crude he certainly is, but young stand-up Russell Howard says: "I remember seeing Johnny Vegas a few years ago do a gig in Bath that lasted two and a half hours. It had everything. People were gut laughing, crying, listening, smiling. He held the audience in a trance."

Michael Pennington, as he was born, was brought up in a strict Catholic family and spent a year and a half in a seminary before moving to London to study ceramics. He soon realized there was not much call for "teapot menders" though, as Johnny Vegas, he has incorporated live pottery into his act, even demonstrating his skills once at the Victoria and Albert Museum.

The northern comic only started being professionally funny in 1995, when he was 24. Initially, he died but, ironically, became a winner by pretending to be a loser. As he shrewdly noted: "At the end of the day, what makes it all work is that I'm a much sadder person than you." In 1997, he became the first newcomer to be nominated for the main Perrier Award. With a dash of live pottery, a sing-song or two and loud banter with the audience, Vegas gigs were memorable, though not always for their quality.

The same could be said of Vegas's screen output, which received a huge boost after he appeared alongside a woollen monkey on adverts for the ill-fated ITV Digital channel. On the plus side, there were regular spots as a panellist on *Shooting Stars*, appearances in Paul Whitehouse's *Happiness* and the BBC's 2005 production of *A Midsummer Night's Dream*, and the lead role in BBC3's weed-fuelled sitcom *Ideal* in 2006. These were balanced by two poor British comedy films, *Blackball* and *Sex Lives Of The Potato Men*, the latter of which, despite the promising title, has been described as "the worst film ever".

 Who's Ready For Ice Cream? (2003). A stand-up set dressed up in a loose plot. Ignore the plot and concentrate on Vegas's erratic but entertaining set, featuring some great repartee with the audience, in Edinburgh's smoke-filled Stand comedy club.

Tim Vine

1968–

Tim Vine is the current world record-holder for the most number of jokes told in one hour and is appropriately tagged the "joke machine gun". His puns provoke inescapable guffaws, striking the audience as ludicrous and inspired.

Examples include: "So I was getting into my car, and this bloke says to me 'Can you give me a lift?' I said 'Sure, you look great, the world's your oyster, go for it'." Or: "Apparently, one in five people in the world are Chinese. And there are five people in my family, so it must be one of them. It's either my mum or my dad. Or my older brother Colin. Or my younger brother Ho-Chan-Chu. But I think it's Colin."

These jokes gained infamy when they appeared in 2001 in a global email attributed to Tommy Cooper. There was no doubting the similarity in style but most of these killer gags and puns proved to belong to Vine.

Dressing akin to Freddie Starr – and very much a fan of such old-school comics as Les Dawson, Ken Dodd and Norman Collier – Vine started in comedy after visiting the Comedy Café in Shoreditch.

His steady crawl up the comedy ladder was finally recognised in 1995 when he won the Perrier Best Newcomer Award. Since then he has found work in various TV shows: Channel 5's quizzes *Whittle* and *Fluke* and BBC1's *Housemates*. By far his most successful outing was in ITV's *The Sketch Show*, which was since remade for US television with Kelsey Grammer.

Vine is the younger brother of Jeremy Vine, the former presenter of *Newsnight* now filling Jimmy Young's old slot on BBC Radio 2. Of their divergent career paths, Vine says: "He's more grown up. I'm essentially making a living from mucking about. The other day I was doing this joke where I was asking: 'Is it possible to change the world?' and I say yes, 'I've changed the world' and I take out this cube-shaped world. When I was cutting up the box to make it and sticking the map to the sides of it I thought, this is my job, it's ridiculous but I love it."

The firmly rooted Tim Vine

 Tim Vine Live (2004). Vine's constant stream of gags guarantees value for money. The extras include Vine talking the viewer through his act and reminding himself of the jokes he forgot to tell.

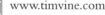 www.timvine.com

The Guinness Book Of Records' comedy record-holders

Fastest talking female stand-up Fran Capo, who has been credited as talking at a speed of 603.3 words per minute.

Most jokes in one hour 499, Tim Vine.

Highest average punchline delivery 12 punchlines per minute, Phyllis Diller.

Longest continuous comedy variety performance 28 hours by The Comedy Factory, Edmonton, Canada, who set the record with continuous stand-up, ventriloquism, improvisation, magic and juggling in September 2002.

Longest running comedy show *NewsRevue*, the satire show at London's Canal Café Theatre was first launched in 1979.

Longest non-stop joke-telling 60 hours by Derek Denniss and John Evans, in Sandton City, Johannesburg, South Africa in September 1988.

Most stand-ups performing on stage continuously 150. At the Dancehouse Theatre, Manchester in October 2003. Comedians included Quentin Reynolds, Hazel Humphries, Gavin Webster, Toby Foster, Susan Murray and Johnny Vegas. Each comedian who took part in the 2003 Manchester Comedy Festival had two minutes each on stage (apart from Johnny Vegas who was allowed to go on longer).

Largest audience watching one solo comedian 10,108. The audience that watched Lee Evans at the MEN Arena in 2005, breaking Eddie Izzard's previous record of 8700. However, Izzard's representatives are trying to record his audience at the MEN arena in 2003, believed to be around 13,500, as the official record.

Mark Watson

1980–

Though born in Bristol, Mark Watson appears on stage as a rather quirky, absurdist and frenetic Welshman, purveying his own brand of cerebral, lyrical comedy.

Watson may have only started performing stand-up in 2002 but he has two Edinburgh shows, two comedy tests of endurance (a 24-hour show and another lasting 2005 minutes or 33 hours) and two novels under his belt.

Watson has demonstrated that he is a force to be reckoned with when it comes to hecklers: "I once got a heckle concerning sheep-shagging where the person made baa-ing noises. I said something about how it was odd he should accuse me of being a sheep-shagger by pretending to be one, thus soliciting sex."

He believes that passion is at the heart of good stand-up ("though, having said all that, I've seen people be massively successful with fairly superficial acts") and refines his act partly by

The overambitious Mark Watson

doing a lot of gigs and seeing what works: "I tend to see jokes as the footballers with me as the manager – always give a joke three games to prove itself."

The two tests of comic endurance that he set himself in Edinburgh, *Mark Watson's Overambitious 24 Hour Show* in 2004 and his show *2005 Years In 2005 Minutes*, produced inspired moments from him and from the many fellow comedians who helped him.

As well as writing novels (a screenplay of his fictional debut *Bullet Points* is under discussion) Watson has several radio and television projects in development. His previous TV experience has seen him appearing as an extra in several North American sitcoms while living in Toronto, including three episodes of the US version of *Queer As Folk*.

Nick Wilty

1958–

"My sex life is like a fairground; it only happens twice a year and on some waste ground." Nick Wilty – his stage surname is an acronym for Would I Lie To You? – is a short, solid-looking man with solid, punchy lines who is feted on the comedy circuit. Mel Smith describes him as "The best warm-up comedian in England".

Wilty doesn't have a rich heritage of one-hour Edinburgh shows because he has been busy globetrotting, having gigged on every continent except Antarctica (though he did get to Tierra del Fuego). Wilty's wanderlust started young. He hitchhiked the world when he was 18; two years later he joined the Signals Regiment and served in the Falklands. After leaving the army, Wilty kept travelling and discovered comedy at an open spot night in Vancouver where he made his debut after accepting a dare from another member of the audience. He was voted best international comedy act in San Francisco in 1996. Once, in Singapore, he was told he couldn't make jokes about sex, politics or religion and to list ten subjects he would joke about. He suggested the badger population of southeast Kent but, realizing that his minder didn't understand much English, did his usual act.

The public speaks

We live in an age dominated by polls and top tens, but what do the statistics tell us about the state of comedy in the eyes of the British public? In the last few years there have been a rash of such polls and, broadly speaking, they tell us that we like something old, something new, something borrowed and something blue.

On the subject of the nation's favourite stand-up or individual comic, *FHM* put Peter Kay top, followed by Ricky Gervais and Jimmy Carr, and rather unkindly suggested that the funniest woman was "none of them". Kay was also voted top by the sex- and sports-obsessed lads' mag *Zoo*, although such stalwarts as Bill Bailey and Lee Evans

also figured. Other polls, such as the one chip-makers McCain conducted for Comic Relief in 2005, put more emphasis on the old guard with Tommy Cooper top and Peter Sellers, Eric Morecambe and Benny Hill in the top ten. A *Reader's Digest* poll, sampling an older readership, put Cooper first and relative new boy Peter Kay second.

But just who is the funniest of them all? For this you might need to ask the comedians themselves, which is exactly what Channel 4 did in 2005, putting, predictably, Peter Cook top. Groucho Marx, at number five, might well have suggested that any poll that had him as a member was not worth having.

Channel 4 comedians (2004)

1. Peter Cook
2. John Cleese
3. Woody Allen
4. Eric Morecambe
5. Groucho Marx
6. Tommy Cooper
7. Laurel and Hardy
8. Billy Connolly
9. Vic Reeves and Bob Mortimer
10. Richard Pryor

FHM best stand-up (2005)

1. Peter Kay
2. Ricky Gervais
3. Jimmy Carr
4. Jack Dee
5. Harry Hill

McCain/Comic Relief (2005)

1. Tommy Cooper
2. Eric Morecambe
3. Peter Sellers
4. Benny Hill
5. John Cleese
6. Spike Milligan
7. Leonard Rossiter
8. Sid James
9. Tony Hancock
10. Peter Cook

Reader's Digest funniest Briton (2004)

1. Tommy Cooper
2. Peter Kay
3. Billy Connolly
4. Morecambe and Wise
5. Bob Monkhouse
6. Ken Dodd
7. Roy "Chubby" Brown
8. (equal) Norman Wisdom
8. (equal) Les Dawson
10. Lee Evans

Zoo funniest person (2006)

1. Peter Kay
2. Ricky Gervais
3. Lee Evans
4. Eddie Izzard
5. Billy Connolly
6. Dylan Moran
7. Bill Bailey
8. The Mighty Boosh
9. Jimmy Carr
10. Matt Lucas and David Walliams

Wilty may come across as a regular laddish comedian, an old-school stand-up – he has no props, no deformity and no amusing tales of the time he worked in a graveyard – but he likes to surprise his audience with clever wordplay ("Bush put the oops into troops and took the style out of hostile") and the range of his subject matter.

Despite his enormous experience, he admits he doesn't always have the audience eating out of the palm of his hand: "I was taking part in a Black Variety Night at the Hackney Empire and was so excited at being on the same stage as Charlie Chaplin and playing to a full house. But it all went pear-shaped and even the clapometer stayed below zero."

Wilty has appeared in televised stand-up shows, interviewed a string of celebrities (including Dennis Hopper, Tom Jones, Robbie Williams and Kylie Minogue) for the TV series hosted by radio DJ Steve Wright and worked as a warm-up for a special edition of *The Comedians*, ITV's long-running showcase for mainstream comedians. One performer gave him a lift back to London after the show. Wilty recalls the comedian saying to him: "You had some good lines there, I can't wait to put them in my act."

www.geocities.com/nickwiltywebsite

The Canon:
50 essential comedy shows

Tony Robinson and Rowan Atkinson strike a pose in their *Blackadder Goes Forth* costumes

The Canon:
50 essential comedy shows

Today's TV executives spend their waking moments in an anxious, never completely satisfied quest for shows that create what they call "water cooler moments". It's a pity that many of them have forgotten that comedy, just as much as soap, reality TV and cops and robbers, can provide that communal experience. Monty Python's legendary "Four Yorkshiremen" sketch, though stale now from repetition, was one of the first great water cooler moments, with David Brent's dance in *The Office* being one of the most recent and most memorable.

Does it matter that, as Armando Iannucci pointed out in his Oxford University lecture in March 2006, the top five sitcoms were watched by 14.7 million people in 1986 but, in 2001, by just 6.9 million? Does it matter, in a digital multi-channel universe, that the amount of hours devoted to original comedy programming on the four main channels has slumped from 264 in 1984 to 172 in 2004?

Actually, it does matter. It's not enough for viewers, producers and writers to take comfort in the quality of product on offer. Quality comedy relies on quantities – the amount of screen time that allows shows to develop and the level of funding needed to attract the best performers and writers. British television – and Britain itself – would be much poorer if, in a decade's time, every televisual water cooler moment came from a manufactured confrontation in Albert Square or a grumpy maverick cop apprehending a villain.

Sitcoms

The word "sitcom" isn't glamorous, but since the alternative comedy revolution of the 1980s, some of British television's most talismanic programmes have been sitcoms. Not just *The Office*, but *Father Ted* and *Blackadder*. Better still, the sitcom universe is much more varied than it used to be. Alternative comedy has, through such inspiring writers as Ben Elton and Graham Linehan, refreshed the sitcom, finding room for farcical and surreal situations which, in the right hands, somehow feel utterly appropriate.

The best of these sitcoms are discussed here, alongside a few – such as *Shelley*, *Rising Damp* and *The Fall And Rise Of Reginald Perrin* – that predate the alternative comedy boom but continue to make their presence felt. The success of quirky fourth wall sitcoms like *Black Books* suggests that, despite some predictions so gloomy even *Dad's Army*'s Private Frazer might chafe at their pessimism, the traditional sitcom can coexist with more naturalistic products such as *Spaced*, *Peep Show* and *Nighty Night*.

Absolutely Fabulous

1992–2003

Irreverent and anarchic like *The Young Ones*, though more sassy than surreal, *Absolutely Fabulous* more emphatically put girls on top than the sitcom of that name. Dawn French, Jennifer Saunders and Ruby Wax, all writers and performers on *Girls On Top* (ITV, 1985–86), were again the driving force behind this glorious sitcom. Born out of a French and Saunders sketch,

Ab Fab was arguably the logical culmination of the double act's work.

Saunders played Edina Monsoon, strongly rumoured to be based on legendary PR guru Lynne Franks. Though Franks could see the resemblance, she loved the show and didn't see Edina as her fictional alter ego. But then Edina and her best friend "fash mag slag" Patsy (Joanna Lumley) were hedonists of the highest order, indulging in an orgy of drugs and drink and, in Patsy's case, men, swinging as enthusiastically as they had in their 1960s heyday. Rich and famous after profiting from Britain's obsession with fashion and celebrity, they could be as brash and as rude as they liked, particularly towards Edina's mother (June Whitfield) and her chronically square daughter Saffy (Julia Sawalha) whom Edina constantly rebukes: "I don't want a moustachioed virgin of a daughter, now for heaven's sake do something about it!"

Apart from the sharp, un-PC repartee and nifty one-liners (Patsy, a fashion guru, insists: "Y'know, one snap of my fingers and I can raise hemlines so high the world's your gynaecologist") there were some great moments of visual comedy. In the series two finale, Patsy, having burnt the kitchen down, is found amid the smouldering ruins, stuck by her cigarette to a charred surface.

There was a six-year hiatus between the third and fourth series of *Ab Fab* (it came back for a fifth – and last – run in 2003). Saunders had wanted to call it quits after the third series ended in 1995 but new ideas for the characters just kept on coming. For some critics, the later series were forced and lacked timing. That didn't stop

These were good too...

Absolute Power
2002–05

The PR world got a very different comedy makeover in this pointed BBC2 sitcom starring Stephen Fry and John Bird. The shenanigans at Prentiss McCabe included inventing an illness for a celebrity client to suffer from. There are plenty of cracks about celebrities, with characters often supposedly embroiled in embarrassing phone conversations with such stars as Kylie Minogue.

Hardware
2003–04

Hardware was Simon Nye's rather claustrophobic ITV sitcom revolving around the personality clashes in a hardware store. This may sound like an overlong *Two Ronnies* sketch but the show was helped by some fine ensemble comedy acting from *Spaced*'s Peter Serafinowicz as the self-satisfied Kenny, Martin Freeman from *The Office* (once again the employee distancing himself from the chaos around him) and Ken Morley, playing a comic variation on his Reg Holdsworth role in *Coronation Street*.

The High Life
1994–95

Camp capers 30,000 feet up were the order of the day in *The High Life*, a shortlived BBC2 sitcom that derived from a character duo called Victor and Barry performed by Alan Cumming and Forbes Masson. Cumming's Sebastian Flight played the super-camp air steward to Masson's sex-crazed colleague, Steve McCracken. Most of the duo's time was spent trying to avoid the disciplinarian chief stewardess Shona Spurtle, (Siobhan Redmond). Slick and fast-paced, this sitcom earned Cumming a ticket to Hollywood.

If You See God, Tell Him
1993

Veteran comedy writers and on-off partners Andrew Marshall (*2 Point 4 Children*) and David Renwick (*One Foot In The Grave*) created four episodes for BBC1 themed around a man (Richard Briers) with a 30-second attention span. The title had a dual meaning. God was short for Briers' character name Godfrey and the name of the show alluded to a popular British Gas slogan ("If you see Sid tell him"). To the consternation of wife Muriel (Imelda Staunton) and son Gordon (Adrian Edmondson), Godfrey's attention span means he can only focus on adverts, providing the cue for some seriously black humour and a critique on mass communication.

Nightingales
1990

This must be the strangest sitcom actor Robert Lindsay has ever played in. Lindsay was one of three security guards – along with James Ellis and David Threlfall – in a high-rise office block. The revelation that the trio are covering up the death of a colleague so they can share his wages gives some idea of the absurd nature of this Channel 4 sitcom. While borrowing from Harold Pinter in style, this odd series gave itself scope to suggest that, for example, the Virgin arriving on Christmas Eve to give birth to a goldfish is all in a day's work.

the show inspiring two Patsy and Edina–styled Muppets on *Sesame Street* and anticipating the raunchy comedy of *Sex In The City*.

All five series of *Absolutely Fabulous*, plus *Absolutely Special* and the feature-length *Gay*, are available on DVD.

Agony
1979–81

Before Kelsey Grammer's Frasier Crane truly claimed the radio phone-in show as rich comedy territory, Maureen Lipman was dividing her time between radio and newspapers as glamorous agony aunt Jane Lucas.

Agony was created by an actual agony aunt Anna Raeburn and American sitcom writer Len Richmond. The show's semi-autobiographical feel was heightened by Lipman's performance, which often aped Raeburn's dry delivery and succinct morality. Despite the daring suggestion of depravity in some storylines (swingers, drugs, porn movies), Lucas ultimately toed a fairly firm moral line, earning the nickname "Citizen Jane".

Her stint at Radio 242 proved more fertile comedy ground than her role at *Person* magazine thanks to Peter Blake's lecherous, burnt-out hippy DJ Andy. The agonizing irony for Lucas was that her personal life was complex enough to fill many problem pages. She was separated from her roving husband Laurence (Simon Williams) with whom she had a predictably on-off relationship. A psychiatrist, Laurence used the couch as much for sexual as therapeutic ends. Jane's stereotypical Jewish mother was interfering and ever-present while her magazine boss was a pseudo-Thatcherite Sloane Ranger and her secretary was friendly, but useless. Jane drew strength from her gay neighbours Rob and Michael, who, in a shocking departure for a 1970s sitcom, weren't as camp as a row of John Inmans. But that support was cruelly removed when Michael killed himself in the third and final series.

Because of the characters and issues involved, *Agony* had a contemporary, progressive feel.

Lipman made the most of some sassy one-liners (when her fashionable bohemian style is criticized for being reminiscent of Bob Dylan she replies: "Well we're both trying to make a comeback") but some of the ensemble acting was wooden and melodramatic.

Black Books
2000–04

Black Books centred on the dysfunctional trio whose lives intertwined around a bookshop that defied the laws of economics. The show was an immediate cult success, uniting the immense comic gifts of Dylan Moran (Bernard Black) and Bill Bailey (Manny), giving Tamsin Greig her big break as Fran and drawing on the considerable writing talents of Moran and the *Father Ted* team (Graham Linehan and Arthur Mathews).

Bernard Black is a loveable misanthrope who drinks on the job, and would prefer not to have customers or, at the very minimum, have customers that didn't force him to restock by buying something. He reluctantly takes on the kind-hearted Manny, whose serenity stems from the fact that he accidentally swallowed *The Little Book Of Calm*. Fran, Bernard's only friend, is on hand to aspire, pointlessly, to normality, social life and a boyfriend. The three are implicated in a series of charming, bizarre adventures involving nude male modelling, Stalinist children's stories and vintage wine.

Though not as far-fetched as *Father Ted*, Linehan's signature is clear. Bernard Black's irreverence is matched by the casual treatment of sitcom rules. There is no straight man, no sustained love interest, no resolution or reason for events, but the show did have regular high-profile cameos from such stars as Omid Djalili, Johnny Vegas, Lucy Davis and Kevin Eldon, who played a contract cleaner character in the style of *The Matrix*.

One of the sitcom's most striking achievements is to find room for two established stand-ups. Moran recalls: "We had jokes that came and went. Jokes in sitcoms only work when they're not conspicuous and reveal character. The characters can't be wittier than people in real life. They have to be character witty."

Bailey commends the programme for sharing some qualities with his stand-up act: "Everything that goes on is based on something that could vaguely happen. In this way, it is heightened reality rather than strictly surreal stuff. It isn't about floating bananas. It is rooted in plausibility."

Billy Bailey, Dylan Moran and Tasmin Greig, standing outside the *Black Books* shop, set aside the usual sitcom rules

 All three series of *Black Books* are available separately on DVD, or as a complete DVD box set.

Blackadder

1983–89

Blackadder rightly pushed *Only Fools And Horses* all the way in BBC's 2004 poll to choose the best sitcom. The programme is so cherished it's easy to forget that the first series, *The Black Adder*, was nearly the last. Michael Grade, then running BBC1 programming, felt "there weren't enough laughs to the pound". The first series did lack spark but it won an Emmy and the award

– along with a promise to reduce expensive location shooting – persuaded Grade to reluctantly recommission it.

When it returned, as *Blackadder II*, Rowan Atkinson relinquished writing duties, allowing Ben Elton to collaborate with Richard Curtis in a comedy writing dream team. Elton relished the series' poetic licence and bolstered it with some fine repartee ("A man may fight for many things. His country, his friends, his principles, the glistening ear on the cheek of a golden child. But personally, I'd mud-wrestle my own mother for a ton of cash, an amusing clock and a sack of French porn.") and toilet humour that worked brilliantly in the bawdy court of Miranda Richardson's girly Elizabeth I. Elton and Curtis worked the same magic in the third series, aided by Hugh Laurie's buffoonish George IV. The comedy was helped by the decision to toughen up Edmund Blackadder's character, replacing the pathetic

Will the real Hugh Grant please stand-up?

Long before his mutually beneficial friendship with Richard Curtis, his floppy fringe and the world's most publicized blow job, Hugh John Mungo Grant – Hughie to his friends – was a member of the cult comedy troupe The Jockeys Of Norfolk, alongside the less famous Christopher Lang and Andrew Tayler. After a trot around the paddock of their alma mater Oxford University, the 23-year-old Grant and the Jockeys played the London pub comedy circuit, often billing alongside a young Canadian comic living in London, Mike Myers. They also played the Edinburgh Festival, but sold just six tickets on their opening night. This gig did lead to a slot on Russell Harty's chat show and that led to a pilot TV show, but as their comedy suited theatre more than television, they were never offered a contract. The Jockeys went their separate ways soon after.

wimp with a sneering misanthrope who was a joy to watch.

Apart from regulars Tony Robinson (Baldrick) and Tim McInnerny (Percy in series one and two, and Captain Darling in four), superb supporting turns were provided by Stephen Fry as the conspiratorial Lord Melchett in *Blackadder II* and the insane General Hogmanay Melchett in *Blackadder Goes Forth*, and by Rik Mayall as the oversexed, overconfident Lord Flashheart (in *Blackadder II* and *Blackadder Goes Forth*). Flashheart had many of the best lines, once comparing a woman to his plane: "Treat your kite like you treat your woman … get inside her five times a day and take her to heaven and back."

The final series, *Blackadder Goes Forth*, set in World War I, achieved a level of empathy with the characters rare in any sitcom before or since. Edmund's character was, in these terrible circumstances, more paternal and the final scene where he goes over the top of the trenches with George (Laurie), Captain Darling and his ever-faithful manservant Baldrick had the audience in actual tears, rather than tears of laughter.

 All four series, plus the *Millennium Back And Forth Christmas Special* and *Comic Relief Cavalier Years* are on DVD.

The Comic Strip Presents…
1982–2000

Unlike the nearby Comedy Store, The Comic Strip club, financed by theatre impresario Michael White (who brought *The Rocky Horror Show* to the stage), featured a regular group of performers honing their acts every night. The venue was more a theatre than a club and was home to Alexei Sayle, Arnold Brown, Peter Richardson and Nigel Planer (as The Outer Limits), Rik Mayall and Ade Edmondson (as Twentieth Century Coyote) and French and Saunders.

Peter Richardson, later to write and direct *Stella Street*, led the charge that saw the main members – the pair of double acts – end up on the new Channel 4. The channel's founding genius Jeremy Isaacs had watched the troupe and six films were rapidly commissioned. The first, the splendid *Five Go Mad In Dorset*, was aired on C4's opening night in 1982. This Enid Blyton parody typified the group's cheeky style, sending up the posh kids' racist, homophobic and superior attitudes.

In all, 37 films were made for TV by the Comic Strip production company (which included Robbie Coltrane). There was a switch to BBC2 in 1990, a five-year hiatus after 1993 and finally a return to Channel 4. There were also two feature-length films, *The Supergrass* (1985) and *Eat The Rich* (1987), though in the latter the regulars only have bit parts. Two storylines that especially caught the imagination, giving domestic political strife the Hollywood treatment, were *The Strike* and *GLC*. In *The Strike* Richardson plays Al Pacino playing Arthur Scargill while in *GLC* Coltrane plays Charles Bronson playing Ken Livingstone.

Other shows, like the Famous Five sequel, *Five Go Mad On Mescalin*, were less impressive and others now look decidedly dated. Yet, alongside *The Young Ones*, *The Comic Strip* was the standard-bearer for alternative comedy drama on 1980s television.

A DVD of the complete *The Comic Strip Presents…*, minus Keith Allen's parody *The Bullshitters*, is available.

Desmond's

1989–94

A sitcom set in a barbershop in Peckham, starring a mainly West Indian cast, screened on Channel 4 may not have seemed like a recipe for success but *Desmond's* reached a mainstream audience both in the UK and in the US.

The secret of the show's global appeal owed a lot to the barbershop, a casually convenient environment for characters to interact in. The characters were strong too, especially the grumpy but likeable owner

Desmond (played by experienced actor Norman Beaton, who died shortly after the series ended), and his supportive wife Shirley Ambrose (played by the equally celebrated black actress Carmen Munroe). She was justifiably proud of *Desmond's*, saying: "We have successfully created a space for ourselves, where we can just be a real, honest, loving family, with problems, and we can present that with some degree of truth and not lose the comedy."

The rest of that extended family was made up of the Ambrose children, Gloria, Sean and Michael, as well as hairdresser Tony (one of two white characters) and several drop-in characters. Desmond's old friend Porkpie (Ram John Holder) and local student Matthew (Gyearbuor Asante) often popped in to put the world to rights. The rapport between the African Matthew and the Guyanan Porkpie provided another interesting interracial dimension to the show's dynamic.

The warm barbershop comedy of *Desmond's*

Desmond's was invented on the bus. Taking the bus to meet the producer Humphrey Barclay, writer Trix Worrall noticed staff in a barbershop leching at schoolgirls. A plot hatched in his head. Worrall drew on his childhood in Peckham and his Guyanan roots to flesh out the rest and pitched the concept to Barclay straightaway.

Worrall followed *Desmond's* with a sitcom based around the Porkpie character and named after him. The series started with Porkpie winning the lottery and deciding how to handle his new wealth. In a fitting tribute to the character of Desmond – and the man who played him – Porkpie helps fund a community centre in Brixton bearing Desmond's name.

Early Doors
2003–04

Craig Cash's show is probably the best bar-room sitcom since *Cheers* although, given the quality of the competition, that may be damning *Early Doors* with faint praise.

Like *The Royle Family*, which Cash co-created, *Early Doors* centred on one room, the bar, with occasional forays to the parlour and living quarters upstairs. The pub's regulars put each other and themselves down in a sardonic manner ("I hope you don't do what I did on my first date with my Tony, it was dead embarrassing." "What was that?" "Got pregnant."), and swap puns (retiring tortoises that don't come out of their shell) and innuendoes (gags about polishing someone's trophies).

Though it's still a rarified atmosphere, the mood in the bar is much freer and less sombre than in the Royles' living room. The ambience

is lighter for one very literal reason – the bright *mise en scène*, where the pub is bathed in an early evening glow ("early doors" is a term describing the bustle of customers when pubs reopen), while at night, the pools of light give the set a cosy feel. The show's extended family makes the programme feel less intense than *The Royle Family* and, by creating more scope for subplots, helps segment the show.

All the characters are accessible and likeable, in their way, but not one-dimensional. Ken is a traditional landlord who looks after his regulars. His gossipy mother lives upstairs, looked after by the wily, cheeky carer Winnie, while Ken's attractive adopted daughter Melanie (Christine Bottomley), a student, lives in the pub and helps in the bar. The regular barflies are factory worker Joe (Cash) and his friend Duffy (Phil Mealey with whom Cash created the series when his *Royle Family* collaborator Caroline Aherne became unavailable); Tanya, the sometime punter, sometime barmaid; Tommy, the elderly misanthrope; and the somewhat simple Joan and Eddie. In the parlour lurk Phil and Nige; two incredibly indolent, spliff-smoking policemen who avail themselves of Ken's hospitality and whisky, use the rest of the thin blue line to help them cheat at pub quizzes and say "crime won't crack itself" a lot.

Both series of *Early Doors* are available on DVD.

The Fall And Rise Of Reginald Perrin
1976–79

Could there be a better example of middle-aged and middle-class malaise than David Nobbs'

> ## "I didn't get where I am today…"
>
> Here are CJ's five greatest maxims:
>
> "…by selling ice creams tasting of bookends, pumice stone and West Germany"
>
> "…without knowing there's no fun in getting where I am today"
>
> "…by everything smelling of Bolivian unicyclists' jockstraps"
>
> "…by sleeping with sweaty, Caledonian chefs"
>
> "…by thinking"

sitcom? In *American Beauty*, Kevin Spacey throws his life deliberately out of kilter to escape mundanity. And so – across the Atlantic, two decades earlier on the small screen – did Reginald Iolanthe Perrin, a pen-pushing malcontent at confectionery company Sunshine Desserts.

Reggie was embodied by Leonard Rossiter whose vocal inflections and facial posturing stole scenes left, right and elsewhere. In one particular repeated sequence, he imagined his mother-in-law as a hippopotamus. The imminent appearance of this footage was obvious from the look in his eye, so the one time when he anticipated the footage and it never came was a classic variation on the running gag.

Reggie's workplace, where he routinely arrived at least eleven minutes late on the train ("Escaped puma, Chessington North" he explained once), was peopled by the sycophantic duo Tony and David, who sucked up to boss CJ (John Barron), who was constantly reminding everyone pompously and ever more surreally: "I didn't get where I am today by…". Reggie's secretary Joan (Sue Nichols) held a strong sexual

allure for him. But Reggie remained faithful to his optimistic wife Elizabeth (Pauline Yates) and, indeed, fell in love with her again when he famously faked his own death and adopted a new identity at the end of the first series.

The faked death replicated the disappearance of the politician John Stonehouse, who fled to avoid investigation into his financial affairs – his vanishing act, oddly, was staged after Nobbs had written the book but before it had been published.

In the second series – not quite as successful as the first – Reggie sets up Grot, a shop selling useless items that, to his chagrin, is such a success that the venture becomes another Sunshine Desserts.

Spinning off from the show was *Fairly Secret Army* (Channel 4, 1984–86), featuring a character pretty much like Reggie's brother-in-law Jimmy (Geoffrey Palmer). In *Fall And Rise*, Jimmy wanted to establish a coalition against lefties but Reggie tells him: "You realise the sort of people you're going to attract, don't you Jimmy? Thugs, bully-boys, psychopaths … fascists, neo-fascists, crypto-fascists, loyalists, neo-loyalists, crypto-loyalists." To which Jimmy replies: "Do you think so? I thought recruitment might be difficult."

 The complete collection of *The Fall And Rise Of Reginald Perrin* is available in a DVD box set.

Father Ted
1995–98

"That whole loaves and fishes thing is a bit mad. You're not supposed to believe it are you Ted?" One of the many qualities that made *Father Ted* so magical was Ardal O'Hanlon's divine eejit, Father

Dougal, eternally troubled by theology, bishops and the tiring challenge of keeping track of Ted's schemes. Stupid characters are the lifeblood of many sitcoms but O'Hanlon's artfully incredulous expression – and the superb variations on the theme devised by writers Graham Linehan and Arthur Mathews – made Dougal one of the greatest chumps in sitcomland.

Yet in the madcap household of priests on Craggy Island, Dougal almost seemed normal. Father Ted (Dermot Morgan) had vainglorious, backsliding tendencies, tempered only by an inconsistent desire to do the right thing, while Father Jack (Frank Kelly) drank anything

Craggy Island's surreal clerical household: Fathers Dougal, Ted and Jack with housekeeper Mrs Doyle

in sight and, if he wasn't saying "Drink! Girls! Feck!", might sagely observe: "That would be an ecumenical matter". This trio were very loosely held in check by Mrs Doyle (Pauline McLynn), the batty tea-obsessed housekeeper, famous for saying "Go on, go on, go on, you will, you will, you will…"

The trio's series of surreal adventures took such affectionate swipes at the Catholic Church that, after the first episode was screened, one viewer complained it was anti-Catholic, while another complained it was pro-Catholic. But Catholicism was only part of the comedy – above all *Father Ted* was a highly imaginative romp where ludicrous coincidences and mishaps ran riot.

Arguably the most memorable episode involved Father Ted accidentally offending a hitherto unknown Chinese community on Craggy Island. The series of misunderstandings, which include a hilarious accidental Hitler impersonation, results in a hastily put-together celebration of the Island's diversity and a botched attempt at political correctness.

O'Hanlon helped found Ireland's first alternative comedy club, The Comedy Cellar, in Dublin in 1988 and still tours as a stand-up. *Father Ted* paved the way for further television exposure, most painfully in the terminally mainstream BBC comedy *My Hero*.

Writer and director Linehan is now a key figure in the world of British TV comedy. His other credits include *Big Train*, *Black Books* (as writer and director) and *Little Britain* (as a director). Dermot Morgan had always said that the third series was to be his last and it was, though not in the way he had imagined: he died of a heart attack, aged just 45, shortly before it went on air.

All three series and the Christmas special are available on DVD.

15 Storeys High

2002–04

Sharp-suited and booted comic Sean Lock's easy-going demeanour and sheepish wit beguiles audiences and fellow professionals alike. But when Lock, a quick-witted panellist on shows such as *QI*, and co-author of Mark Lamarr's BBC2 show *Leaving The Twentieth Century*, wrote and starred in his own sitcom *15 Storeys High*, the show was much more downbeat than his cheery charm might have led fans to expect.

15 Storeys High centred around Lock's mean on-screen character Vince and his tolerant Chinese flatmate Errol (Benedict Wong). Delusional, miserable, Vince has many bad habits and particularly enjoys taking other people's stories and making them his own, fooling nobody in the process. The highlights in Vince's life include rescuing dilapidated furniture and special offers down the supermarket, while working at the local swimming pool gives him only occasional food for thought. Lock's misanthropic Vince can be fascinating to watch as he tries, not too hard, to clamber out of a life he has made for himself through inaction and isolationism.

Vince's neighbours in the tower block – wife-swappers, lap-dancers, even a boy band – provide some weird and wonderful distractions. The mix of misanthropy and quirkiness made for an enjoyable show, albeit, as Lock can be on *QI*, a little too understated at times.

Mark Lamarr joined the writing team of Lock and Martin Trenaman for the second series but the bleak, funny show always mainly reflected Lock's obsessions with the petty irritations of everyday life.

 Only series one of *15 Storeys High* has been released on DVD so far.

Green Wing

2004–

Green Wing came from the team behind *Smack The Pony* and bore the hallmarks of that snappy, surreal sketch series. The Channel 4 show is part sitcom, part sketch show, with actors actively encouraged to improvise in some set pieces. One of the writers James Henry says: "Often only about a tenth of a scene is improvised – but gallingly, that tenth can get 90 per cent of the laughs."

The show is set in a hospital but, unlike *No Angels*, *Only When I Laugh* and *Scrubs*, the location

The 4077th

Although the sitcom *M*A*S*H* (BBC2, 1973–84) was not as dark as the Robert Altman movie – or Richard Hooker novel – it sprang from, the early episodes (before Wayne Rogers was replaced as Alan Alda's sidekick by Mike Farrell) could be dark, sardonic and cruel, with lines like: "Every war has its cute things, World War II had nice songs, the War of the Roses had nice flowers." Alda, as gifted rebel surgeon Hawkeye Pierce, brought believable indignation to some fine set pieces, once ranting: "I will not carry a gun, Frank. When I got thrown into this war I had a clear understanding with the Pentagon: no guns. I'll carry your books, I'll carry a torch, I'll carry a tune, I'll carry on, carry over, carry forward, Cary Grant, cash and carry, carry me back to Old Virginia, I'll even hari-kari if you show me how, but I will not carry a gun."

is incidental to the comedy. Stuart Kenworthy, another writer on the show, has rebuffed the frequent comparisons to *Scrubs*, saying the show has more in common with *M★A★S★H*. *Green Wing* is, first and foremost, about the idiosyncrasies and peculiarities of a group of distinct characters played by an experienced cast of comic actors that includes Sarah Alexander, Tamsin Greig and Mark Heap.

In a show that never puts too much emphasis on plot, the "story" starts with the first day at work for Dr Caroline Todd (Greig), who is set up by permanently randy male doctor, Guy Secretan (Stephen Mangan). Todd is immediately sucked into this perverted world, forced to blackmail Secretan to stop her reputation being besmirched. And so the peculiarity party starts with two characters involved in a not-so-secret sadomasochistic affair – played out by Dr Alan Statham (Mark Heap) and Joanna Clore (Pippa Haywood) – a doctor who likes to ride his motorbike down the corridors and much egomaniacal and romantic gamesmanship.

On top of this intrigue, the creators have piled plenty of sight gags and a few gross moments that owe something to their hospital context – notably the famous scene where one character mistakes eczema for macaroons. The show's generally unorthodox approach, running at over an hour including adverts, split viewers, though it is loved in the comedy industry and by most critics. But *Green Wing* did well enough to earn a second series, not as acclaimed as the first, in 2006.

Both series of *Green Wing* are available on DVD.

The Hitchhiker's Guide To The Galaxy
1981

Douglas Adams' masterful creation has been successful in every media from radio, where it made its debut, to television, theatre and most recently the movies although the film was only successful in a commercial sense.

The destruction of Earth and Arthur "we're all going to die" Dent's voyage of discovery afterwards is a tale that spans media and genres, working as science fiction, comedy and as a saga that, in a light-hearted way, provokes its audience to ask philosophical questions.

Through Arthur (played by Simon Jones on radio and TV) we see Earth's puny existence. Experienced interplanetary traveller Ford Prefect (David Dixon on TV) puts the planet in the context of a random galaxy. And Marvin the Paranoid Android (David Learner on TV) proves knowledge doesn't necessarily bring happiness.

Aficionados generally cite the radio show as the original and best incarnation but the TV series was a treat, with colourful characters such as space cowboy Zaphod Beeblebrox gloriously comic in three dimensions. The occasional touch of delicious savage satire – with the inheritors of the Earth depicted in one scene as a bunch of ghastly yuppies – was a delight. The chemistry between characters, particularly the key relationship between Arthur and Ford, worked well and the narration of Peter Jones as the guide provided more continuity between the radio and TV series.

The series had some telling and poignant moments. Once seen, the woman in the Rickmansworth café who works out the meaning of life just as the Earth is destroyed is hard to forget – as is the farcical discovery that the answer to that eternally debated question is 42.

The secret to the success of the radio show, books and TV series was the imagination and literary craft of the late Douglas Adams who had been a script editor for Tom Baker's *Doctor Who*. Adams, who died in 2001, when he was 49, had a very different idea of what his contribution to comedy might have been in a parallel universe: "I wanted to be John Cleese, it took some time to realise the job was in fact taken."

 The whole mini-series is on DVD, as is the 2005 movie version.

Kelly Monteith

1979–84

Kelly Monteith (1943–) may have been born in St Louis but for much of the 1980s he was an adopted British comedian. After several successful appearances on *Des O'Connor Tonight* in 1977–78, Monteith was given his own self-titled series by the BBC, starring in a spoof show-within-a-show years before the idea occurred to Garry Shandling.

Monteith teamed up with veteran comedy writer Neil Shand and together they devised a semi-autobiographical collection of sketches, situations and observations centred around the life of a Monteith-alike stand-up. Although there were no other principal characters other than Monteith's on-screen wife (Gabrielle Drake, who was often mistaken for his real wife), the scenario anticipated *Seinfeld* by a decade.

The show gave new life to some fairly obvious domestic situations. When Monteith was kicked out by his wife, his possessions were thrown out of the window one by one, until his teddy bear hit him on the side of his face as he pulled a delightful resigned expression. (Ironically, given the show's blurring of life and art, Monteith's real wife left him at this time.) The series also illustrated his thoughts and daydreams, with such short sketches as imagining a soldier having to make an appointment with his enemy's secretary (sat at a desk in the middle of a battlefield) to attack him.

Soon after the UK series ended, Monteith returned to the US, with his second wife and child, and had to "virtually start all over again" as a stand-up. The fact that his sitcom is not available on video or DVD simply reflects the neglect this pioneering show has suffered.

Knowing Me, Knowing You ... With Alan Partridge / I'm Alan Partridge

1994–2002

After training as an actor at Manchester Polytechnic, Steve Coogan hit the comedy circuit as a stand-up and impersonator. He got work doing voice-overs for adverts and satirical puppet show *Spitting Image*.

First appearing on Chris Morris's *On The Hour* as sports reporter Alan Partridge, Coogan's monstrous creation made the same journey from radio to television. *Knowing Me, Knowing You ... With Alan Partridge* aired in 1994, the same year as *On The Hour*'s TV spin-off *The Day Today*.

Sycophantic, patronizing, irritating, tactless and hapless, Partridge was a monstrously cringeworthy creation. *Knowing Me, Knowing You* gave

More cock and bull

In his 2005 film *A Cock And Bull Story*, director Michael Winterbottom again unites some of the biggest names in British comedy, as he had done in his "Madchester" epic *24 Hour Party People*. Steve Coogan and Rob Brydon, *24 Hour* veterans, were joined by Dylan Moran, David Walliams, Mark Williams, Ronni Ancona and Stephen Fry as well as actress Gillian Anderson. The starry cast brought to life Laurence Sterne's supposedly unfilmable, rambling eighteenth-century novel *Tristram Shandy*.

The action continually switches between the actual story to a making-of-the-movie plot in a knowing, self-referential style that invokes inevitable comparisons to Larry David's *Curb Your Enthusiasm* and Ricky Gervais's *Extras*. While the mixing of character persona and actor persona pleasantly confuses, the double act between Coogan and Brydon, who, as rival actors onscreen, argue over everything from billing to who does the better Al Pacino impression, provides the best lines.

(Sally Phillips) hides from him. Partridge's tragi-comic existence makes for compelling, nauseating, painfully funny car-crash television.

Things improve for Partridge in the final series, aired five years later, when he is fronting a digital TV clip show of car crashes called *Crash, Bang, Wallop! What A Video!* and has penned *Bouncing Back!*, a celebratory memoir about his return to fame.

Cementing the Alan Partridge legend is far from Coogan's only comedy legacy. He has founded his own production company Baby Cow (with fellow performer Henry Normal) which has been responsible for *Marion And Geoff*, *Nighty Night* and *The Sketch Show*.

 All six episodes of *Knowing Me, Knowing You* and the Christmas special are available on DVD.

Both series of *I'm Alan Partridge* are available on DVD.

The League Of Gentlemen
1999–2002

In taking *The League Of Gentlemen* to their hearts the British public showed a taste for that rare fusion of comedy and horror that Hammer Horror films achieved by accident rather than design.

The troupe (Jeremy Dyson, Mark Gatiss, Steve Pemberton and Reece Shearsmith) enjoyed a rapid rise. They started out on the London fringe theatre circuit in 1995, won the Perrier at the Edinburgh Festival in 1997 and had, by then, already recorded a radio series for the BBC in the belief that it would transfer to the small screen. The first series aired on BBC2 in 1999; a year

him a cheesy studio, complete with house band, in which to interview guests, all of whom had to endure the ritual of completing the Abba song lyric in the show's title (the correct response being "Ah – haa"). The guests were played by *Day Today* regulars Rebecca Front, Patrick Marber and Doon Mackichan, while the show was produced by Armando Iannucci. Dave Schneider played the BBC executive who cancels Partridge's show, banishing him to the media wilderness.

Three years later, in 1997 in *I'm Alan Partridge*, our uncharismatic hero resurfaced in the Linton Travel Tavern, having stooped to an early morning slot on Radio Norwich. His only real company is his unflagging, loyal, long-suffering PA, Lynn (Felicity Montagu). Even the hotel receptionist later it won a BAFTA. By 2005, when the movie *The League Of Gentlemen's Apocalypse* was released to reasonable acclaim, it would have come as no great shock to discover they owed their success to a Hammer Horror-style pact with the devil.

The League of Gentlemen took their name from a Jack Hawkins movie, while Royston Vasey, the fictional Peak District town where their characters lived, was the real name of old-school Middlesbrough comic Roy "Chubby" Brown, who appeared in the second series as the town's outspoken mayor.

Heading Royston Vasey's cast of dysfunctional misfits and loons are Edward and Tubbs, who run the shop, which is very definitely for local people – as passing customers from out of town would testify if they hadn't been killed by the couple. Strangers were given fair warning. A sign at the edge of the town reads: "Welcome to Royston Vasey. You'll Never Leave!" Visitors might well pass this sign in the cab of Barbara Dixon – surely a pun on the Scottish singer – who regales customers with graphic tales of what it's like to have a sex change. Meanwhile, there's a Sweeney Todd-style butcher, a vet who accidentally kills his patients and Pauline, an officious job-training officer, who must have inspired Marjorie Dawes in *Little Britain*.

One of the most popular later characters is Papa Lazarou, a freaky circus ringmaster and stealer of taps and wives. He was based on Mr Papalazarou, a former landlord of Steve Pemberton's and Reece Shearsmith's, who directly inspired the catch phrases "Is Dave there?" and "This is just a saga now".

All three seasons, the Christmas special and the movie are available on DVD.

Marion And Geoff
2000–03

Rob Brydon has exacted more mileage from the character of cuckolded taxi driver Keith Barrett than his character ever clocked up on his meter. The Welshman first appeared unto the whole nation in ten-minute slices of self-deprecation and unnatural grace in the face of adversity before his inner pain filled 30 minutes in a second series. As his marriage disintegrates, Brydon's cabbie tries to put a brave face on things: "I don't feel I've lost a wife, I feel I've gained a friend. I'd never have met Geoff if Marion hadn't left me."

Barrett then found solace in other people's marital adventures in *The Keith Barrett Show*, which, live and on TV, portrayed a man who had come out fighting after his wife left him and his children turned against him. New, improved Keith could hold his own in chat-show land and attack the institution of marriage in a way that the humiliated cabbie in *Marion And Geoff* would never have dared.

In the early days, Brydon's character had to take suffering sitting down, as he poured his woes good-naturedly into a camera mounted on his cab dashboard. As the series progressed, Barrett's predicament was revealed to be bleaker and bleaker, requiring all of Brydon's gift for understating pathos.

Keith Barrett, a character Brydon developed while working in radio, has made him. He has since appeared in *Little Britain* and continued to collaborate with Steve Coogan, notably on Michael Winterbottom's well-received movie *A Cock And Bull Story* (2005).

Both series of *Marion And Geoff* have been released on DVD.

The ups and downs of lad lifestyle: Gary (Martin Clunes) has some explaining to do to Deborah (Leslie Ash), Tony (Neil Morrissey) and Dorothy (Caroline Quentin)

Men Behaving Badly

1992–98

Men Behaving Badly was the seminal mainstream sitcom of the 1990s. It combined the traditional fourth wall sitcom format and a timely look at lad culture, becoming a huge popular hit by rebuffing all that nonsense about "new men".

The first series aired on ITV and starred Harry Enfield as Dermot, replaced by Neil Morrissey as Tony in the second series. Enfield was not right for the role but he persuaded Martin Clunes to take the part of Gary. By the third series (it ran for six series and there were quite a few specials) the show had transferred to the BBC, after ITV's unfortunate decision not to recommission.

The regular cast on BBC was Morrisey, Martin Clunes, Caroline Quentin and Leslie Ash, with other regular characters at various times including John Thompson as the absent-minded barman Ken.

The show focused on the hapless laddish antics of emotionally stunted flatmates Gary (Clunes) and Tony (Morrissey), who spend most of their free time on their sofa, swilling beer, talking about birds and pontificating on all manner of trivia which, in Gary's case, often end with him beaming like an idiot and saying "Kylie!" Though perfectly suited to the franker, more laddish, male culture rife at the time, *Men Behaving Badly* was no blatant "lad ad", poking fun at the downside of such a lifestyle. The series was just as popular with women, with Dorothy (Quentin) and Deborah (Ash) empathetic characters – Dorothy because she desperately wanted Gary to grow up and Deborah usually repelling Tony's attentions.

Simon Nye wrote *Men Behaving Badly* as a novel first, based on university acquaintances. The book spawned the series which then spawned novelty books. The Christmas 1998 special wrapped up the show's history with Dorothy giving birth to Gary's baby.

All seven series are available separately on DVD, and series 1–6 are available as the *Men Behaving Badly 6 Pack* box set.

The New Statesman

1987–92

"I'm the right B'stard to shake Maggie" screamed the *Daily Mirror* headline in 1987 above an interview with Rik Mayall about his latest character, Alan B'stard MP in *The New Statesman*. This outrageous political sitcom my not have brought down the Conservative government but it poked fun mercilessly at the regime's greed and malevolence.

The New Statesman's writers Lawrence Marks and Maurice Gran, whose other credits include much less in-your-face shows, were asked by Mayall to write something for him. Capitalizing on his energy and quick wit, they gave him licence to be zany and delightfully over the top.

The show's premise is that B'Stard was elected with a huge majority for the constituency of Haltemprice (echoing the real constituency of Haltemprice and Howden, where David Davis, darling of the right, was elected in the same year, though that is where the similarity ends). A head-on car crash, engineered by B'Stard, sidelined the Labour and SDP candidates. To avoid police investigation, he promised to push through a bill allowing them to carry guns – weapons he planned to sell to them.

B'Stard's reign was littered with such twisted double-dealings. He dupes and defrauds, thinks nothing of dumping nuclear waste in a playground and openly admits his recreational activities are: "Making money, drinking, driving, dining out on other people's expenses, boogying, bonking, droit du seigneur, grinding the faces of the poor."

Supporting B'Stard to one degree or another were his lapdog fellow MP Piers Fletcher-Dervish (Michael Troughton), who would inevitably be caught up in B'Stard's devilish schemes, and his wife Sarah (Marsha Fitzalan), who was as unfaithful as he was, if not more so.

The show's feel, though not as formal as the Whitehall classic *Yes Minister*, was helped by the fact that it used a House of Commons set, previously used for a serialization of the political novel *First Among Equals* by another great Tory opportunist, Jeffrey Archer.

The maverick MP got his comeuppance at the end of the second series but inevitably staged a comeback, initially as a Euro MP for the German constituency of Ubersaxony and, in 2006, as a New Labourite in a West End show.

All four series are available separately on DVD or as a four-disc box set.

Nighty Night
2004–

In television comedy, the 1990s was an era where clowning for laughs was frowned upon. The likes of Steve Coogan and Chris Morris were finding out just how close to the bone you could go and still get a laugh. This approach took comedy closer to being an art form but could prove too nauseating to be entertaining.

Julia Davis, who wrote and starred in *Nighty Night*, has had to climb some considerable hurdles to become an icon of black comedy. While studying English at York University she developed glandular fever and spent two years bedridden at home in Bath. After that, she had several nondescript jobs before joining an improv troupe with Rob Brydon and Ruth Jones.

A role in a Radio 4 comedy with Arabella Weir introduced Davis to *Father Ted* writers Graham Linehan and Arthur Mathews, who cast her in their *Big Train* sketch show. She also met Chris Morris and collaborated with Steve Coogan on his 1998 tour. Coogan's company Baby Cow was responsible for developing *Human Remains* and *Nighty Night*, both of which Davis has written and starred in.

Human Remains (BBC2, 2000), in which Davis co-starred with Brydon, was a series of six mockumentaries on the hideous and embarrassing relationship between six different couples from widely differing social backgrounds. *Nighty Night*, which could almost be described as a West Country *Fatal Attraction*, was altogether more brutal.

Davis' character, beauty store owner Jill – "mid-20s widow with a lust for life and a flexible spine" – is Machiavellian and malevolent. After her husband Terry (Kevin Eldon) is diagnosed with a terminal illness, she asks: "Why does everything happen to me?" Terry reassures her, saying: "Look, love, it'll be okay. It's not really that bad. It's me who's got the cancer." Cheered, Jill declares his early demise and sets her sights on her new neighbour Dr Don Cole (Angus Deayton), even though he is married to Cath, an MS sufferer.

Jill woos Cole shamelessly, re-enacting Sharon Stone's most infamous scene from *Basic Instinct* at a party and exercising in her underwear outside his house. The show feels part surreal sitcom, part documentary, retaining as it does a rough-cut edited feel and realistic background sound.

 Series one and two of *Nighty Night* are on DVD.

No Angels

2004–06

No Angels is one of Channel 4's string of contemporary comedy drama products, though, unlike the comparable show *Shameless*, it veers more towards sitcom than drama.

No Angels centres on four cheeky, sassy and – you guessed it! – sexy nurses in a Leeds hospital: Anji (Sunetra Sarker), Beth (Jo Joyner), Lia (Louise Delamere) and Kate (Kaye Wragg). The foursome live a raucous, irreverent life, the burden of work made bearable by sex, drugs and alcohol. An indiscretion by Kate, the highly organized acting sister on her male-dominated ward, kicks off the series. She sleeps with senior house doctor Jamie. His subsequent aloofness throws her and he blames the death of a patient on her distracted attitude.

Tragedy and comedy are never far apart, though comedy usually wins out, with the patients often cruelly mocked for their ailments and predicaments. MRSA inevitably makes an appearance, but in this show such topical allusions don't feel intrusive.

Although the women's antics are the focus of the show, the male character of McManus (Francis Magee) is a stereotypically arrogant, dictatorial, buffoonish caricature of a NHS senior consultant who, it must be said, is a beacon of efficiency when compared to some of the younger male medical staff.

More daring than hospital dramas of yesteryear, with the title pointedly distancing the show from BBC1's seminal 1970s nursing potboiler *Angels*, the show does borrow from them and, at times, from the *Carry On* and *Doctor* movies. The nostalgic flavour of *No Angels* is enhanced by the show's Motown soundtrack. The truly chilling aspect of this show is that many of the incidents are drawn from real life.

 Series one and two (of three) are available on DVD.

The Office

2000–03

One quality that defines a great sitcom is the creation of a character who is adopted by the entire nation. And in David Brent, the smug, leering,

Extra helpings

Following *The Office* was never going to be easy and Ricky Gervais and Stephen Merchant's *Extras*, a sitcom set in the world of showbiz, was an easy target for critics keen to suggest the earlier smash was a one-off.

Gervais played David Millman, a bit-part actor, who was closer to his own persona than Brent but used, he said, "the same voice and facial muscles". The show attracted most attention because of its celebrity cameos – from the likes of Kate Winslet, Ben Stiller and, er, Les Dennis – but the sitcom, though more gentle than *The Office*, had a few genuinely laugh-out-loud moments. No one who saw the scene where Les Dennis suddenly shouts out "Oh Mavis!" at the moment of sexual climax will ever forget it.

platitudinous, excruciatingly grotesque boss from hell, Ricky Gervais and Stephen Merchant's *The Office* created a monster all the more entertaining because, as Gervais admitted, there is a bit of Brent in all of us.

As the office manager of a paper merchants in Slough, Brent suffers from the delusion that he is a people's person ("friend first, boss second, entertainer third") although only Gareth, the office's Territorial Army-obsessed nerd, holds Brent in anything approaching esteem. Even he, as the show progressed, began to distance himself from Brent.

As with *People Like Us*, the sitcom is made as a fly-on-the-wall documentary. This device is actually less important than the ribaldry and rivalry between the characters. Memorable set pieces included the "fixed" company quiz night, the lecherous outing to a nightclub and, most famous of all, that David Brent dance.

The love story between Tim (Martin Freeman) and receptionist Dawn (Lucy Davis, daughter of Jasper Carrott) helped maintain viewer loyalty. The romantic potential between them was akin to the on-off Ross and Rachel saga in *Friends*, but less contorted. Their budding romance gave warmth to a show that would have been too monotonously cringeworthy with only Brent's boorish antics and the staff's childish sniping.

That said, it is Brent's antics and faux zen wisdom ("Never do today that which will become someone else's responsibility tomorrow" and "There may be no 'I' in team but there's a 'ME' if you look hard enough.") that the series is most remembered for. The series – especially after it was remade in the US – propelled Gervais, once an aspiring pop star, into comedy superstardom, launching him as a stand-up and winning him his own episode of *The Simpsons*.

Both series and the Christmas special are on DVD.

Peep Show
2003–

David Mitchell and Robert Webb were another comedy marriage made at Cambridge University. As president of Cambridge Footlights, Mitchell revelled in the role to the detriment of his studies, admitting: "Out of comedy, drinking and history I could have done any two. And I didn't choose comedy and history." Webb was a year ahead of Mitchell but the pair formed a lasting duo that won plaudits in Edinburgh and writing credits with sketch shows *Armstrong And Miller*, *Big Train* and *Bruiser*.

Mitchell and Webb's *Peep Show* was refreshingly brazen about human self-interest. As flatmates

Mark and Jez, Mitchell and Webb's thoughts were audible to the audience and action was often played out from the actors' point of view, involving portable cameras for some scenes. The duo's thoughts were usually covetous or conniving. Jez was preoccupied with his self-styled rebel image and future in the music business and Mark was obsessed with coupling up – primarily with his office colleague, Sophie (Olivia Colman).

At times, the show was like watching a scripted fly-on-the-wall documentary revealing the inner workings of the human mind. The difference between what people say and mean was delightfully exposed. Choice lines such as "She's got the magic combination of beauty and low self-esteem" were thought, while equally outrageous lines such as "Who do you support? Mark's Israel.

I'm Palestine. Makes the news more interesting" were outspoken in both senses of the word.

Peep Show was nominated for a BAFTA award. A third series was commissioned in 2005, though Mitchell and Webb have pursued solo projects, with Webb landing a lead role in *The Smoking Room* and Mitchell appearing on many chat and quiz shows.

The first two series (of three) have been released on DVD.

Rising Damp
1974–78

Despite the dark, claustrophobic sets, the melodramatic delivery of some lines and the fact that, more than thirty years since its first run, it is finally looking a bit dated in parts, *Rising Damp* is still a classic, simply the best sitcom ITV ever produced.

Leonard Rossiter as Rigsby is a comic turn to savour. His clever portrayal of a bigoted, racist, unscrupulous, yet loveable, landlord has survived the ravages of political correctness and beyond. Rigsby's teasing of black student Philip (the sublime Don Warrington) showed the landlord struggling to cope with Britain's changing culture and provided a great excuse for boarding house bawdiness:

Rigsby: Is it true that your women are much more … you know…
Philip: Oh yes, much more.
Rigsby: Yes, I'd heard that.
Philip: It's a medical fact. They get much more excited.
Rigsby: Yes … ours are always getting headaches. Do yours get headaches?
Philip: No, I don't think so.

Rising Damp's comedy character quartet (and baby): (from left) Frances de la Tour, Leonard Rossiter as bigoted, unscrupulous landlord Rigsby, Richard Beckinsale and Don Warrington

The ten worst TV comedies ever

Trippers Day
1984

After Leonard Rossiter's work in *Rising Damp* and *The Fall And Rise Of Reginald Perrin*, this lame tale of a supermarket manager struggling to control his staff was almost heartbreaking to watch. The jokes hit the floor with a heavy thud.

Up The Elephant And Round The Castle
1983–85

Worse even than Jim Davidson's dubious talents as an actor were the scripts for this sitcom which made his character's birds and booze quests far less diverting than Davidson's tabloid escapades.

Yus My Dear
1976

Spun off the dire, racially stereotyping sitcom *Romany Jones*, named after veteran comic actor Arthur Mullard's lame catch phrase, this was so hideously unfunny even ITV yanked it off air after one series.

Take A Letter, Mr Jones...
1981

This sitcom was a vehicle for *Are You Being Served?*'s camp hero John Inman (Mr Humphries) but a one-dimensional plot about him being the secretary (and not a woman) flagged halfway through the first episode.

Mr Bean
1990–95

Though successful, with even a smash movie spin-off, there's only so much face-gurning you can take from Rowan Atkinson.

The Upper Hand
1990–96

This dull remake of the popular US sitcom *Who's The Boss*, had a one-joke premise that everything else fell around: the will they, won't they, who cares anyway issue of whether widower/housekeeper Charlie (Joe McGann) would get it together with his employer Caroline (Diana Weston).

Keeping Up Appearances
1990–95

Though attracting devoted fans in number this comedy of manners had nothing on its sparkling predecessor, *The Good Life*.

Babes In The Wood
1998–99

Samantha Janus and Denise Van Outen were easy on the eye for male viewers but this hackneyed young, free and single "birds on their own" premise was looking decidedly jaded by this point in comedy history.

Coupling
2000

A shrill exploitation of the *Friends* formula, this retread had the same number of characters as the US sitcom but one sixth of the charm and guile.

Shane
2004

A disappointingly middle-of-the-road outing for Frank Skinner, almost as cheesy as Jim Davidson's *Up The Elephant And Round The Castle* (above).

Rigsby and Philip had something in common. As the show's writer Eric Chappell noted, "They were both outsiders for different reasons". Completing the quartet were Richard Beckinsale, beautifully sunny and naive as the student idealist Alan, and the classically trained actress Frances de la Tour as the proper but scatty spinster Ruth Jones, whom Rigsby adored.

Miss Jones – Rossiter always said her name in a way that suggested he was slightly out of breath – only had eyes for Philip, who used her adoration to wind up Rigsby.

De la Tour, Rossiter and Warrington had all been in the cast of *The Banana Box*, the stage play by Chappell on which *Rising Damp* was

Five characters sitting around a TV – the essence of *The Royle Family*

based. Two of the show's principals were simultaneously appearing in acclaimed BBC1 sitcoms: Rossiter was Reginald Perrin and Richard Beckinsale played another young idealist, Godber, in *Porridge*. But Beckinsale tragically died from a heart attack shortly after quitting the show after its third series, when he was just 31.

Rising Damp represented an almost perfect match of cast and script. On the rare occasions that Chappell's lines weren't quite up to par, it was enough simply to watch Rossiter's grimacings, shufflings and nervous twitches. He used his full repertoire of physical tricks in the sitcom – including his trademark corkscrew head movement – but never even looked in danger of going over the top.

All four series are available as a DVD box set, and you can also buy a best-of selection, the first series and the movie on DVD.

The Royle Family
1998–2000

Like that other inspired sitcom about working class life, *Till Death Us Do Part*, *The Royle Family* could have split the country along the north/south divide but instead won almost universal admiration. The show had a warm, homely feel, accentuated by such touches as the mother's secret biscuit drawer. The extraordinarily effective pacing of episodes made such a simple setup – five characters sitting around a TV and talking – feel mysteriously richer than more frenetic sitcoms.

One reason often trotted out for the decline of the British sitcom is the quality of the acting. It's true that sitcoms like *Dad's Army* were helped immeasurably by the casting of such experienced, gifted actors as John Le Mesurier. The casting on *The Royle Family*, bringing in two *Brookside* veterans (Sue Johnston and Ricky Tomlinson) and the experienced comic actress Liz Smith, was simply superb.

Caroline Aherne, who co-wrote the show, was marvellous as daughter Denise, while her writing partner Craig Cash made the difficult role of Dave, Denise's boyfriend, a character, not a cipher. Ralf Little was utterly believable as put-upon son Anthony, while Liz Smith, as Nana, extended the range of the comedy. The central pairing of Johnston as mum Barbara and Tomlinson as dad Jim was crucial. The sitcom's relentless focus on births, deaths, marriages, shopping catalogues and betting on *Antiques Roadshow* could have paled but Johnston and Tomlinson gave performances of such nuanced charm that it was impossible to look away.

The dialogue was usually downbeat but punctuated by raucous punchlines, usually delivered by the irascible Jim ("I paid a quid for these underpants, I've got 50p's worth stuck up me arse", he complained once). Jim's vitriol would often be directed at the television: "Anne Robinson, my arse! *Watchdog*? I am watching a bloody dog!"

The show had pathos aplenty but in later series Jim's ire towards Nana, Denise's impending motherhood and the introduction of Anthony's useless friend Darren subtly varied the comedy. For all their failings there was plenty of warmth and love in this Royle family, making the clever title even more double-edged.

 All three seasons are available on DVD, and you can also buy a three-disc box set and *The Very Best Of The Royle Family*.

Shameless
2004–

Shameless by name, shameless by nature. The exploits of bad dad Frank Gallagher involved a television orgy of drugs, sex, violence and dodgy goings-on, yet the comedy/drama was hailed as a triumph of "dramedy" as critics became so enthused, they invented a new mini-genre.

Frank (David Threlfall) has six children and, when his wife leaves him, turns to drink, leaving the children to fend for themselves. His eldest daughter Fiona becomes head of the family. Frank's drinking problem is so immense that in one episode he wakes up in France after a bender not knowing how he got there. Further proof of Frank's utter lack of shame is the opportunism with which he moves in with rich, sex-starved neighbour Sheila when her husband leaves her. Frank had been sleeping with Sheila's daughter, Karen, who had also dated Lip, one of Frank's sons.

In the infamous Christmas special (for which The Smiths' Johnny Marr provided the music) Frank leads his neighbours into a riot when the army seal off their estate after a food poisoning outbreak – caused by abandoned meat sold by Lip and Frank's mate Kev.

The Gallagher clan's anarchic adventures on the Chatsworth Estate, a shabby fictional housing area in Manchester, were based on writer Paul Abbott's childhood experiences. Abbott's early life was even darker than the series suggested. When he was 11, Abbott and his 17-year-old sister looked after the other eight children in their family after their parents abandoned them. Surviving a rape and a suicide attempt when he was 15, Abbott was sectioned before going into foster care. His interest in writing was nurtured at meetings of Burnley Writers Circle and his professional writing career began after he graduated from the University of Manchester with a psychology degree. Abbott became the youngest ever script editor on *Coronation Street* at 24 and his other credits to date include political thriller *State Of Play*, *Touching Evil* and *Clocking Off*.

By writing the outrageous *Shameless*, Abbott acknowledged there had been good times in his youth: "Imagine a teenage party where your parents clear out to give you run of the house – but for six years! I remember us once spending about half our household budget on that week's top ten singles, just so we could open the windows, whack up the volume and make the street think we were loaded. What parent would have countenanced that?"

Series one and two and the Christmas special have all been released on DVD.

Shelley

1979–92

Rather like Tony Hancock's comic persona, Shelley (Hywel Bennett) took everything life threw at him and responded with sarcasm and disdain. As with Hancock, Shelley believed the world ought to revolve around him and was disappointed whenever this proved not to be the case.

But James Shelley was an even more unlikely sitcom hero than Hancock. He began as a 28-year-old undergraduate determined not to become part of the system and ended up, more than seventy episodes later, older, no wiser and keen to avoid responsibility even though his girlfriend Fran had become pregnant.

Shelley's sardonic, world-weary views were mostly inflicted on the authoritarian landlady of his North London bedsit, Mrs Hawkins (Josephine Hewson). Shelley had a knack of getting people caught up in his observations about the world and their role in it, once showing up a doctor and a double-glazing salesman as useless and neglectful, although the two men still enjoyed Shelley's company.

While Shelley always had a line for every situation, he cast a pall over proceedings. His personal life was similarly dulled when Fran left him and took their daughter Emma with her, judging Shelley, always without a steady job, incapable of supporting a family. Shelley left for America and that appeared to be that. Four years later, in 1988, came *The Return Of Shelley* complete with new characters and new challenges for Shelley in yuppie Britain, a place that felt, to him, like a foreign country.

The *Buffy* meister

Joss Whedon, the creator of *Buffy The Vampire Slayer*, was educated in Winchester, Hampshire, and the influence of English humour is reflected in the fact that he wrote two English characters into *Buffy*, one of the few American shows to match *Spaced* with the breadth and depth of its pop cultural references.

Whedon was born into comedy – his father Tom wrote for *The Golden Girls* – and started out writing on *Roseanne*. *Buffy* is technically not a comedy but between 1997 and 2003, the genre-bending show using humour and irreverence to debunk many archetypes, including the Broadway musical. The show's unusual attitude to the genres of horror, romance and comedy mark it as an obvious precursor to *Shaun Of The Dead* and will probably inspire future comedy crossovers.

Writer Peter Tilbury drew on his memories of the dole queue to create Shelley, though Guy Jenkins and Andy Hamilton, who would later create *Drop The Dead Donkey*, ably assisted him. In 1997, Shelley returned for six episodes on Radio 2, with Stephen Tomlinson – Damien from *Drop The Dead Donkey* – as the philosophical idler.

Spaced
1999–2001

If *This Life* was the flat-sharing drama of the late 1990s, *Spaced* was the flat-sharing comedy for the same generation. Number 23, Meteor Street, Tufnell Park, North London was the focal point for a collection of charming misfits and

Flat-sharing comedy for the 1990s: Daisy (Jessica Stevenson) and Tim (Simon Pegg) in *Spaced*

wannabes watched over by daunting chain-smoking, alcoholic landlady Marsha Kelin (Julia Deakin). The occupants were Tim Bisley (Simon Pegg), a wannabe comic-strip writer, Daisy Steiner (Jessica Stevenson), a wannabe writer, Brian Topp (Mark Heap), a wannabe artist and finally the legs – for that is all we ever saw – of Marsha's rebellious daughter Amber. Tim's best friend Mike, a Territorial Army fanatic, moved in for the second series.

Most of the group's everyday adventures referred imaginatively to popular culture. There is a particularly significant scene where Tim says a prayer for his future job success and the camera pulls back to reveal he has been invoking *Buffy The*

Vampire Slayer. Like *Buffy*, *Spaced* plays irreverently with genres and popular culture. When Daisy gets a job in a kitchen, the strict working conditions are presented as if the staff were characters in *One Flew Over The Cuckoo's Nest*.

Some shows were completely jam-packed with references. In *Art*, in the first series, there are nods to *Poltergeist*, *Evil Dead 2*, the computer game *Resident Evil 2*, George A. Romero's zombie films, and the Francis Ford Coppola movie *The Conversation* – all in the first five minutes! Some of the characters appeared to be direct lifts. Tyres, a dance-music-crazed bicycle dispatch rider, was a dead ringer for the *Viz* character Ravey Davey, while Tim's boss, played by Bill Bailey, is called Bilbo, an obvious Tolkien

The old-school stand-up

If you ever wondered what *Phoenix Nights* would be like without the irony, cast your mind back to – or catch a digital rerun of – *The Comedians* (ITV, 1971–93), a no-nonsense, does-what-it-says-on-the-tin showcase for generations of stand-ups that represented everything alternative comedy was trying to get away from.

The show featured a veritable roll call of old-school stand-ups – including Bernard Manning, Charlie Williams, Tom O'Connor, Jim Bowen, Frank Carson, Mike Reid (before his fame in *Eastenders*) and, latterly, Russ Abbott, Stan Boardman and Roy Walker – who were distinguished, if at all, by their personalities not their material. Their gags – often of the traditional mother-in-law or Englishman, Irishman and a Scotsman variety – were sometimes racist and sexist and so similar as to feel shared.

In retrospect, the most intriguing member of the group was Charlie Williams, a black comedian from Barnsley who divided the black community on how much a black man telling stereotypical jokes could be considered a role model. For Lenny Henry, Britain's most iconic black comedian, Williams was a hero: "As soon as he opened his mouth and talked about his childhood in the 1930s, of the war, of terraced houses, of outside lavs, of ordinary British life, we knew he was from right here. Anyone with half a brain could see that. And we loved him for it."

Trevor Griffiths' 1975 play *Comedians*, which anticipates politically correct comedy, was inspired partly by a meeting with some stars of the ITV show. For all the play's ideological import – it compares the political strategies of social democrats and revolutionaries – the play was also a sideswipe at the then established comedy regime.

---

allusion that echoes Bailey's appearance and his stand-up shtick.

There was an intriguing romantic tension throughout between Tim and Daisy, who had to pose as a couple to live in the flat. There were several other loose ends to tie up too and plenty of twists and turns before the show's final resolution.

Simon Pegg and director Edgar Wright teamed up again for *Shaun Of The Dead*, the 2004 zombie comedy movie starring *Spaced* actors Nick Frost and Peter Serafinowicz, *The Office* star Lucy Davis and Dylan Moran.

 Both series are available separately on DVD, or together, with a host of extras, on a three-disc collector's edition box set.

That Peter Kay Thing/ Phoenix Nights

2000–02

Peter Kay's entrance into comedy could have been the subject of one of his own routines – he took a stand-up module in his Media and Performance HND. Laughable though that sounds, by his second gig Kay had won the North West Comedian Of The Year Award. In 1997 he was nominated for a Perrier Award and in 1998 he filmed a one-off programme for Channel 4's *Comedy Lab* series that became the basis of *That Peter Kay Thing*.

That Peter Kay Thing (Channel 4, 2000) was a series of six spoof docusoaps centred around his native town of Bolton. The main male and female characters (all played by Kay) had dead-end jobs and their own special idiosyncrasies. Binding the series together was the narration of Andrew Sachs (Manuel in *Fawlty Towers*) and a running joke about the appearance – or not – of "celebrity Bob Carolgees". The show helped fill Kay's trophy cabinet by winning best comedy series at the British Comedy Awards.

Peter Kay's Phoenix Nights, which started in 2001, was foreseen in an episode of *That Peter Kay Thing*. Co-written with fellow stand-up Dave Spikey and Neil Fitzmaurice, the show depicted the ruses and rivalries involved in running a social club in – where else? – Bolton. Kay's main role was Brian Potter, the petty, conspiring wheelchair-bound owner, while Spikey was the club's MC, Jerry Sinclair, and Fitzmaurice was cheesy DJ Ray Von. Perrier-winning stand-up Daniel Kitson had a role as glass collector Spencer. Kay also played bouncer Max, who along with his colleague Paddy (Patrick McGuinness) would do the odd turn, performing the Tony Christie hit *(Is This The Way To) Amarillo?* which Kay re-released as a duet with Christie for Comic Relief. Kay featured the pair in the spin-off *Max And Paddy's Road To Nowhere*, which lacked the charm and enjoyable ensemble acting of *Phoenix Nights*.

By the time the second *Phoenix Nights* series aired in 2002, Kay was already a national comic icon, who sold out several big live tours, even though his television comedy and tour itinerary focused exclusively on the north of England.

That Peter Kay Thing and *Peter Kay's Phoenix Nights* are both available on DVD in their entirety.

The Thick Of It
2005–

While the Stephen Fry sitcom *Absolute Power* (BBC2, 2002) did a good job satirizing the spin of public relations, *The Thick Of It* offered a more ruthless and brutal take on political spin.

Centre of attention in *The Thick Of It* was the hapless government minister Hugh Abbott (Chris Langham), whose career was kept afloat by his advisers. Pulling most of the strings was Malcolm Tucker (Peter Capaldi), a thinly veiled take on New Labour's spin doctor extraordinaire Alastair Campbell, both of whom could list swearing as a hobby in *Who's Who*. In one episode, Tucker says with simple eloquence: "Come the fuck in or fuck the fuck off." Buckling under the weight of Malcolm's edicts were Abbott's staff, Glen Campbell (James Smith) and Olly Reeder (stand-up Chris Addison, making his small screen breakthrough). Providing the (largely ignored) voice of reason and conscience was press officer Terri Coverley (Joanna Scanlan).

The sitcom embroils Abbott in many potential contemporary political traps. He creates policy on the hoof – inventing a whole new policy in forty minutes – and becomes dangerously involved with a focus group member who he tries to use to publicly endorse another policy.

Framing the action is the same juddery hand-held camera technique that had followed Langham in *People Like Us*. The overall feeling of the show hung somewhere between *People Like Us* and *The Office* but with a dose of the knowing political savvy that creator Armando Iannucci had previously brought to *The Saturday Night Armistice* and *The Day Today*.

The show won two British Comedy Awards in 2006, including best comedy actor for

Langham, just reward after a career of ups and dramatic downs. His triumph was overshadowed by an even more dramatic down a few days later when it was announced that Langham had been arrested during an investigation into Internet child pornography. The actor maintained his innocence and the whole bizarre affair seemed as if life were imitating a very dark sitcom.

 The first six episodes of *The Thick Of It* are available on DVD.

The Young Ones

1982–84

The Young Ones might never have been made had it not been for the threat that Channel 4 would snap up the new comedy talent the BBC had tapped into. Though the Comic Strip gang of comedians Peter Richardson, Nigel Planer, Rik Mayall, Adrian Edmondson, Jennifer Saunders and Dawn French did end up on Channel 4, the BBC was wise enough to nurture an idea from Mayall, his partner Lise Mayer and Ben Elton called *The Young Ones*. The scripts – a never entirely seamless fusion of Mayall and Mayer and Elton's comedy – gave the series much disjointed, unpredictable charm.

The show's student digs housed a formidable array of boisterous and anarchic characters. Mayall and Edmondson (Rik and Vivian) took roles similar to those in their *The Dangerous Brothers* act, likewise Planer's drippy hippy Neil echoed half of his cabaret double-act with Peter Richardson. Actor Chris Ryan was thrown in as Mike, a kind of Fonz authority figure. The many cameos included, most significantly, appearances from Emma Thompson, Robbie Coltrane, Dawn

French, Jennifer Saunders and Arnold Brown. Alexei Sayle, who played the Eastern European character he used in his act, dropped in whenever the quotient of mayhem seemed likely to run low and even used excerpts from this act in the programme.

It's often forgotten that the show had several puppet characters such as Vivian's cantankerous Geordie hamster and the never-used household cleaning implements under the stairs who took the roles from domestic drama *Upstairs, Downstairs*. The puppet characters – and the comedy's knockabout edge – attracted, to the chagrin of some parents, many younger viewers.

The group's cartoon antics extracted laughs from such seemingly mundane events as the visit of the TV repair man or funny pastiches such as their unexpected appearance on *University*

Challenge (an episode featuring Griff Rhys Jones and Stephen Fry). There was a lot of slapstick violence, a cricket bat being Vivian's weapon of choice, when his head wasn't being severed from his body.

Among the many memorable moments of the show was Vivian's rant against *The Good Life*, a funny, telling moment indicative of the wider shift that was taking place in television comedy in the early 1980s.

Both series are available separately on DVD, or combined in a box set called *Every Stoopid Episode*.

Sketch shows

British sketch comedy has its roots in music hall and reviews like *Beyond The Fringe*. The genre is almost as diverse as comedy itself, varying from the zany antics of Kenny Everett to the verbal duelling of Fry and Laurie and the surrealism of Spike Milligan and *Big Train*. Traditionally, sketch shows featured unrelated skits but, today, it is more common for a show to have a definite theme (the girl-powered *Smack The Pony* or the sketch show-cum-sitcom *Green Wing*).

The sketch show has also given us some iconic characters – from Dick Emery's "Oooh you are awful" blonde in the 1970s to Kenny Everett's Cupid Stunt and *The Fast Show*'s Ralph and Ted. Sometimes, with programmes like *A Bit Of Fry And Laurie*, the comedy is more about harnessing the personalities involved.

its time, with wacky moments that predated *Vic Reeves' Big Night Out* but owed an obvious debt to the mainly Scottish sketch show *Naked Video* (BBC2, 1986–91) and *Monty Python*.

The *Absolutely* group cohered around Jack Doherty and Moray Hunter, who had written for *Spitting Image* and *Alas Smith And Jones*. They were later joined by Peter Baike (mainly a composer of TV music), John Sparkes (from *Naked Video*), Gordon Kennedy and Morwenna Banks,

Absolutely

1989–93

Effectively a Scots product, albeit made for Channel 4, *Absolutely* had little trouble crossing the border and achieving cult status. One of Channel 4's best-kept secrets, *Absolutely* was one of the more refreshing comedy products of

Wry humour

On 31 December 1978, BBC Scotland offered an alternative to the usual televised tartan teuchterama of Hogmanay with the much treasured sketch show *Scotch And Wry*, that some devotees insist is better than *Absolutely*. Starring light entertainment veteran Rikki Fulton, the show's best remembered comic characters are the useless traffic cop and the Presbyterian minister the Rev. I.M. Jolly, author of the bestselling tome *How I Found God And Why He Was Hiding From Me*. The annual skits helped introduce such talent as Miriam Margolyes and Tony Roper and Gregor Fisher. The latter pair would become better known as Jamesie and Rab in the sitcom *Rab C. Nesbitt*.

whose previous writing and performing credits included *The Lenny Henry Show* and *French And Saunders*.

One of its longest-running and most successful sketches, "Stoneybridge", was untypical of the show's content. In the sketch the councillors of a tiny village, Stoneybridge, strive to put it on the map as a vibrant, exciting metropolis with the catch phrase: "Stoneybridge has facilities and … facilities, so come to Stoneybridge!"

Sketches such as "Old Man: Bert Bastard" and, to a lesser extent, "Naughty Kids" crossed over and resembled Harry Enfield classics "Old Gits" and "Kevin And Perry" – proof, if nothing else, that great comic minds can think alike. The repugnant Frank Hovis, who delivered his mono-

Parodying pop culture: Adam Buxton and Joe Cornish in *The Adam And Joe Show*

logues from the toilet and had a nasty phlegm problem, also seems a forerunner for *The Fast Show*'s Bob Fleming.

The Adam And Joe Show
1996–2001

This irreverent, late-night sketch show opened up the imaginative world of the stereotypical student bedsit to the public, acquiring a cult following among the Friday night just-back-from-the-pub audience partly by offering some of the funniest, most concise parodies of popular culture seen on Channel 4.

Adam Buxton and Joe Cornish had worked together on short films since meeting in their early teens and their obsessions were delightfully pubescent. Various pop culture skits were facilitated via *Star Wars* figurines, including one of *Stars In Their Eyes* where C3PO and R2D2 become The Pet Shop Droids. The use of stuffed toys, apart from being usefully cheap, hinted at shared childhood memories, gently warming the comedy.

The films *Trainspotting*, *Showgirls*, *The English Patient* and *American Beauty* all got the stuffed toy treatment. The sight of toys in compromising positions or unlikely situations (for example, the Geoffrey Rush character from *Shine* playing a Wham tune on the piano) usually raised a laugh. The spoofs – especially the send-up "Saving Private Lion", which included the immortal line "everybody knows the Second World War was won by American actors" – were a superb opportunity to expose the pretensions of stars and filmmakers.

Another regular feature was Adam Buxton's father, alias BaaadDad, reviewing the latest music releases. He memorably dismissed The Prodigy's "Firestarter" as "unnecessarily loathsome". Adam and Joe provided musical interludes of their own (sometimes aided by Zac Sandler). These were usually simple ditties inspired by anything from football (with the irritating chorus: "ball, ball, ball, footy, footy, footy") to Bob Hoskins, where cockney rhyming slang is made up from his film titles.

Some sequences were filmed outside their Brixton bedsit (in reality, a performance space above a Body Shop). The duo pretended to be street portrait artists, knocking up school-boy paintings and passing them off to tourists, while, in another episode, people paid to see Hollywood movie scenes enacted by manne-quins. The programme was extremely formulaic, something that was only tweaked in the fourth, penultimate series. By and large, the formula worked very well.

The Adam And Joe DVD, a collection of clips from the show, is available on DVD.

Big Train
1998–2002

Created by *Father Ted*'s Graham Linehan and Arthur Mathews, *Big Train* was so puzzling, funny and surreal that the strange three-year hiatus between the first and second series seemed weirdly appropriate. Today, though the show was a winner at the 1999 British Comedy Awards, the sketch series is probably best

The Tate gallery

Catherine Tate parlayed supporting roles in shows like *Big Train*, a lead opposite Dawn French in *Wild West* and a relatively brief career in stand-up into her very own primetime sketch series. The sketches varied in quality but five of Tate's creations struck a national chord: the office worker goading her colleague to guess about everything; the apparently loveable granny who is really a foul-mouthed racist; the dim couple who think everything's funny; the mother who is so scared her baby might wake she stays in the car with it when they visit friends; and the schoolgirl who is continually asking: "Am I bov-vered?" Not a bad strike rate for a show that first aired on BBC3 in 2004.

remembered for the wealth of comic talent it helped develop.

Apart from Linehan and Mathews, the writer/performers included Simon Pegg, Mark Heap of *Spaced* fame, Julia Davis and Kevin Eldon (*Nighty Night*) and Catherine Tate. The writing team included Robert Webb and David Mitchell, creators of the successful *Peep Show* series and, occasionally, Adam Buxton and Joe Cornish.

As in Chris Morris's *Jam*, sketches were often set in tense situations. Among the ludicrous creations devised by this talented team were a bomb disposal team who used a flamenco dancer to carry out controlled explosions. Unlike in *Jam*, the atmosphere was never so brooding that the humour was lost, even in the maudlin sur-roundings of an operating theatre. In the many workplace sketches, Simon Pegg had an extended storyline as a man who couldn't refrain from making puns during meetings. Watching his character try to refrain from golden opportunities was funnier than hearing the original puns.

Other quirky sketches involved a tortoise who spoke fluent French, a foul-mouthed mermaid and a woman who leaves her husband for a set of traffic lights. The only long-term fixture was an animated staring competition narrated by Phil Cornwell and sports commentator Barry Davies.

An acquired taste, *Big Train* had many moments of brilliance. Some found it totally unpalatable. Gordon Wallace, TV critic of Scotland's *Daily Herald*, managed to be both harsh and unfair when he said of the second series: "How this nonsense ever got back on track for a return journey is a complete mystery to me. To be fair, only some of the sketches were bad, the rest were truly awful."

Both series of *Big Train* have been released on DVD.

A Bit Of Fry And Laurie

1986–95

By the time of *A Bit Of Fry And Laurie*, Stephen Fry and Hugh Laurie had been working together for five years, having met in 1981, their last year at Cambridge, when Laurie needed help writing a panto. The dynamic between the two meant that their performances were good to watch just on a technical level. Their occasional unscripted lapses into giggles and out-of-character moments and asides made this polite, but cutting, show seem all the funnier.

Though Fry and Laurie played out a wide variety of characters, in various guises and in various settings their comic personas remained constant. Laurie was the sweet, indignant fool with a gift for facial expressions, while Fry was controlled and controlling, impassive and

irreverent, a genius of the bon mot and implied innuendo.

The show retained a residual feel of the Cambridge Footlights. Some sketches feel rather stagey and old-fashioned (notably the skits based on ludicrous Pythonesque names or terribly polite spies) but there was a live feel about some of the action and the show covered all comic bases. Not content to rely on Fry's poetic command of the English language, the duo often threw in some slapstick and gratuitous slapping and hitting.

Cliché-ridden executives ("Mccolleague…") were a particular target, often given extended sketch time. In between longer sketches there were short vox pops about nothing in particular. These usually featured Fry and Laurie in their most diverse guises, notably Laurie's policeman who doesn't speak English and Fry's string-vest-wearing dad.

This series established the Fry and Laurie brand name as a double act. They worked together on other programmes such as *Jeeves And Wooster* and more loosely on *Blackadder* but have done so much in their own right on stage, on film and on the page that they have, unlike many other double acts, survived without being inextricably linked.

 The first two series (of three) have been released on DVD.

Bo Selecta!

2002–04

Leigh Francis so successfully buried himself in the character of Avid Merrion that his real name is hardly referred to in discussing *Bo Selecta!* or any of the characters arising from it.

Francis started his character as a *Big Brother* obsessive in adverts for the reality show on E4 before Avid came into his own on *Bo Selecta!*. Merrion dubs himself the "number one superfan here in the world" though he is more like the world's number one celebrity stalker, wearing a neck brace after an altercation with Lisa Tarbuck. His home life is suitably dysfunctional. He has his dead mother locked in one cupboard and Craig Phillips, from the first *Big Brother*, chained up in another. In his desperation to get close to his heroes, Merrion uses various ruses, such as posing as a lesbian to ingratiate himself with pop sensation TaTu who, understandably, were left totally bewildered.

The show's celebrity caricatures are as twisted as Merrion and have a cruel surreal quality. His take on Mel B from the Spice Girls was to make her older, much more Northern and totally crass while his Michael Jackson was played like an older crankier impersonator. The show's title came from a song by another victim, Craig David. Merrion also sends up Davina McCall, the woman credited for discovering him, changing her *Big Brother* catch phrase – "You're live on Channel 4 please don't swear" – to "...and remember don't say fuck or bugger..." On the writing team for *Bo Selecta!* was Channel 4's favourite stand-up presenter Jimmy Carr.

In later series, the focus switched to another of Francis's creations, The Bear, a teddy bear whose interview techniques were based on Ronnie Corbett's cosy fireside chats, but who would invariably get an erection during the interview thanks to a female guest or mention of an attractive female celebrity.

All three series and the Christmas special are available on DVD.

The 11 O'Clock Show
1998–2000

The most amazing thing about *The 11 O'Clock Show* (Channel 4) was that anyone escaped with their career intact from this satirical mess. Ironically the biggest victim was imposing anchorman Iain Lee who held the proceedings, always variable in quality, together admirably. Yet Lee, after acquiring a reputation as a tricky customer to work with, came out of the series all dressed up in a sharp suit with nowhere to go. Daisy Donovan (who, like Lee, appeared in all but the last series) fared better. Her gift for innuendo-laden celebrity interviews and the striking combination of her butter wouldn't melt looks and sharp tongue earned Donovan her own show, *Daisy Daisy* (Channel 4, 2001), and a job keeping panellists in check on Channel 4's *Does Doug Know?*.

The menagerie the duo were in charge of included several stand-ups (Rich Hall, Fred Macaulay and Brendon Burns) used with varying degrees of success; Ricky Gervais, whose misanthropic reportage was hit and miss, sometimes within two sentences; and fellow *Office* star Mackenzie Crook, who, in series two, was laughable, for all the wrong reasons, as a third anchor. East End comic and ex-boxer Ricky Grover appeared in the fifth and final series as Buller, his tough convict alter ego but it was Sacha Baron Cohen's "street spoof" Ali G character that made the show a cult hit for a while.

Legendary heavy metal DJ Tommy Vance gave a dramatic and lewd round-up of the news headlines that was one of the show's highlights for four series. Meanwhile the final series was fronted by Sarah Alexander, who had impressed in *Smack The Pony*, and John

"Since then, he's just chilled?"

In all the hype that surrounded Sacha Baron Cohen's creation Ali G – including the unresolvable debate over whether he wasn't or was racist – it's often forgotten that he could be subtly funny, memorably asking a bishop, who had just insisted that God created the universe, "and since then he's just chilled?".

His shtick of humiliating celebrities by lulling them into absurd interviews didn't always work. Donald Trump, who didn't get where he is today by suffering fools gladly, dismissed Ali and his idea of an "ice cream glove" in an instant. But the creation has made Cohen globally famous. He has wed Australian model Isla Fisher and starred in NBA ads directed by Spike Lee. His latest character, a spoof Kazakhstani journalist called Borat, upset the Kazakhstan government and the Anti-Defamation League, which accused Cohen, who is Jewish, of anti-Semitism – after he sang a spoof Kazakh country song which included the line "throw the Jew down the well" on US TV. The bad news for the Kazakhstan government is that Cohen is already filming a movie, tentatively entitled *Borat*, directed by *Seinfeld* writer Larry Charles. For Cohen, fame and controversy go hand in hand.

Holmes, now best known as a writer for *Dead Ringers* amongst others.

Though the material was uneven – at its worst neither funny nor intelligent – and the show was sometimes just brash, *The 11 O'Clock Show* groomed some of the best talent in British comedy and tried to treat the news agenda in a way that spoke to a younger generation.

The Kenny Everett Television Show

1981–88

Kenny Everett made his name in the 1960s as a popular DJ on pirate radio and jumped ship to Radio 1 when the government closed the pirate stations. His lively, zany character landed him in hot water when he was sacked – though later reinstated – by Radio 1 for joking that Mary Peyton, the wife of the then transport minister, had bribed her instructor to pass her driving test. After his return to Radio 1, Everett moved to Capital Radio where he is credited with helping to make Queen's "Bohemian Rhapsody" a massive hit.

Everett made his TV debut in 1968, alongside Germaine Greer on a Granada TV show called *Nice Time*, and appeared in the satirical review *Up Sunday* (BBC1, 1972), with Willie Rushton. But he didn't appear consistently on the small screen until *The Kenny Everett Video Show* (ITV, 1978–81) and *The Kenny Everett Television Show* (BBC1, 1981–88).

The *Video* and *Television* shows cemented Everett's reputation as a versatile comedy performer. Backed by a writing team that included comedy perennial Barry Cryer and, on BBC1, David Renwick and Andrew Marshall, Everett had the confidence to ad-lib, sometimes even taking physical control of the camera. His characters included the daringly named Cupid Stunt, a gauche film star eternally being interviewed by a cardboard cut-out Michael Parkinson, who always did things "in the best possible taste", a catch phrase she accompanied by crossing and uncrossing her legs in a way that would make Sharon Stone blush. Elsewhere quickie puns or traditional one-liners would be delivered by punk characters

Gizzard Puke and Sid Snot or proclaimed by spoof gospel minister Brother Lee Love, a creation Everett famously took to a Conservative Party rally, an appearance he was later to regret.

Meanwhile longer skits could have equally corny endings, such as Tarzan returning home and exclaiming to his wife: "It's a jungle out there". More effective was his "Sherman Tank" sketch which demonstrated the vehicle's advantages when it came to finding – or rather making – a parking space. His unsubtle, but dead-on, spoof of Rod Stewart singing "Do Ya Think I'm Sexy?", with his backside inflating to ludicrous proportions, made it even harder to take the Scottish rocker seriously ever again.

In 1984, Everett made the horror movie spoof *Bloodbath At The House Of Death* which, despite the presence of the likes of Vincent Price, Pamela Stephenson and Don Warrington in the cast, was stymied by a lack of decent jokes. That was the first harbinger of disappointments to come, and his comedy fell increasingly out of favour in the late 1980s.

 Kenny Everett: The Naughty Bits, actually a compilation of *The Kenny Everett Video Show*, is the only DVD currently available.

The Fast Show
1994–2000

If one of the signs of a successful comedy programme is the number of catch phrases it bequeaths to the nation, *The Fast Show* should live long in the annals of TV comedy history.

Creators Paul Whitehouse and Charlie Higson had known each other since university and collaborated with friend-of-a-friend Harry Enfield

on Stavros and Loadsamoney, the *Friday Night Live/Saturday Live* hits as well as *Harry Enfield's Television Programme* where Whitehouse made his name as a performer. A fast-cut promo for Enfield's show inspired Whitehouse and Higson to write short sketches where characters would appear, say something funny and make way for the next character.

Along with regular cast members Simon Day, Mark Williams, John Thomson, Arabella Weir and

Brisk character sketch comedy with depth: estate worker Ted and country squire Ralph shared a tender relationship in *The Fast Show*

Caroline Aherne, the duo created such characters as the sublime Geoffrey Norman MP, who would deny everything including his taxi fare; Swiss Toni, the car salesman for whom everything was like making love to a beautiful woman; the very, very drunk Rowley Birkin, QC; Louis Balfour, the Jazz Club presenter, for whom everything was "nice!", "great!" or "cool"; Jesse of "This week, I have mostly been eating…" fame; and music hall legend Arthur Atkinson who constantly exclaimed: "Where's me washboard?" Some characters were known just by their catch phrase, such as the enthusiastic "Brilliant!" kid.

Set pieces like foreign television station Channel 9 (from which the catch phrase "Scorchio" was derived) and Ted and Ralph got longer airtime. Ted and Ralph, acclaimed for its touching portrayal of a repressed homosexual country squire's love for his Irish estate worker, even spawned its own TV special.

The Fast Show ended its run in 2000 but there were several specials afterwards mainly featuring the Ron Manager character ("jumpers for goalposts") including *Match Of The World Cup*, in 2002. That same year, the *Fast Show* team toured the UK with their live show, which had its first outing in 1998 with members of the *Shooting Stars* team.

All four series – and *The Last Fast Show Ever Part One* and *The Farewell Tour* – are available on DVD.

Goodness Gracious Me

1998–2000

When sketch show *Goodness Gracious Me* started its run on Radio 4 in 1997, it signalled the entrance of Asian comedy into the mainstream.

The first black-made sitcom on British TV, *No Problem!* ran for three series on Channel 4 from 1983 to 1985. The show's creator, Farrukh Dhondy, also wrote *Tandoori Nights* (Channel 4, 1985–87), the first real Asian sitcom. Dhondy's tale of rival Indian restaurants had a conventional sitcom structure and didn't deal with such issues as arranged marriages, religious purity, patriarchal struggles and cultural differences. On *Goodness Gracious Me*, these matters were the source for humour that appealed to Asian and non-Asian audiences.

Goodness Gracious Me were: writer and performer Meera Syal, a veteran of *Tandoori Nights* and *The Real McCoy*, the successful 1990s black sitcom; Kulvinder Ghir, another *The Real McCoy* star; Sanjeev Bhaskar, spotted by producer Anil Gupta while performing a double act called *The Secret Asians* with Nitin Sawhney (who appeared in the show's Radio 4 series); Nina Wadia; and the show's "token" white man Dave Lamb.

Lamb had many supporting roles, most memorably as the waiter in the English restaurant sketch. This skit, the group's most famous, drew, knowingly or unknowingly, on previous material by Billy Connolly and Rowan Atkinson and featured a group of badly behaved drunken Indians at an English restaurant, reversing the normal stereotype of drunken Englishmen at an Indian restaurant. Among the regular sketches were: "Mr Everything Comes From India", "The 'I can get you that' Uncle" and "Smeeta Smitten Showbiz Kitten", who grew more distinctive as the series progressed.

After *Goodness Gracious Me*, Bhaskar and Syal appeared in *The Kumars At No 42*, an amusing sitcom-cum-chat show featuring an Indian family from Wembley, that attracted guests of the calibre of Michael Parkinson, Minnie Driver, Melvyn Bragg, Leslie Phillips, June Whitfield,

Jerry Hall and Stephen Fry. Steve Punt of Punt and Dennis was on the writing team.

 All three series and a complete three-disc box set are available on DVD.

The Innes Book Of Records

1979–81

Neil Innes was thrown out of art school in 1963 for spending all his time playing music but his distraction paid off when he became a cult comedy musician. With fellow art students he formed The Bonzo Dog Doo-Dah Band, originally The Bonzo Dog Dada Band in honour of the surrealist movement. The group clocked up a hit with "I'm The Urban Spaceman" in 1968; meanwhile another song, "Death Cab For Cutie", featured in the Beatles movie *Magical Mystery Tour*. Sometimes known as "the seventh Python", Innes was the only non-Python, apart from Douglas Adams, to contribute both sketches and songs to the celebrated series.

The Beatles were the subject of one of Innes' most successful ventures, The Rutles, a parody band who appeared on *Rutland Weekend Television*, a TV comedy series created by Innes and Monty Python's Eric Idle. The Rutles' creation spawned two TV films – the lauded *All You Need Is Cash* (1978) and the dodgy remake *Can't Buy Me Lunch* (2002) – and a hilarious spoof of the Beatles' *Anthology* CD box set.

The Innes Book Of Records placed as much emphasis on humour as comedy, though comedy stars such as Rowan Atkinson, Michael Palin and fellow Doo Dah band member and cult figure Viv Stanshall (known for his Sir Henry at Rawlinson End character) all appeared. The musical skits that peppered the show sometimes resembled pop videos. There were also pastiches where classical composers met rock'n'roll ("Blue Suede Schubert") and a Bob Dylan parody ("Protest Song"), that featured the oft-quoted line "I've suffered for my music, now it's your turn". Although Innes often behaved as if he would rather have been the fifth Beatle than the seventh Python, watching his musical parodies involved no great suffering.

 No DVDs have been released, but two CDs are available.

Little Britain

2003–

The vacancy for iconic comedy show created when *The Office* finished in 2003 was filled almost immediately by *Little Britain*, a sketch show that captured the nation's imagination with characters who ranged from surreal to hapless, while the incomprehensible chav Vicky Pollard touched a nerve as a precise social parody. Not everyone is a fan though. Creators Matt Lucas and David Walliams were famously heckled at a *South Bank Show* awards bash by director Ken Russell for "spitting in the face of the public" and the third series provoked a minor media backlash.

Lucas and Walliams met at the National Youth Theatre and collaborated on *Sir Bernard Chumley And Friends*, the Edinburgh show featuring Lucas as the legendary knighted raconteur and actor, a character he had launched on the comedy circuit in 1992, when he was just 18. Chumley made his TV debut in 1999, while Lucas made regular appearances with Vic Reeves and Bob Mortimer in *Shooting Stars*, *Bang, Bang It's Reeves*

And Mortimer and the remake of *Randall And Hopkirk Deceased*.

Lucas and Walliams kept working together, scoring a hit with *Rock Profiles*, a spoof pop star interview programme televised in 2001, the same year *Little Britain* started on Radio 4. Two years later the sketch show transferred to BBC2, quickly becoming a cult smash.

Some of the show's characters have more obvious ancestors than others. Hopeless transvestite Emily Howard is straight out of the Dick Emery school of comic character while Marjorie Dawes, the tyrannical head of the Fat Fighters diet club, has more than an echo of cruel job centre maven Pauline in *The League Of Gentlemen*. Lou and Andy, named after Lou Reed and Andy Warhol, were among the most popular characters. Lou was the long-suffering friend and carer to the wheel-chair-bound Andy, who, unbeknown to Lou, is perfectly mobile. Then there's the aforementioned

The full Monty

All sketch acts get compared to Monty Python, it's a fact of comedy life. Fused together by prolific and influential comedy writer Barry Took, Graham Chapman, John Cleese, Terry Gilliam, Eric Idle, Terry Jones and Michael Palin, Monty Python became a global comedy icon and Britain's premier comedy export.

The four series of *Monty Python's Flying Circus* ran on the BBC from 1969 to 1974 (John Cleese missed the last series having left to develop *Fawlty Towers*) and provided a wealth of classic sketches still quoted to death today. They include "The Dead Parrot", where customer and shopkeeper argue over the sale of a dead bird; the sex-obsessed "Mr Nudge Nudge"; and the "Four Yorkshiremen", where each character tries to outbid each other's experience of childhood poverty. The latter sketch was written for ITV's *At Last The 1948 Show*, whose stars included Marty Feldman, Tim Brooke-Taylor, John Cleese, Graham Chapman and Eric Idle. The rest of the Pythons came from ITV's children's sketch show *Do Not Adjust Your Set*.

These classic sketches were conventional compared to the zanier exploits of, to take just one example, The Spanish Inquisition riding around on buses in full fifteenth-century garb. This motley crew were one of the troupe's many clever ways of linking sketches. Python also used Gilliam's animations and a whole host of capers that segued proceedings or toyed with

televisual conventions by, for instance, cutting to a completely different show.

The show's success inevitably inspired several spin-offs, including various movies – the best being *Monty Python And The Holy Grail* (1975), though *Monty Python's Life Of Brian* (1979) was nearly as good – and the concert *Monty Python Live At The Hollywood Bowl* (1982). On television, as well as *Fawlty Towers*, individual Pythons contributed to several other ventures. The best, arguably, was the fabulous *Ripping Yarns* (BBC2, 1976–79), a Palin/Jones collaboration. These nine imaginative comedies featured such classic scenes as the nailing of public schoolboys to a wall, and the ritual breaking of household ornaments after the umpteenth defeat of a football team slavishly followed by one of Palin's greatest characters.

By creating their own bizarre world, full of in-jokes, allusions and surreal send-ups of exaggerated, but recognizable, characters, Monty Python made comedy cool in the 1970s. Their influence is summed up by the oft-quoted adage that the team were "the Beatles of comedy", having cracked America like their musical counterparts (albeit with some bother in the courts about how American broadcasters edited the series) and having talented members who succeeded outside the celebrated group dynamic. It can't be denied, we loved them, yeah, yeah, yeah.

Vicky Pollard, the teenage mum who had more catch phrases ("Don't go giving me evils" being one of the oddest) than some rival shows.

Narration between scenes by Tom Baker lent proceedings a comic gravitas and there were some great comedy in-jokes, such as naming a school "Kelsey Grammar" after the *Frasier* star.

In the third series, the strain of a small writing team started to show. The BBC1 primetime slot elicited more press and with it accusations, some well-founded, that the show was out to shock, not entertain.

 Both series are available on DVD (with the first series becoming Britain's biggest-selling DVD ever upon its release).

Not The Nine O'Clock News

1979–82

Not The Nine O'Clock News successfully filled the gap left by Monty Python as a fast-moving and influential sketch show. Unlike Python, *Not The Nine O'Clock News* was largely satirical, albeit in the widest sense, without being overtly political. The show, a must-see on the nation's campuses, helped plug a gap in topical comedy that wouldn't be properly filled until television seriously exploited alternative comedy in the mid-1980s.

The team most viewers will know – Rowan Atkinson, Pamela Stephenson, Mel Smith and Griff Rhys Jones – was only arrived at after a few permutations. Rowan Atkinson and Chris Langham were survivors from a pilot that was never transmitted because of the 1979 general election and concerns about content. Producer/writers John Lloyd and Sean Hardie (who had been co-opted

The "classic" NTNON line-up: Griff Rhys Jones, Rowan Atkinson, Mel Smith and Pamela Stephenson

from BBC current affairs) went back to square one while on the hunt for a female star. Victoria Wood, Alison Steadman and Susan George were considered before a chance meeting with Pamela Stephenson ended the search. The first series aired with Atkinson, Langham and Stephenson, with Mel Smith making up the quartet.

A second series was commissioned but without Langham who, it was agreed, did not fit with the rest of the team. He was replaced by comedy actor and radio producer Griff Rhys Jones, who had played supporting roles in the first series. Each star brought different skills to the show. Atkinson was a skilful physical comedian with great verbal dexterity, Stevenson an excellent mimic, as showcased in her spoofs of newscasters (especially her parody of Jan Leeming trying to pronounce African leaders' names correctly), while the soon-to-be double act of Smith and Jones raised laughter through fairly straight acting, never needing to ham it up.

The cast, except for Stephenson, all wrote for the show. An open-door policy meant that virtually anyone could contribute sketches. Those who did include: Richard Curtis, Rory McGrath,

Peter Richardson, Nigel Planer, Clive Anderson and Ruby Wax. Among the memorable skits was the gorilla sketch, a TV interview with an educated talking gorilla called Gerald (Atkinson) and his trainer (Smith). Trainer: "When we captured Gerald he was absolutely wild." Gerald: "Wild? I was absolutely livid!" Another featured a Miss World contestant (Stephenson) who, when asked why she wanted to win the competition, replies: "I want to screw someone famous." Some of the musical spoofs were sublime, especially "Ayatollah Khomeini Closer And I'm Going To Lose My Cool".

Two volumes of *The Best Of Not The Nine O'Clock News* are available on DVD.

Henry The First

Saturday Live and *Friday Night Live* were a showcase for a galaxy of comedians but Lenny Henry (1958–) was the only performer who could also boast that he had been the first member of the *Black And White Minstrel Show* to have actually been black.

Henry's career is a fascinating illustration of the sea change in British comedy reflected in shows like *Saturday Live*. He started in working men's clubs in the 1970s, often doing material that would now be deemed racist, but made his name on *Tiswas*, the anarchic Saturday morning ITV show that ran from 1974 to 1982 and led to a brief, but cult, adult version *OTT* (ITV, 1982), in which Henry co-starred with Alexei Sayle. He also acted alongside Norman Beaton in *The Fosters* (ITV, 1976–77), the British reworking of the black US sitcom *Good Times*.

Henry made his mainstream TV debut as a pure comedian with the sketch show *Three Of A Kind* (BBC1, 1981–83). With a reasonably innovative format and three very different strands of comic performers – Henry shared the billing with David Copperfield and

Tracey Ullman – *Three Of A Kind* was a good, fast-paced sketch show that was significantly ahead of its time. Jokes zipped across the screen in Teletext type, doing for comedy what *The Chart Show* did for pop nearly a decade later. The sketches and characters were effective, if uncontroversial, and Henry perfected characters that would later have their own show.

Influenced initially by *Tiswas* co-host Chris Tarrant's anarchic humour, Henry had begun to produce new material, a process accelerated by a visit to The Comedy Store: "I realized I didn't have to do impressions so much, I could be funnier doing my own material." His new approach was cemented when he fell under the influence of Ade Edmondson, Rik Mayall and Dawn French, who he later married.

Though Henry's subsequent career has had its ups and downs – he is now a national institution as much for helping found Comic Relief as for sitcoms like *Chef!* – he was a key figure in the shift to a new kind of TV comedy, even if his career hasn't really benefited from that revolution.

Saturday Live/Friday Night Live

1985–88

No other television show has captured alternative cabaret, or for that matter, cabaret, as successfully as *Saturday Live* (Channel 4, 1985–87) and *Friday Night Live* (Channel 4, 1988). The man behind the show, BBC producer Paul Jackson, had already established his track record promoting new wave comedy with *The Young Ones*. With *Saturday Live*, a variation on America's *Saturday Night Live*, he perfected a formula that captured the imagination of a new generation of comedy fans.

Mixing rock and pop bands with the best comedians and cabaret acts in the UK and US, Jackson produced a lively show that rode the crest of the burgeoning comedy circuit and made stars of Ben Elton and Harry Enfield.

Elton was undoubtedly the focus of *Saturday Live* while Enfield was the main attraction of *Friday Night Live*, with his crass plasterer-on-the-make Loadsamoney and his more loveable Greek kebab shop owner Stavros. Elton's legendary motormouth rants and jokes about The Thatch (then prime minister, Margaret Thatcher) made him loved and loathed by viewers and agitated the right-wing press.

The programme's participants run like a *Who's Who* of comedy with the home-grown acts including Dawn French and Jennifer Saunders, Jeremy Hardy, Lenny Henry, Helen Lederer, Rowan Atkinson, Angus Deayton, Morwenna Banks, Julian Clary, Josie Lawrence, Paul Merton, Nigel Planer, Steve Punt and Hugh Dennis, Stephen Fry and Hugh Laurie, Bob Mills, Moray Hunter and Jack Doherty, Lee Evans and Jo Brand. Such luminaries as Emo Philips, Rita Rudner, Will Durst and Steven Wright dropped in from the other side of the Atlantic.

Both programmes celebrated some of comedy's great old-timers. Among the elder statesmen invited to appear were Peter Cook, Spike Milligan, Dame Edna Everage, Frankie Howerd and Jasper Carrott, who was chastized by Ben Elton for telling gags about women drivers.

Smack The Pony

1999–2003

Together Doon Mackichan, Fiona Allen and Sally Phillips have done as much as any female act to prove that, yes, women can do comedy.

A huge army of writers supplied fast-paced sketches covering a range of scenarios – calamitous relationships, unrequited lust, incompetence and competitiveness in the office – and short surreal skits with outrageous stunts or gimmicks for this Channel 4 show. Running gags included mock dating agency videos and spoof music videos, including a hilarious take on indie music.

Two *Smack The Pony* routines featured in a Channel 4 poll of the fifty greatest comedy sketches. "Singing Match" featured two office workers going to ludicrous lengths to prove who has the best voice while singing along to the radio. The other sketch involved three friends, a man and two women, saying goodbye to each other. The man can't let go of one of the girls, mauling her, oblivious to the conversation. It turns out, in a superb final twist, that he is the other girl's boyfriend.

The show won Emmys for best popular arts show in 1999 and 2000. Apart from the regular trio, Sarah Alexander (*Coupling*, *Green Wing*) and Darren Boyd made frequent appearances, while musical comedian Jackie Clune sang the theme tune.

The main cast members went on to do a variety of work. Fiona Allen played Mike Baldwin's love interest in *Coronation Street* for a while. Doon Mackichan has cropped up in *Brass Eye* and in the Canadian sitcom *Bromwell High*, which featured a significant number of British stand-ups. Sally Phillips has appeared in both Bridget Jones films, but was unfortunate to have her role in *Notting Hill* cut. She also shone in *Rescue Me*, an average comedy drama that was not re-commissioned by the BBC.

The Best Of Smack The Pony is available on DVD.

Spitting Image
1984–96

This puppet-powered satirical show ran for twelve years, became a national institution – at its peak, it was a more effective critic of Thatcherism than the Labour Party – and numbered among its writers and performers the cream of British alternative and post-alternative comedy talent.

The puppets were voiced by, among others, Steve Coogan, Robert Newman, Harry Enfield, Rory Bremner, Alistair McGowan and Chris Barrie. The writing team included Richard Curtis, Ian Hislop, David Baddiel, Steve Punt, Jack Doherty and Moray Hunter.

No one was safe as the rubber puppets (created by Roger Law and Peter Fluck) savagely parodied the royal family, and British and American politicians and celebrities. Much to tabloid horror, the Queen Mum was invariably portrayed with an "eeh bah gum" accent and a bottle of Gordon's

Comedy feeding on itself: *Spitting Image* satirizes Joanna Lumley's character, Patsy Stone, from the sitcom *Absolutely Fabulous*

gin in her hand. Meanwhile, the pope was awarded rock star status, Madonna had a singing belly button, Joanna Lumley became her chain-smoking, champagne-guzzling *Absolutely Fabulous* caricature and Ronald Reagan was always searching for his brain. Despite such biting portrayals, the rich and famous were often flattered to be parodied, deeming it an honour much as, later, appearing on *The Simpsons* would become.

The most striking parody was of Margaret Thatcher. Her puppet toughened as her policies hardened, many viewers joking that it was hard to tell them apart. One of the most famous Iron Lady sketches was set in a restaurant where the PM is dining with her Cabinet. The waiter asks Thatcher for her order and she replies "Raw meat". The waiter asks: "And for the vegetables?" to which she replies: "Oh, they'll have the same." Thatcher's replacement by the grey man John Major, and the arrival of satirical rival *Have I Got News For You?* would eventually weaken the show.

Spitting Image inspired several spin-offs, including *Les Guignols* in France and *DC Follies* in America, where the original format had unsuccessfully piloted. "The Chicken Song", an appalling parody of the Black Lace party hit "Agadoo" became a number-one hit from the show in 1986.

One poor *Spitting Image* DVD is available, but the *Best Of* video is a better bet.

Reality comedy

The vogue for reality comedy, mockumentary and an altogether more naturalistic approach can be traced back to the late 1970s with such unlikely pioneers as Kelly Monteith's sitcom. But in the last decade, these shows have been developed in such quantity and quality that this approach has almost now become the mainstream.

This shift has given us some great comedies such as *That Peter Kay Thing, People Like Us* and *The Office*, and enabled such maverick geniuses as Chris Morris and Mark Thomas to give their comedy a sharper political edge. The baiting of celebrities – by Louis Theroux, Caroline Aherne as Mrs Merton and Paul Kaye as Dennis Pennis – became an international sport while, in his own offbeat manner, Dom Joly dressed up to give his own twist on real life.

Anyone For Pennis?

1995–97

Paul Kaye's irreverent creation Dennis Pennis, a cheeky, geeky American celebrity interviewer,

put stars in excruciatingly embarrassing situations pointing the way to Ali G's subsequent exploits. The outrageous appearance of both characters seemed to attract then repel stars who, too late, realized they had been trapped. While Ali G was gangsta style, Pennis chose the errant schoolboy look with a red Dennis the Menace style blazer clashing with his shock of dyed red hair.

Pennis owes a great debt, as Kaye freely acknowledges, to Australian actor Garry McDonald, whose 1970s comic creation Norman Gunston was the original celebrity torturer, famously ruffling Muhammad Ali's feathers at a press conference before the "Thriller In Manila" world title fight in 1975 and saying to Paul McCartney's wife Linda: "That's funny, you don't look Japanese."

Pennis was just as successful at making the rich and famous frown, scowl and sneer. Some of his best moments came with British politicians where his wacky America approach and their British reserve clashed very nicely indeed. He asked the bouffant Michael Heseltine whether there was more harmony in his hair than there was in the Tory Party. Labour politicians were

The art of Cookery

Chris Morris's comic hero Peter Cook (1937–95) was the Leon Trotsky of British television comedy. Brilliant but, after a brief golden era, condemned to exile and accused of wasting his gifts, Cook was spared the ice pick but not much else, pronounced comedically dead before he physically died. His friend Stephen Fry rebuked the media: "Why commentators have to talk about extraordinary people as if they are composing school reports is beyond me: 'A fair term's work, but Peter must concentrate more on writing stage plays this year'." Michael Palin acknowledged Cook's influence, saying "He laid the basis for the new comedy of the 1960s and 1970s." Inspiring the Pythons and others, Cook was a grandfather to alternative comedy.

The most dazzling talent in the 1960s satire boom, Cook starred in the trailblazing revue *Beyond The Fringe*, set up a comedy club, The Establishment, which introduced Lenny Bruce to the UK and revived Frankie Howerd's career, and helped found *Private Eye* magazine. He did all that even before teaming up with Dudley Moore for the acclaimed BBC1 sketch show *Not Only But Also* and the bizarre, scatological, yet often uncomfortably hilarious Derek and Clive albums. Through Derek and Clive, he became an unlikely punk hero, hosting a TV pop show called *Revolver* where he royally slagged off bands like XTC.

His iconic stature was reflected in appearances in *Saturday Night Live*, *The Comic Strip Presents...* and *Whose Line Is It Anyway?*. But his career as Sven, a fake Norwegian fisherman calling up London radio stations between 1988 and 1992, anticipated later stunts by Chris Morris and Mark Thomas. His final glory was his four characters for the price of one performance on *Clive Anderson's Talk Show* in 1993, a last *tour de force* from a man who, for all his gifts, was probably one of the world's ten worst actors.

---

held to account too. Tony Benn took it all very seriously before it dawned on him that he was being sent up.

More glamorous targets included Helena Christiansen who failed to get Pennis's joke: "Why was the supermodel staring at the carton of orange juice? Because it said concentrate!" Long before Michael Moore goaded Charlton Heston in his film *Bowling For Columbine*, Pennis perplexed the movie legend with a series of questions that punned on the actor's name. "What do you think of Suzanne, Charlton?" was not, as Heston thought, an inquiry about his views on Paul Cezanne but a pun on Heston's name and that of BBC weather girl Suzanne Charlton.

In 1997 Kaye killed off the character to concentrate on other things. He took a more dramatic role in television series *Two Thousand Acres*

Of Sky, appeared in the critically panned comedy movie *Blackball* about a rogue bowls player (directed by Mel Smith) and had a tiny uncredited role in *Shaun Of The Dead*. He has since experimented with other characters – including a foul-mouthed American lawyer – but none have had the impact of Dennis Pennis.

 The Pennis From Heaven compilation is available on DVD.

The Day Today/Brass Eye
1994, 1997

The elusive giant of comedy Chris Morris was famously fired from BBC Radio Bristol for letting off a canister of helium in the news studio, one of many pranks that have punctuated his career.

Breaking away from his supposedly straight radio career Morris focused on comedy with his *On The Hour* show (Radio 4, 1991–92) gathering the talents of Armando Iannucci, Steve Coogan and Patrick Marber to produce a ground-breaking media spoof that crossed over to television as *The Day Today* (BBC2, 1994) and, in just six episodes, had a serious influence on television comedy. The show beautifully satirized the foibles of newscasters and reporters, building a comic chemistry with, for example, the mutual disdain between Chris Morris's overbearing, oily anchorman and Coogan's blustering, patronizing sports editor Alan Partridge.

While Coogan would develop Partridge with *Knowing Me, Knowing You* and *I'm Alan Partridge*, Morris morphed *The Day Today* into *Brass Eye*, a Channel 4 spoof news magazine show that allowed him to return to his prankster ways. Celebrities (including Paul Daniels, Noel Edmonds and Rolf Harris) and politicians were duped into warning against a new, fictitious drug called "cake". By far the most infamous outing for *Brass Eye* was the paedophilia special in 2001. Here celebrities – including Phil Collins and Gary Lineker – backed a campaign against paedophilia called "Nonce Sense". The programme received a record number of complaints. The controversy, fuelled by the tabloids and involving condemnations from government ministers who later admitted they hadn't seen the programme, arose largely because of the scene where Morris confronts a pro-paedophile spokesman (played by Simon Pegg) and demands to know if he wants to sleep with his son.

Morris continued to explore, albeit less controversially, the darker side of comedy and dealt with themes like death, torture and madness in *Jam* and the remixed late-night version *Jaaaaam* (both in 2000). Sometimes the line between comedy and drama was so fine it was arguable whether it was comedy at all. Morris returned to the public consciousness in 2005 with his poorly received sitcom about trendy media types *Nathan Barley*.

 The Day Today and *Brass Eye* are both available on DVD (except for the *Brass Eye* paedophilia special).

Chris Morris in *Brass Eye* in sensationalist oily anchorman mode

The Mark Thomas Comedy Product

1996–2002

The fact that the word "comedy" was dropped from the title of Thomas's show in later series highlights the difficulty of balancing political content and laughter. Ben Elton, who tiptoed on a similar tightrope in the 1980s, was often accused of preaching and losing the plot while such heavily politicized comics as Jeremy Hardy were sometimes deemed too earnest. With his cheeky schoolboy grin and laddish persona, Mark Thomas succeeded in making political comedy extremely accessible while imparting useful and radical information about the institutions that govern us.

Thomas attended Bretton Hall drama school in Wakefield, after which he worked for his father, a builder, and performed stand-up by night. His father was, Thomas later said, a "working-class Thatcherite before Thatcher" and was pro-life, a movement Mark mercilessly attacked.

Thomas's boyish brand of political humour earned him spots as support comic on *The Mary Whitehouse Experience* in the late 1980s and appearances on Radio 1's *Loose Talk* before his own show started in 1996. The programme, including specials, ran until 2003 when Thomas and Channel 4 parted company over how far they were willing to go on the issue of corporate manslaughter legislation.

Combining stand-up and investigative journalism, Thomas has scored several coups. He has managed to get Indonesian military chiefs to admit on camera that their government tortured dissenters to "protect the security of our society" and exposed a loophole that required art collectors to exhibit some works publicly if they wanted to avoid paying tax on them. Rather than face hordes of people demanding to see his etchings, Sir Evelyn de Rothschild decided, after being outed by Thomas, to pay the tax.

Thomas found himself at the centre of an alleged Whitehall smear campaign when an official purporting to be acting on behalf of the then trade and industry minister Richard Caborn sent an email trying to solicit "background dirt" on Thomas.

His greatest contribution, as an activist, may be helping to block the Ilisu hydro-electric dam in southeast Turkey which would have displaced up to 78,000 people, mostly Kurds, with inadequate compensation or consultation.

Parallels have inevitably been drawn between Thomas's work and that of the American activist, humorist and filmmaker Michael Moore. Their careers have flourished in sublime synchronicity. Though less high-profile than Moore, Thomas has had the advantage of never seeming quite as self-seeking as the American but Thomas has welcomed Moore's contribution and the impact made by Moore's movie *Fahrenheit 9/11*.

People Like Us

1999, 2001

People Like Us represents the apogee of the fascination with fly-on-the-wall-style comedies in the last decade or so. The show ran on Radio 4 between 1995 and 1997 and jumped to BBC2 in 1999. The central figure was filmmaker Roy Mallard (Chris Langham), who was always crossing the line between being "merely an observer" and being drawn into the various situations he was exposing.

Mallard shadowed several professional people, interviewing, among others, an estate agent, a police officer, a vicar and an airline pilot. During the interviews, Mallard was only just out of sight. Various comments by interviewees would suggest he was somehow unattractive and Mallard took the interviewees' offhand comments and pushed them to unintentionally amusing conclusions.

Langham's career has touched upon some great comedy programmes and productions. He was the sole British writer for *The Muppet Show* and was airbrushed out of *Not The Nine O'Clock News* after the first series. Despite this hiccup and some personal difficulties, Langham has clocked up appearances in Ben Elton's *Happy Families* (BBC1, 1985) and a spy spoof *The Preventers* (ITV, 1996), and wrote the above-average mainstream sitcom *Kiss Me Kate* (ITV, 1998), starring Amanda Holden and Caroline Quentin and set at a psychotherapy clinic. On a similar theme, Langham starred as the psychotherapist to an array of Paul Whitehouse's patient characters in *Help!* (BBC2, 2005). But Langham's biggest subsequent success has been the political mockumentary sitcom *The Thick Of It*.

Series one is available on DVD and series two is to follow.

Trigger Happy TV
2000–03

Dom Joly's great comic achievement is to prove you can use the public imaginatively to provoke laughter rather than gratuitously winding them up in the tedious manner of *Beadle's About*.

Joly's pranks did ruffle a few feathers, sometimes literally, since, alongside spoof celebrity interviews and other surreal scenarios, giant puppet animals were a favoured ploy of his. Joly famously trailed mayoral candidate Ken Livingstone dressed as a gorilla with a sign saying "Vote Monkey, Get Monkey". During the stunt a scuffle broke out between Joly and a Livingstone aide. Later, Livingstone admitted he found Joly's work funny but criticized the "cruel streak" in the comic's humour that led him to pick on older people.

The sketch the London mayor presumably had uppermost in his mind featured Joly as a park warden admonishing pensioners for acts of vandalism. Joly countered criticism by suggesting that it was patronizing to say that anyone over 50 should be excluded, that the participants were fully compos mentis and that they did all sign a consent form after filming.

Joly served an interesting apprenticeship before becoming the twenty-first century's prankster-in-chief. He grew up in Lebanon, attended boarding school in England but returned to war-torn Beirut for holidays: "I hated going back to Lebanon because I was petrified all the time, but I much preferred being there than boarding school, which I loathed even more." After completing his politics degree at London University's School of Oriental and African Studies, he worked as a junior diplomat in Prague – in the year the Communist regime collapsed before the Velvet Revolution – before working at ITN organizing interviews with politicians. He used this post to start surreptitiously initiating stunts, once getting children to kick a ball at David Mellor.

Though fascinated by politics, Joly had a more scattergun approach than Mark Thomas, with whom he next worked on the *Comedy Product* show. His reward for a stint producing publicity stunt shorts for the Paramount Comedy

Channel, including sending strippers to William Hague's party and placing a mini-Dome in Peter Mandelson's garden, was his own Channel 4 show.

Perhaps best known for his gimmick of producing a giant mobile phone in various social settings and shouting "Hello!", Joly's *Trigger Happy TV* inspired many similar series including Channel 4's *Little Friends* and more recently *I'm Spazticus*, a disabled prankster show.

The best of series one and all of series two and three are on DVD.

Britcom on celluloid

Television comedy has always been a starting point for ambitious comedians dreaming of movie stardom. In the past, the preference was to expand a successful sitcom to feature length, even at the risk of simply cobbling together several well-worn plots to create an uneven whole, a method most popular in the 1970s (see the films of *Dad's Army*, *Man About The House*, *Porridge* and *Rising Damp*). There has, more recently, been a trend for TV stars to expand and riff on their television personas to create something new and unexpected. This has led to the *Spaced* team battling zombies and The League Of Gentlemen physically struggling with their comic creations.

But the most consistent motto, as comedy shows migrate from TV to cinema, has been "if it ain't broke, don't fix it", with everyone from the Monty Python team to Mr Bean extracting commercial gain by moving their well-tested TV shtick from the small to the silver screen. Unfortunately, the same trick can go badly awry, as anyone who watched Rik Mayall and Adrian Edmondson try to extend their *Bottom* personas to feature length in *Guest House Paradiso* (1999) can testify. As for Garth Jennings' *The Hitchhiker's Guide To The Galaxy* (2005), making the film of the TV series of the book of the radio show was never going to be easy and the movie ranks as the biggest disaster since the Vogons demolished Earth in order to build an intergalactic bypass.

What follows is a selection of the best – and most significant – comedy films to spin off from TV in chronological order.

 ...And Now For Something Completely Different
dir Ian Macnaughton, 1971, UK, 88m

The first feature-length film outing by Cleese, Chapman, Jones, Gilliam, Idle and Palin was a ragtag assortment of reshot greatest hits from the first two series of *Monty Python's Flying Circus*, including the "Dead Parrot" sketch and "The Lumberjack Song". The film's budget was roughly £100,000 – which didn't go that far even in 1971 – and much of the film was shot on an abandoned dairy farm, because a sound stage would have cost too much.

Monty Python And The Holy Grail
dir Terry Gilliam and Terry Jones, 1975, UK, 90m

Arguably the Python collective's funniest feature film. The cast and crew struggled admirably against budget and location constraints, Graham Chapman's raging alcoholism, and a distinct lack of horses. Although the end result is a little sloppy in places (especially in the cop-out ending), the film is marked by an ingenious silliness that still makes it fresh after thirty years, when so much other comedy from the 1970s has dated and wilted. The movie's sketchiness ensures that everyone has their favourite set piece, from the discussion of swallows and coconuts to the limbless knight who won't give up the fight.

The Likely Lads
dir Michael Tuchner, 1976, UK, 90m

The classy sitcom *Whatever Happened To The Likely Lads?* (BBC1, 1973–74), a sequel to the original series *The Likely Lads* (BBC1, 1964–66), spawned this ninety-minute feature as a last hurrah for the Tyneside twosome Bob Ferris and Terry Collier (Rodney Bewes and James Bolam). In this outing, Bob, now settled down with his wife Thelma (Brigit Forsyth), has a mid-life crisis that his slacker friend Terry tries to remedy with a caravan holiday in Northumberland. The mid-1970s northeastern setting gives the comedy a decidedly gritty feel, with the lads' favourite pub and family homes torn down to make way for cheap, crime-ridden tower blocks.

Are You Being Served?
dir Bob Kellett, 1977, UK, 95m

When the Grace Brothers department store closes for refurbishment, the entire staff go on holiday to Costa Plonka (hold onto your sides), and general hilarity abounds. Sort of. Viewed nowadays, the film is a fascinating timepiece, recalling all the tawdry glory of 1970s British TV comedy and set in an era when holidaymaking, especially overseas, was a new concept. So the film entertains us with corrupt inept Spaniards, "Krauts" monopolizing the poolside space, "greasy foreign muck" that is suspiciously different from bacon and eggs, revolutionaries, and admirably tortuous connections made between a pet cat and a vagina. Those were the days.

Porridge
dir Dick Clement, 1979, UK, 93m

This good-in-parts feature-length addition to the Ian Le Frenais and Dick Clement sitcom came towards the end of *Porridge* and near the start of its spin-off, *Going Straight*. Norman Stanley Fletcher (Ronnie Barker) and his sidekick Lennie Godber (Richard Beckinsale) find themselves having to break back into prison after they inadvertently escape during an inmates' football match.

Monty Python's Life Of Brian
dir Terry Jones, 1979, UK, 93m

Controversial upon release, this movie is now often remembered for a series of catch phrases ("Welease Woger", "He's not the Messiah, he's a very naughty boy",

et cetera, ad nauseam…). But *Life Of Brian* still packs a punch, exposing the hypocrisy of fanaticism and the downright silliness of many aspects of organized religion, giving the film a surprising political resonance today. All that and there's a cracking Shirley Bassey/James Bond theme spoof to boot.

Rising Damp
dir Joe McGrath, 1980, UK, 98m

Leonard Rossiter reprises his role as Rigsby, the lecherous landlord, and Frances de la Tour returns as Miss Jones, the object of his desires. Denholm Elliot plays Seymour, a smooth ex-RAF conman out to swindle Miss Jones. The other plot strands are mainly recycled from the TV series but this time without Richard Beckinsale, who had died in 1979. The sub-plots are given a tacked-on happy ending, including a surprising twist from self-styled African prince Phillip (Don Warrington) and an unlikely tête-à-tête between Rigsby and Miss Jones. All this is made bearable by the ever-excellent cast, led by the superb Rossiter.

The Meaning Of Life
dir Terry Jones, 1983, UK, 90m

The Python team returned to the sketch format in a patchy, but at times hilarious last hurrah, tackling the seven stages of life with typical irreverence. Highlights include the song-and-dance routine "Every Sperm Is Sacred", the gluttonous Mr Creosote – a darker riff on the Basil Fawlty persona – and the gory "Organ Donor" sketch, in which people must donate their vital organs whilst alive.

Kevin And Perry Go Large
dir Ed Bye, 2000, UK, 83m

Harry Enfield and Kathy Burke reprise their roles from *Harry Enfield And Chums*, as Kevin and Perry, two teenage boys whose main aim in life is to lose their virginity. Their desire to "do it" and become DJs takes them to Ibiza with Kevin's parents in tow, where they run into legendary dance guru Eyeball Paul (Rhys Ifans). Will they be able to get their mixtape played in a club, and seduce two ladies? On quite a slim budget, Enfield and director Ed Bye had a noticeable hit with the film, which made over £10 million in the UK alone.

Shaun Of The Dead
dir Edgar Wright, 2004, UK, 99m

From the team that brought us the sitcom *Spaced* comes the world's first romantic comedy with zombies, or ZomRomCom for short. Dumped by his girlfriend (Kate Ashfield), stuck in a dead-end job and lumbered with a layabout friend (the ever-excellent Nick Frost), Shaun (Simon Pegg) then finds himself in the middle of an attack of the undead. With its loving references to zombie films and creative direction from Edgar Wright, this was a quirky sleeper hit.

The League Of Gentlemen's Apocalypse
dir Steve Bendelack, 2005, UK, 91m

The characters of Royston Vasey come to life to terrorize the League of Gentlemen (Mark Gatiss, Steve Pemberton, Reece Shearsmith and Jeremy Dyson), who are trying to distance themselves from the characters and make a Restoration drama. Though not as well regarded as the TV series, the film proves that Gatiss, Pemberton and Shearsmith have an incredible range, with each playing half a dozen parts, often appearing in scenes opposite themselves, and includes some impressive set pieces and moments of real pathos.

Funny Business: the craft of comedy

Peter Kay's physical comedy amuses the
fans outside the 2003 BAFTA Awards

Funny Business:
the craft of comedy

The various secrets of comedy can be brought down to instinct and a shared knowledge between joke teller and audience. There are no hard, fast, scientific rules but a few vital guidelines define the difference between a joke being painfully funny and just painful...

Monty Python coined the phrase "what have the Romans ever done for us?" Well, they may have given us the seven tenets of comedy, although Aristotle might argue the case, having speculated in *Poetics* that comedy started with the *komos*, a rollicking, eroticized precursor of morris dancing in which singing men cavorted around the image of a large phallus. Sex certainly lies at the root of much humour but it doesn't help us define the types of comedy. Everyone may have a slightly different idea of what the tenets of comedy are, and they may give different importance to differ-

ent types of comedy. But the tenets would seem broadly to be:

• **Farce** A light dramatic work in which highly improbable plot situations, exaggerated characters and slapstick elements are used for humorous effect. Most episodes of *Frasier* and *Fawlty Towers* work on this basis.

• **Irony** The concept of irony has been spectacularly over-used and misunderstood but for comedians, irony is usually defined as an expression or utterance in which apparent and intended meaning are deliberately different. Irony is a favoured tool of stand-ups wanting to deflate politicians, while pointing out ironies of fate or unintentional ironies is also popular. Alanis Morrisette's song "Ironic" is ironically full of situations that aren't ironic but provided Ed Byrne with a memorable routine who noted, for example: "Rain on your wedding day is only ironic if you're marrying a weatherman and he set the date."

• **Non-sequiturs** A statement that does not follow logically from what preceded it – pretty much anything Eddie Izzard has ever said.

Freud clearly not in a discharging sort of mood

• **Parody** Imitating the characteristic style of an author or a work for comic effect or ridicule, as French and Saunders' movie spoofs do so brilliantly.

• **Pastiche** Consciously imitating work by other artists. Bill Bailey's act features many musical pastiches such as a West Country tribute to Madonna called "Moozak", a take on her hit "Music".

• **Satire** The use of irony, derision and wit to humorously attack folly, vice or individuals. The British satirical tradition – dating back at least to seventeenth century poet John Dryden – has prospered through *Beyond The Fringe* to puppet caricatures *Spitting Image* and Chris Morris's *Brass Eye*.

• **Slapstick** A boisterous form of comedy – the word comes from the stick with which comic entertainers used to slap or strike each other in the seventeenth century – marked by chases, collisions and crude practical jokes. *Father Ted* was notable for inspired, surreal, knockabout comedy while Dom Joly is a master of the practical joke.

On top of that list, there are various tools that service each genre, such as: exaggeration, surprise, truth, brevity, word-play (e.g. made-up words, puns), double entendre, bathos, contrast, black humour, incongruity, affirmation (e.g. stereotypes), aggression and juxtaposition.

Tenets and categories only take us so far. American humorist E.B. White insisted: "Humour can be dissected, as a frog can, but the thing dies in the process, and the innards are discouraging to any but the scientific mind." That hasn't prevented a plethora of theses, usually spiced up with topical references to the latest hit comedy, on every aspect of laughter, ranging from the Freudian theory of tension release to the science of what's funny and what isn't.

Sigmund Freud argued that jokes, rather like dreams, helped order the human mind. Jokes, he argued, were a "discharge of physical energy" stored up by suppressing feelings about a subject. Sex and death usually come top of the suppressed list, as Woody Allen has so amusingly proved.

Physiologists describe laughter in all its physical manifestations such as expelling air and twitching muscular motions. In his 1860 article *The Physiology Of Laughter*, British philosopher and sociologist Herbert Spencer tried to identify the cause of laughter. His suggestion that "nervous excitation always tends to beget muscular motion" sounds remarkably Freudian.

Robert Storey, in his 1996 article *Comedy, Its Theorists, And The Evolutionary Perspective*, sees laughter as an evolved response that strengthens the human gene pool: "As patterns of behavior, tragedy and comedy are strategies for the resolution of conflicts … When faced with polar opposites, the problem of comedy is how to resolve conflict without destroying the participants."

In not dissimilar terms, John Morreall, professor of religion at the College of William and Mary, Virginia, believes laughter is a coping mechanism that indicates danger has passed. For example, a woman threatens to leave her husband claiming she can make £400 a night for what she does to him in bed. He says he wants to tag along to see how she will live on £800 a year. With the wife deflated, the danger subsides.

It's possible – as suggested by the works of Plato, Aristotle and Thomas Hobbes – that we laugh to assert that we are on the same level as people around us or, more likely, a higher level. Research has indicated that bosses tell more jokes than their employees, while, in social situations, women allegedly laugh much more when they're with men and men tell more jokes when they're with women. Although men apparently laugh more quietly around women than with other men.

Research by Paul E. McGhee, who runs a US company called The Laughter Remedy, promotes the idea that, as the *Reader's Digest* notoriously suggested, laughter really is the best medicine, applying humour to various ailments from muscular stress relief to cancer where laughter can improve the immune system. "They who laugh, last" is his message.

Stand-up Chris Addison says the analysis of Freud, Storey and McGhee is irrelevant to most comics: "Comedians are often reluctant or unable to examine the process by which jokes are created. For most of us, it doesn't happen in a formal, conscious, way. And there's always the fear that in making the unconscious conscious you ruin it."

Writing comedy either for live performance or for television – with the pressure to churn out sitcom episodes or write a new Edinburgh set – can become a quasi-industrial process. The challenge and the pleasure is finding new spins on old methods, a task that is urgent today. Many mainstream comics who dominated our stages, piers and screens in the twentieth century shared a heritage of mother-in-law jokes, "There was an Englishman, Irishman and a Scotsman…" gags, and suggestive limericks. Today, with that heritage fractured by alternative comedy, it is more common to borrow/steal an idea and adapt it so the punchline is different.

Ultimately, comedy is about finding your own style without reinventing the wheel. The rules are, there are no rules – except there are…

Stereotypically funny

Stereotypes (conventional, formulaic and oversimplified conceptions, opinions or images) arise from divisions, whether racial, sexual, regional or national, and from observed repeated behaviour where the law of averages may be on the side of the observer but where the repetition of a stereotype makes it harder for exceptions to be recognised.

Stereotypes are often of their time, a defensive response to social change. Immigration into Britain from the 1950s triggered a backlash of racist humour, with gags exchanged in pubs or passed around the club circuit between acts. Building on the example of Bernard Manning and his ilk, Jim Davidson's Chalkie character paid the West Indian community the tiresome back-handed compliment that they were all well-endowed. The response from black comics on the circuit now, such as Stephen K. Amos, to Davidson's gag is simply to cheekily say: yes, of course it's true.

Alternative comedy hasn't ended stereotyping but racial and sexual stereotypes have ultimately, in the post-alternative phase, shifted towards social stereotypes. As John Byrne and Marcus Powell suggest in their book *Writing Sitcoms*, there are plenty of stock characters to play with: "The uptight, pedantic office manager, the opinionated cab driver, the lazy council worker, these stereotypes are as old as the hills, yet are constantly reworked and included in the sharpest contemporary sitcoms."

As the old-school jokes about the Irish and blacks diminished, new targets have emerged, notably – and for no obvious reason – the Welsh, while gags about chavs have become so common as to suggest there's something in the theory of superiority.

The scrapes Jimmy Carr's jokes have got him into prove that the stereotype is still with us. For example, Carr made this joke on Radio 4's *Loose Ends* show in January, 2006: "The male gypsy moth can smell the female gypsy moth up to seven miles away – and that fact also works if you remove the word 'moth'." When the Gypsy Council complained, the BBC said the joke should never have been broadcast, but there are no such checks, pre-emptively or retrospectively, in most comedy clubs.

The terrifying art of stand-up

The stand-up comedian is the observer, the commentator, the myth-exploder, the therapist, the propaganda destroyer, the scourge of etiquette, the man or woman who laughs in the face of convention and reveals shared truths about themselves or the world around them – that's if they are doing their job properly.

There is often something about a comedian's private life, a disability, a disturbing experience, that maintains the anger that fires their comedy. Matt Lucas had a soap opera's worth of trauma as a youngster, losing his hair after being hit by a car when he was six, struggling with a weight problem and, finally, seeing the father he idolized jailed for fraud.

Whatever a stand-up's motivation or persona (be it classic observational, deadpan observational, political, surreal, raconteur or in character), they must frame their ideas so that what they think is funny is understood to be just that by an audience. A stand-up is on a constant quest for inspiration from current affairs, pop culture or social behaviour.

The mental process of crafting a joke can be approached from various angles. Jim Pullin, who has written for Jack Dee and Jonathan Ross, says: "Basically, comedy writing is sitting in a room and staring at a blank piece of paper until your forehead bleeds."

But there are ways to minimize the blood loss. Some things beg to be parodied. For example, John Major's crusade for family values, launched by a government littered with ministers whose peccadilloes filled the tabloid press. These jokes are simple but effective; the object itself amuses even before the punchline arrives.

Other routes are less obvious. The death of Pope John Paul II in 2005 was not off limits to comedy. For example, there was the uncredited gag: "The pope spent his life kissing the ground and now finally he's going to be buried in it – that's like the longest act of foreplay ever."

Some jokes drew attention to unfortunate juxtaposition. The fact that the new pope is announced by smoke billowing from a chimney and that Pope Benedict XVI had belonged to Hitler Youth encouraged an obvious allusion to the Nazi concentration camps. Such gags, though not in the best possible taste, amusingly highlighted the incongruous past of such a powerful figure. As veteran comic Arthur Smith says: "One of the tricks of the funny person (and the historian) is to remind people of the thing from earlier that they'd all forgotten."

The language of comedy

Live comedy is not shrouded in a haze of mysterious language. Many of the words regularly used to describe a show are obvious, such as **headliner** to describe the final and main act on the **bill** (or programme). Headliners and supports will be introduced to the audience by a compere or **MC** (Master or Mistress of Ceremonies) who is literally in control of the mike or **mic** (microphone). Comedians, like musicians, will call the evening a **gig** and hope they **kill** or **storm the gig** (do well) rather than **die** or **bomb** (do badly) or get **gonged off** (a term meaning "made to leave the stage", referring to the Comedy Store's initial way of handling acts, later enshrined in *The Gong Show*).

Doing well involves a comic delivering good **punchlines** (the end of a joke that usually inverts the first part or setup), a **topper** or **capper** (a joke that betters a previous joke) and avoiding **hecklers** (people who call out to the comic, usually insults),

unless they thrive on them and can **ad lib** (improvise a joke) from the heckle. A comic may have a repeated phrase that is their trademark or **catch phrase**, or use running gags (the same joke retold during the comedian's act or set) or **callbacks** (a joke that refers to another told earlier). They may rely on **innuendo**, an indirect, often derogatory, suggestion, sexual or otherwise, or a **double entendre**, an ambiguous statement with one intended, unsubtle meaning, usually sexual. A comedian's particular use of these elements will define their **shtick** (trademark comedy style). Each element of an act requires a **segue** or link to flow, while **sight gags** (visual jokes) may be involved. Either way the comic will hope for a high **lpm** (laughs per minute, a common term in the US), especially those who are just starting out doing **open** or **open mic** spots (unpaid slots for absolute beginners or inexperienced comics).

To arrive at these gags, there is a choice of two routes: the unconscious and the instinctive. The first gag is an instinctive joke where the symbolism of kissing the ground auto-suggests foreplay. The symbolism of the smoke seems initially merely incongruous until gradually the information filters unconsciously into a joke.

Mancunian stand-up Alan Carr says: "I write something that amuses me (e.g. those massage chairs, cat litter trays, tan spray-on booths) and think of ways to include them in my jokes. If you try it the other way, the joke can sound stilted and planned, which it obviously has been."

Ideally, comedians would rather arrive at a joke in one step and build the structure later when thinking about the delivery. Richard Herring, long-time partner of Stewart Lee, says: "I try to write about one funny thing that happened to me or I noticed that day. Otherwise it's just waiting for something to strike you. Reading the papers is good, reading anything can inspire, but it's basically about staying observant and spotting things that might work. Most of the hard work is done on stage. I go on with a basic script, which I improvise with over a few performances. Even when I get something quite set, I like to muck around with it and usually discover some new avenue to explore."

The rhythm method

How you deliver the material is crucial. The secret of comedy is usually said to be timing but timing is often dictated by rhythm. Timing is intuitive and, as in conversation, there is a point after which the moment has gone, but a good rhythm can get around that problem.

In his book *Getting The Joke: The Inner Workings Of Stand Up Comedy*, former stand-up Dr Oliver Double says: "The comic seems to talk like a normal person, and laughter appears as if by magic, sparked off by a word or even a pause. It's easier to attribute the laughs to some kind of mysterious atomic clock in the comedian's head than to make sense of the complex process of what's going on behind that word or pause to make it funny."

Rhythm is an integral part of that complex process. The rhythm every comedian wants to hear is: joke-laugh, joke-laugh, ad infinitum, but there are various ways to achieve that. Patterns of rhythm differ from one comedian to another but they are discernible.

American comedian Steven Wright and English comic Jimmy Carr are masters of the one-liner. Wright can distil a joke into one beat, one actual line: "I was once arrested for resisting arrest." Still one line but, with a setup, in two beats is Wright's gag: "If I ever have twins, I'd use one for parts."

Carr, though economical, embroiders by comparison: "My dad's dying wish was to have his family around him. I can't help thinking he would have been better off with more oxygen."

Some of Carr's other gags adhere to the rule of three – establish, reinforce, surprise:

"A woman stopped me with a clipboard in the street.

She said: 'Could you spare a couple of minutes for cancer research?'

I said: 'All right, but we won't get much done.'"

Dr Oliver Double notes: "Perhaps the subtlest rhythms in stand-up are those contained in the sound of the words that make up key lines. The music made by the patterns of vowels and consonants, which a spoken sentence can contain, often holds the key to why it gets a laugh."

To make his point, Dr Double highlights the absurdist comic Milton Jones, infamous for such jokes as: "If you're being chased by a police dog, try not to go through a tunnel, then on to a little seesaw, then jump through a hoop of fire. They're trained for that." Milton tells Double: "You must have the duh-d-d-dum-d-dum-d-durr rhythm worked out, even if it means including an extra word that is grammatically questionable. The rhythm is more important. I dunno what rhythm does, it must be some subconscious thing. I mean obviously, it's to do with timing, and facial stuff as well. You can even move from vocal to physical rhythm…"

Observational and surreal monologues

Some comics move to the beat of different rhythms within the tapestries they weave. Comically raging against life's petty annoyances, Jack Dee can't afford to dismiss a topic with a one-liner, as his act is about working up his frustration and painting a detailed portrait of stupidity with one-liners, put-downs and general sneering observations. For example, his routine about craft fairs is a collection of observations and put-downs, punctuated by visits to separate stalls, culminating in an attack on wicker and the idea that it was devised for the criminally insane. As an observational conversation the piece is much more random than a load of one-liners. While the routine could end without a punchline, Dee leaves the strongest piece until last, letting one observation carry the comedic weight of everything else he has just said.

Jimmy Carr: master of the embroidered one-liner and the rule of three

The routines of Harry Hill and Eddie Izzard are rhythmically more complex. Hill meshes one-liners into longer routines to keep his surreal comedy going. Izzard, often compared to a jazz musician, appears to go off in all directions abandoning the rules completely, showing the skill for free improvisation reminiscent of Lenny Bruce and conjuring up surreal images that hint at a heritage going from Edward Lear or Salvador Dali through The Goons and Monty Python.

As many jazz soloists will tell you, improvisation works better if you know the rules first, and Izzard says he always knows where he is going to end up. But his comic journey gives him immense room for manoeuvre. He is not relying on set joke patterns but uses a series of personifications and flights of fancy, exaggerating them until he ends up somewhere the audience doesn't expect.

In the following excerpt from Izzard's routine *The Rules Of Advertising*, patterns are still discernible among the apparent chaos.

He doesn't go straight into what advertising is like today. The routine is a two-parter with a past-present contrast and both parts rely on a rhetorical "rule of three" – there are three examples of personification given for the effect of advertising. The line about dog food is a separate joke altogether.

The contrast: "So anyway, advertising! Yes, that's what I brought you here to talk about! Yes, advertising … in the old days, before the 1950s, I don't know, it was much more blatant, adverts were more like, 'Come on, there it is! Come on! Haven't got all day, there it is!' … Nowadays we have choice, don't we? So adverts are more subtle, they're the soft sell, much more like: 'Oh, look at that! Those two people like it, and they're shagging'…"

The rhetorical examples: "That's what happens, isn't it? Shagging sells everything! That's it, there's an advert for coffee. You come around, 'Cup of coffee?' 'Ooh, let's shag!' Yes! Adverts for chocolate bars, two bits of chocolate bar, one eats one, one eats the other, 'Oh, let's have a shag!' That stuff for cleaning the floor, clean the floor and then you shag on the floor…

"…Dog food, dog eats dog food … anyway … So … not sure what happens there, but…"

The art of profanity

Some people base their opinion of a comedian on how much they swear, their disapproval rising with each four-letter word. Certainly, profanity, often the easy way out, can be over-used on the circuit. Yet a well-timed word, tingling with the frisson of a broken taboo, can make all the difference. A single word used repeatedly can trigger as much laughter as a gag itself. Jerry Sadowitz's banter is paced by swear words that

Eddie Izzard amidst a flight of fancy

reach a crescendo that is funnier than the joke. Steve Martin's monologue in the movie *Planes, Trains And Automobiles*, in the scene where he is trying to sort out a hire car, is a textbook case of profanity provoking hilarity. The repeated use of the F-word and its variants create mounting tension, almost stifling laughter, with Martin's anger so believable and his delivery so relentless, it is almost like a chant.

The final arbiters

The test-bed of what's funny is an audience. As Richard Herring acknowledges, there is no scientific formula for engineering the expected response: "You have to start with what you think is funny. Then it's about whether the audience agrees. But you've got to try a few audiences because you get different opinions and sometimes you might not perform something well enough. I persevere with something if I think it is really good, even if most people disagree. I prefer making five people in an audience laugh a lot at something the others don't get, to everyone just laughing a bit. Stuff that doesn't work can be turned around by changing a word or an inflexion. It's amazing how much difference that can make."

Scots comic Stu Who once watched a new comedian die on stage, even though he had some promising material. Who told the comedian to change the order of his jokes. The advice worked – for the first two gags, which went down a storm. Then the act stalled again. Baffled, Who asked the comic: "What went wrong?" The beginner replied: "Well, they kept on laughing and it put me off my timing."

Veteran of the comedy circuit Arthur Smith says: "Start with your second or third best joke. End with the best. If you can gather together the strands of what you've done at the end of a show you can create a climax and the audience will be pathetically pleased. As you go along note the things you can reintroduce later. Do not be afraid, occasionally, of a moment of sentiment."

The audience can be sources of inspiration. Great moments may arrive through heckling – if you're quick-witted and thick-skinned enough to handle it – but more lasting changes to an act will come from wandering off in an unplanned direction that, if the audience response is favourable, becomes part of the act.

Jerry Sadowitz perfected his Nelson Mandela joke to wind up the liberal audience at London's Comedy Store. After starting out with the line: "Ladies and gentlemen, Nelson Mandela: what a cunt", he reluctantly acceded to advice that he had to have a punchline. The next night he emerged saying: "Nelson Mandela, what a cunt, you lend some people a fiver and you never see them again."

The physicality of laughter

A stand-up comedian can wear almost anything, from jeans and a T-shirt to the suited and booted personas of Jack Dee and Sean Lock. Famous variations include Ben Elton's sparkly suits and Eddie Izzard's extravagant double-breasted female outfits. Even at the casual end of the scale the look is important. Comedian Adam Bloom said once: "I'd rather wear just a T-shirt. Ironed, because I wanna pay a little bit of respect for the fact that people have paid money to see me. If somebody's wearing a T-shirt that's creased on stage, what they're saying is, 'I don't care about this gig'."

Hecklers and how to survive them

Handling a heckler sounds nerve-racking but, as Dave Gorman says: "If you're having a good gig and you get heckled, the rest of the audience don't suddenly decide they hate you ... they're on your side and the secret is that you can't really lose. If you're having a bad gig and you get heckled, it's a chance to turn it round."

Heckles can enhance the act. Comic Will Smith recalls: "In Southend once, I was closing with my 'List of Men That Could Turn Me' routine, which involves me trying to persuade the audience that every man has a man who he would sleep with if he really had to be gay. Anyway, this enormous man at the front started yelling 'No! No! Fucking no!' I was quite nervous because he looked very hard and very drunk. So I stopped and said, 'Sorry sir, what's the problem?' And he went 'It's wrong mate. Your list of men is just fucking wrong. Where's Sean Bean?'"

By his own account, Jim Tavare has been plagued by some eloquent hecklers. His *Star Trek* routine has been interrupted by the jibe "It's comedy, Jim, but not as we know it", his "I'm a schizophrenic" gag has been greeted with "You can both fuck off" and when he started doing his double bass act, someone shouted "midget with a violin!" when he walked on stage.

Some hecklers just go for the jugular, as Russell Howard, a rising comic, recalls: "A woman at the Ashton Court festival in Bristol marched on stage, pulled a noose out of a wicker bag and handed it to my friend Andy. He said 'What's this for?' and she said 'End my misery and yours'." Others are more cryptic. Richard Herring recalls: "Someone asked me 'Is your hair laminated?'"

Put-downs vary from straight abuse, punctuated with a four-letter word, to something more elaborate. In her short-haired days, cerebral motormouth Natalie Haynes was recalling a time she slept with a sixth-former, when someone shouted "Male or female?". She paused in pure terror and replied: "Do you think I'm a lesbian because I have short hair?" The room stirred uncomfortably before Haynes added: "Because that's probably just what the short-haired girls tell *you*."

Sometimes a comic can do nothing, as Chris Luby discovered when he played Warwick University's Comedy Superstore for the second time in quick succession in 1990. Sound mimic Luby wasn't getting many laughs and a group in the front row decided to take each silence as the cue to rise from their seats and laugh with demonic voracity, becoming much funnier than the act.

Most comedians wear what feels comfortable, although their options will be limited if they play a character. Paul O'Grady, as gaudy gossip queen Lily Savage, had to be caked in make-up and wear outlandish women's outfits that became a visual gag in themselves. In contrast, Graham Fellows' John Shuttleworth delivers his wry, pedestrian tunes in leather jackets and roll-neck sweaters.

Distinguishing physical features give a sense of what makes a particular comedian funny. Jerry Sadowitz's unruly, no-holds-barred act is perfectly symbolized by his unruly corkscrew hairstyle, just as Billy Connolly's shaggy hair is a statement of intent. Wild-man chic advocate Chris Lynam has hair that looks as if his trademark "firework-up-the-bum" act has left a lasting impression. Mark Lamarr's quiff perfectly personifies his slick, tough persona while Bill Bailey's long hair and beard are comedy trademarks defining his hippy/roadie/space cadet look.

"Kinda funny looking…"

Some comics just look funny. Eric Morecambe once said of his double-act with Ernie Wise: "I like to think we make people laugh with our silhouettes." Countless comics have used looks to maximise their fame and humour. Stan Laurel made the world laugh with his crying face, Les Dawson's permanently glum expression made his comic persona stand out, Kenneth Williams' pointed, chiselled features accentuated his camp character, while Marty Feldman's protruding eyes had a life of their own, being very ghoulish (very useful in Mel Brooks's *Young Frankenstein!*) and clownish.

A comic's size can encourage humour either as an inherent quality (as with Oliver Hardy) or from cracks about their weight (Bernard Manning, Omid Djalili, Johnny Vegas, Jo Brand, Peter Kay to name just a few). Thin, wiry and wired types – such as Phil Kay, Chris Addison, Lee Evans, Lee Mack and Lee Hurst – get the laughs too. With different energy levels, they often – but not always – make greater use of the stage than their weightier counterparts. Kay and Vegas are famous exceptions to this rule. Kay's mastery of stage space was at its best when he re-created a Four Tops tribute act singing "Loco In Acapulco" in his *Live At The Top Of The Tower* show (2000).

A comic's movement – extravagant or minimal – can be as crucial to their act as a rock singer's. Usually bedecked in trainers, Geordie improvisational comic Ross Noble bounces around the

Peter Kay: weighty but nimble comedy

stage, scoring almost as high on the stepometer as the gagometer. You need energy and space to explore the idea of a ping-pong-playing Jesus. Luckily for Noble, he is a big enough draw to play theatres and not have to restrain himself in a small club. Jack Dee plays the same theatres but his classic minimalist stand-up uses less space.

With Dee, deadpan and sparing of movement away from the mic, facial inflections, snarls and sneers are all important.

The power of the set

Stand-up usually takes place on a minimal set, sometimes even consisting of just the mic stand. Simple additions may include a stool, an ashtray, a packet of cigarettes and a bottle of beer. Fags and booze were individually introduced to the audience by American comedian Denis Leary when he was extolling the virtues of the vices of drinking and smoking in his show *No Cure For Cancer.*

Comedians famed for having a bag of tricks or props include the comedy magicians Otiz Cannelloni and Jerry Sadowitz, both of whom flourish magic rings or, in Sadowitz's case, a pack of cards. So fond of props is Sadowitz that even doing a purely stand-up show, he parades plastic spiders and such between numerous costume changes that introduce quick characters like Rabbi Burns, a creation that neatly melds his Jewish/Glaswegian origins.

Sometimes objects become part of the act by accident. In 1986, when Robin Williams played New York's Metropolitan Opera House, on stage was a box of props, including a Viking helmet, which the manic comedian just had to use. A backdrop can exert a subtle influence. When stand-up Russell Brand played The Soho Theatre in 2005 his set, a wrestling ring, belonged to the play at the same venue in a different time slot, but proved an intriguing stage space for the gangly comic who makes full use of his long arms and legs.

Learning to be funny

The popularity of comedy – what with it being the new rock'n'roll and all – means you can learn the craft on courses run by comedians, comedy clubs, and universities. To some, learning how to be funny is anathema and such courses attract derision from those comics, agents and promoters who argue that the oral tradition of comedy prevails, that comedy is intuitive and that the only schooling is practice and watching a lot of comedy.

Yet formal instruction in comedy has been, as Dr Oliver Double has noted, around for a century or so. Even comics as gifted as the Marx Brothers went to a vaudeville school as early as 1907. Once a stand-up, Double lectures in the subject at the University of Kent where his course is part of the four-year drama degree, showing how far comedy has evolved as a formal discipline.

The other academic courses involving stand-up are at Middlesex University (where Logan Murray, once partner to Sadowitz in their double act Bib and Bob, teaches), Salford University (where Peter Kay studied) and Southampton Solent University, which offers the world's first full-time comedy degree, led by former stand-up Chris "Doc" Ritchie. But as Ritchie, holder of a PhD in alternative comedy, said when the degree was launched: "Many people have asked, can you teach someone to be funny, and the answer is no. What you can do is identify someone's aptitude towards something and help develop it."

The art of television comedy

Broadcast comedy can start in many ways – as a hole in a schedule, a vehicle for a restless actor, or a compelling idea from a writer or writers. But at the root of great TV comedy is character – as Basil Fawlty, Sergeant Wilson, David Brent, Norman Stanley Fletcher, the principals in *Seinfeld*, Ralph and Ted and Loadsamoney have all proved.

Rob Brydon says there's a lot more Alan Partridge in Steve Coogan than Coogan would like to admit. Therein lies one clue of how to tease a character out of a writer – identify some kind of empathy and build on it. What lies within us may not always be desirable or admirable but, by releasing it through comedy, you may do yourself and the viewer a favour. Certainly, writer Simon Nye believes there is little room for sentiment: "There's no generosity or humanity in writing a sitcom. You can't start off too affectionate about your characters. The common currency of a sitcom is cruelty – it's about one defeat after another."

The other obvious route is to base characters on people you know. Harry Enfield famously did this with his Stavros character. Though the accent and the phrase "Hello, matey peeps" is the first thing people remember, there was much authenticity in the detail – his assessment of Arsenal's 1988 League Cup defeat to Luton and his jibes against the referee replicated real conversations across North London, in kebab houses and hairdressers.

Nye is circumspect about this approach: "I like the idea that I am in control of my characters." Dramas require, he says, two or three fully rounded characters with genuine depth; sitcoms require "tent pegs" who are predictable, at least

initially, so the audience can map things out very quickly.

Predictable doesn't mean boring. In *Friends*, Joey's defining attribute was that he was a bit slow on the uptake. The challenge with Joey was to keep his stupidity believable, loveable and funny. Anything involving maths was a golden opportunity, on-the-spot numeracy not being a quality with which the general public is blessed, so Joey got empathy rather than pity when he counted on fingers, groping for an answer.

A character's inadequacy in one area can be compensated for by another trait and complemented in another character. In Joey's case he was a "himbo", a ladies' man, giving him the edge over Chandler, who used his wit to have the last word on everything else.

Checks and balances and conflict and resolution are essential. "It's all about oppressors and the oppressed, that's the basic dynamic", says Nye. "Characters grow together and suck each other into their own vortex, dragging each other

Oh Mickey!

Rob Long, a writer on *Cheers*, raises what he calls the Mickey Mouse question: why is Mickey Mouse such a big star when he's far less funny than Bugs Bunny? The answer is, according to Long, because people like Mickey. And every sitcom must balance the likeable Mickeys with the manic Bugs Bunny wisecrackers that writers would ideally fill their shows with. The best sitcoms often have one Bugs Bunny-style gag merchant – think Chandler in *Friends* or Walker in *Dad's Army* – but seldom more than one.

down and pulling each other up. You have to have oppositions within your characters and have them rubbing them up the wrong way as much as you have common ground or occasionally, common cause."

Characters must be distinct. Compare *Friends* with British clone *Coupling*. The personalities are much less studied in *Coupling*, the men all exuding general laddishness while the women are shrill, insecure, neurotic harpies. In the great American sitcoms, the differentiation can be ruthless, adapting the comic principle of physical contrasts typified by great double acts like Laurel and Hardy. In *Friends*, the women aren't just differentiated, they are colour-coded by hair, going from brunette to blonde. In *Seinfeld*, the three principal men are completely different physical types: short, stumpy (George), slim, precise (Jerry) and outrageously tall with comically extreme hair (Kramer).

A sitcom will often have a discreet "one-joke character" lurking in the background. In *Friends* we have Gunther behind the Central Perk counter, a latent character only brought out to secretly, hopelessly pine for Rachel. Obscurer still is the partially seen character, such as Marsha's daughter Amber in *Spaced*, who exists, visually, as a pair of legs stomping out of the house after a row with her mother. Finally there's the unseen character, brilliantly epitomized in *Frasier* by Nile's wife Maris, who can be described as a great French cathedral, an El Greco painting and the upper third of Norway magically transformed into a tiny woman – and bear any gag and insult – because we know we will never see her.

Once a sitcom is established, characters can become moulded around the personality of the actor who plays them. Eric Chappell, creator of *Rising Damp*, noted how Rigsby and Leonard Rossiter fused: "When I started, I just wrote a character, based on people I knew from years before. But when Len came into it, after about two or three years you're writing for Len as well, because he's become the character. Sometimes Len would turn to me and say 'No, he [Rigsby] wouldn't say that, Eric'. And I'd think, wait a minute – I wrote this character! Eventually, the actor takes over the part." David Nobbs' *The Fall And Rise Of Reginald Perrin* would have been completely different if Nobbs had had his way and, instead of Rossiter, cast Ronnie Barker as Perrin.

The "sit" in sitcom

At a preview at the Soho Theatre in 2003, Ricky Gervais joked with the audience that the success of *The Office* meant no one could make an office-based sitcom anymore. Though typical of his double-edged arrogance, Gervais was probably right.

Setting is important, but it's not everything. Former Goodie Tim Brooke-Taylor confessed in an interview that he wasn't that keen on *The Office*, explaining: "My children say it is because I've never worked in an office but I was never in the Home Guard and that has never stopped me enjoying *Dad's Army*."

But Gervais and Stephen Merchant's creation was so immersed in the workplace that the office was almost a character in itself. *The Fall And Rise Of Reginald Perrin* was just as successful in portraying the futility of office life but Reggie's home life was almost as crucial in explaining his distracted state of mind. Sitcom locations are normally more narrowly defined. *Fawlty Towers* was, to the chagrin of BBC executives who kept telling John Cleese to open it up, largely confined by the hotel.

Watering holes are almost as much of a prerequisite in a sitcom as in a soap, though remarkably few sitcoms have flourished on the other side of the bar or kitchen. The notable exceptions are the definitive American bar sitcom *Cheers* and Craig Cash's pub comedy *Early Doors*. The watering hole can introduce other characters to break up the story in an off-the-wall manner: John Thompson's quirky amnesiac pub landlord did this perfectly in *Men Behaving Badly*.

It doesn't matter if it's a café, a bar, a pub, restaurant, or reception area, characters need somewhere to congregate to swap stories. Unless, that is, they never leave the house, or, in the case of *The Royle Family*, barely leave the living room. One-room comedy is the sternest test of sitcom writing, representing essentially the same discipline as a one-act play. Claustrophobia cannot suffocate the laughs and often the dialogue must carry pathos and humour. This is where *The Royle Family* and *Steptoe And Son* were so successful. The rag and bone sitcom, by Alan Simpson and Ray Galton, was like a televised Samuel Beckett play, the surroundings were Spartan, with pathos and laughter in abundance. In *Till Death Us Do Part* an odd couple – Alf Garnett and his wife, the long suffering "silly moo" – constantly battled in a confined space, but Alf could escape to the pub. No such release awaited Harold and Albert.

"Establish, tackle and resolve"

Like rhetoric, comedy often follows the rule of three. For stand-up jokes and many sketches, it is "establish, reinforce, surprise"; for sitcoms it is "establish situation, tackle situation, resolve situation."

Location, location, location

The sky is the limit for where you put your characters, as the space antics of *Red Dwarf* have shown. Space, as the final frontier, hasn't inspired that many sitcoms – the most notable have been *Hyperdrive* (BBC2, 2006) and the classic *The Hitchhiker's Guide To The Galaxy*. Some of the odder earthbound sitcom settings have included: a barber shop (*Desmond's*); an aeroplane (*The High Life*); a hospital (*Only When I Laugh*); a funeral parlour (*Billy Liar*); prison (*Porridge*); a D.I.Y. store (*Hardware*); a boxing gym (the 1980s BBC sitcom *Seconds Out* starring Robert Lindsay); and caravans (the second *I'm Alan Partridge* series).

The comedy writer has to ask: what's the worst that could happen? And then top that. For example, in *Fawlty Towers* Manuel's missing pet hamster turns out to be a rat, on the loose just as the health inspector's arrival is imminent.

Evan S. Smith in his book *Writing Television Sitcoms* lists ten scenarios or "predicaments" that sitcom characters often face.

- **Between a rock and a hard place** Poor Jim Hacker in *Yes, Minister* and *Yes, Prime Minister*, treading a fine line between the interests of the country, his party and the power of Sir Humphrey and the civil service.

- **The big lie** Cowardly Rimmer in *Red Dwarf* trying to pass himself off as his much more confident alter ego Ace Rimmer.

- **The big secret** Think of Rachel in *Friends*, endlessly fending off questions about the father of her baby, and countless sitcoms where a character pretends to have a job…

- **Dead body** Basil Fawlty trying to smuggle the dead man out of a hotel room. Sometimes the threat of a body suffices. In *Rising Damp*, the Spooner character fakes death to wind Rigsby up.

• **Misunderstanding** Two very different episodes of *Frasier* revolve around Frasier being mistaken as gay. Almost every *Fawlty Towers* episode features one major misunderstanding with Basil identifying the wrong guest as a hotel inspector, thinking Polly has a lover and giving Sybil the erroneous impression he has forgotten their anniversary.

• **Rocking the boat** The sacking of David Brent in *The Office*.

• **Race against time** In *Spaced*, Tim is desperate to retrieve his portfolio from Dark Star Comics before the boss there sees his unflattering caricature.

• **Sexual/romantic pursuit** Ross and Rachel, Niles and Daphne and, in *The Office*, Tim and Dawn.

• **Surefire scheme** In *Only Fools And Horses*, Del Boy constantly embarks on doomed get-rich-quick schemes, with similarly disastrous results to Fawlty's gourmet night, which ends with Basil thrashing his car with a branch.

• **Trapped** Chandler stuck in the ATM room – although with a sexy model. When the *Dad's Army* platoon get stuck in a flooding room, they have no such diversions.

Different kinds of laughter can be extracted from drastic situations. Frasier being mistaken as gay gives immense scope for innuendo. Misunderstandings often escalate anger, making the use of physical comedy, including slapstick and exaggerated mannerisms, like Fawlty spanking his own bottom and saying "Who's a naughty boy then?", feel appropriate. Unrequited love provides a rich, continuous source of irony where entirely innocent remarks acquire hilarious double meanings.

Jokes in sitcoms should be seamless. The sudden appearance of a club circuit joke would be an incongruity too far in a sitcom unless the setup is very convincing. But the seamlessness means that jokes can be topped in the same conversation. A joke already made can open a door for another – in this case, the first joke is also a setup. In one episode of *Frasier*, Niles is talking about something that, against all odds, sexually excited him and his legendarily frigid wife Maris: "… we pushed our beds together that night … no mean feat – as you know, her bedroom is across the hall".

Back on this side of the pond, Ben Elton and Richard Curtis's *Blackadder* is a fine example of high jokes-per-minute dialogue packed with put-downs, double entendres and the epigrammatic wit that Edmund Blackadder was famous for, in all his incarnations. The "crone" scene from the *Blackadder II* episode *Bells* is one of Ben Elton's personal favourites. Parodying Shakespearean and other historical dramas, Edmund plays with the audience's familiarity with archaic speech patterns:

> **Edmund**: Tell me young crone, is this Putney?
> **Crone**: That it be … that it be …
> **Edmund**: "Yes it is", not "That it be". You don't have to talk in that stupid voice to me, I'm not a tourist.

And, after the crone has proved herself singularly unhelpful, he dismisses her with a typical put-down, "Thank you young crone. Here is a purse of moneys, which I'm not going to give to you."

Running jokes

Running jokes, like returning cameos, should be eagerly anticipated, though some exist to be discovered later by aficionados. The ultimate running gag must be Kenny's deaths in *South Park* – writers and audiences were intrigued to discover what new ways could be found to kill him. Simpler approaches can provide an equally satisfying gag. *The Simpsons* famously burst into life with a whole series of running jokes, with Bart's penance on the blackboard being a particular delight – yet packs in plenty more, notably Homer trying to strangle Bart. Some running gags – for example, the way a shopping cart rolls out of the parking lot, whenever the Try & Save supermarket is shown – are almost subliminal. *Fawlty Towers* is littered with running gags – Sybil on the phone, Manuel's linguistic difficulties, the Major impatiently awaiting the newspapers, the name of the hotel rearranged on the sign in every episode… Sometimes, like Manuel's fractured English, these gags can inspire more jokes, increasing the show's scope for comedy.

The art of sketch comedy

Writing sketches still involves the basic tenets of comedy but the emphasis on character is different. Characters involved in a sketch rarely evolve over a sustained period of time (*The Fast Show*'s Ted and Ralph being an exception to the rule); their role is to serve the joke, be it visual or verbal. This is, of course, also true of running sketches whether that be Harry Enfield's interfering "You don't want to do it like that…" character or the Stoneybridge councillors in *Absolutely*.

Sometimes, actors are even subservient to the props. In one *Smack The Pony* sketch, someone in an office is drinking from a small bottle of water, the person in the next cubicle along is drinking from a bigger bottle and so it goes in an exaggerated fashion. It's a short step from there to outright slapstick – Kenny Everett's Sherman tank, constantly crushing a car so it can park – where you barely see the actor at all.

A Bit Of Fry And Laurie proves that characterization can become peripheral, as long as the dialogue is witty and paced. The disguises and alter egos adopted by Fry and Laurie are thin and never really cover the performers' personas (no Stavros equivalents in this show) so the comedy was often all down to dialogue or mannerisms.

As you might expect from the title, *The Fast Show* team emphasized pace in their sketch comedy, but paid as much attention to the means as to the end. Charlie Higson says: "The traditional sketch is a gag, a funny idea that you show, but those can be a little bit tedious – that was the sort of thing we were reacting against. You start the situation and the setup goes inexorably to the big gag, the payoff or the twist that is revealed. Nine times out of ten the audience is well ahead of the sketch but you're not really enjoying the sketch as it goes along because you're thinking, what's this sketch all about, what's the payoff? What we tried to do was to say it doesn't matter where the sketch ends up, hopefully people will enjoy seeing what the characters are doing which takes away that terrible burden of the punchline."

Devices that make sketches work

Sketches are extremely flexible vehicles for comedy. Among the comedy devices that work well in them are:

• **Catch phrases** count for even more in a short sketch. *The Fast Show* had so many that Paul Whitehouse says he grew used to being told "It's not comedy, it's just a load of bloody catch phrases." Many characters' *raison d'être* was their catch phrase: the innuendo-laden menswear assistants' chorus of "Suit you sir!" which became annoyingly ubiquitous (the test of a really successful catch phrase); the lawyer who was "very, very, drunk"; Swiss Toni, the car dealer for whom everything could be likened to "making love to a beautiful woman" and the "Brilliant!" character whose shtick is stripped down to virtually one word. Still, as one-word catch phrases go, it's not quite up there with Homer's simple, eloquent, cry of "Doh!"

• **Improvisation** is used to build scenes in sitcoms or even – in the case of *Curb Your Enthusiasm* – entire shows, but this tactic is naturally deployed in sketches, most of which start as a loose framework before rehearsals colour them in. This approach has proved especially fruitful on Channel 4's *Green Wing*.

• **Surrealism/juxtaposition** can be especially effective, as Monty Python proved back in the 1960s – in one famous sketch, Terry Jones played a housewife who had nipped down to the shops and bought an internal combustion engine. Python collaborator Neil Innes carried this flavour into *The Innes Book Of Records*, which usually had Innes playing the piano in some unlikely place, while *Big Train* specialized in such odd characters as Mark Heap's flamenco-dancing bomb-disposal expert.

• **A man dressing up as a woman** is a device that was being reused and reinvented even before Shakespearean comedy cemented it as a bona fide theatrical device. Successful comic cross-dressers include Les Dawson, who along with Roy Barraclough played two gossipy old women who, when not pushing up their ample busts, pontificated on matters bodily and sexual. Dick Emery's equally busty Mandy, with her flirty catch phrase: "Ooh, you are awful. But I like you!", has drawn direct comparisons to David Walliams' Emily Howard character in *Little Britain*.

While genre spoofs are evident within sitcoms such as *Spaced*, which often paid homage to sci-fi and horror movies, a self-contained sketch is an ideal vehicle for an outright spoof. *French And Saunders* and *The Adam And Joe Show* are packed with excellent, studied film spoofs and parodies. At their best, these parodies retell the story, packing in sufficient nuances to make it obvious they thoroughly understand the film, and making knowing references to current affairs or to the real lives of the actors concerned. Sometimes – Steve Coogan's cabaret singer Tony Ferrino being a good example – these spoofs focus so hard on being accurate that they forget to be funny.

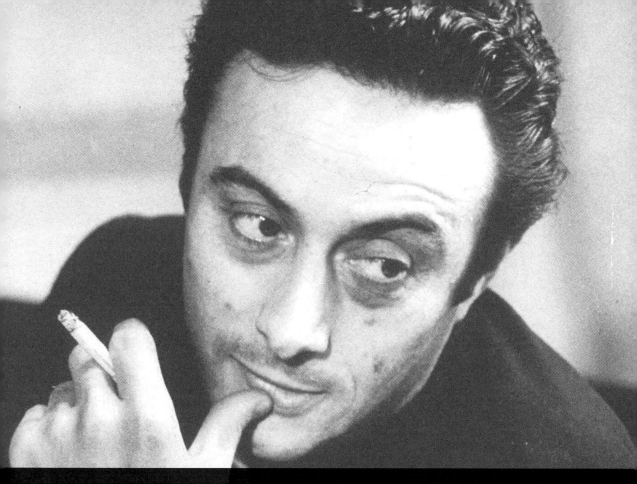

Atlantic Crossings:

the American influence

Lenny Bruce: "the Jesus Christ of
stand-up comedy"

Atlantic Crossings: the American influence

The Americans don't get irony and the British can't laugh because their stiff upper lip keeps getting in the way. But beneath the clichés, the two nations have had a massive influence on each other's comedy.

The roots of American stand-up mirror, in slightly distorted fashion, those of the UK. Stand-up emerged from the late-nineteenth-century tradition of vaudeville, as it was known in the US (music hall in the UK). The fact that in the UK music hall endured until the 1960s, whereas American vaudeville started dying in the 1920s, has affected the countries' approach to stand-up. Such talented monologists and masters of ceremonies as Jack Benny, Milton Berle, Bob Hope and Fred Allen were closer to pure stand-up than British counterparts like Tommy Trinder; their dialogue was much looser, more ad-libbed, and

they abandoned songs and musical skits much more quickly.

As vaudeville died, live stand-up moved to venues associated with Jewish holidaymakers from New York (the Borscht Belt around the Catskill mountains where Danny Kaye and Lenny Bruce started) and the black Chitlin circuit, encompassing venues from nightclubs outside New York to Harlem's Apollo Theatre, which gave civil rights comedian Dick Gregory his break. In the late 1950s, jazz clubs and coffee houses housed cabaret acts and sick comics – a term thrown at Mort Sahl and Lenny Bruce

Jackie Mason

Jackie Mason was the obvious heir to Benny, Berle and Hope until a disastrous appearance on *The Ed Sullivan Show* in 1962. During the broadcast, Mason spotted someone giving him hand signals to wrap his act up. Mason's jokey gesticulations in reply were interpreted by Sullivan as giving him the finger and the humourless host blacklisted the comic. Mason endured by playing the Catskills area, finally making a comeback in 1984 with his show *The World According To Me!*. His direct influence on British comedians is most obvious on sharp, irascible Jack Dee.

because they expanded the range and vocabulary of stand-up and raised political issues in a way that was regarded as subversive.

Though the first actual comedy club, Pip's, opened in Sheepshed Bay, New York, in 1962, comedy clubs only became a national phenomenon in the 1980s. By then, Richard Pryor and Steve Martin had proved comedians could become megastars, playing to huge venues in the 1970s, and stand-up comedians – from Woody Allen to Pryor and Robin Williams – had found fame and varying degrees of fortune in movies and television.

Vive La Difference!

Many American comics – notably Steven Wright, Emo Philips, Joan Rivers, Sandra Bernhard and Bill Hicks – have been greeted with as much, if not more, enthusiasm in the UK than back in the US. But popularity is one thing, influence quite another. For example, Stewart Lee has been likened to Bill Hicks but doesn't name Hicks as

an influence, saying of US comics: "I don't think many of them are as good as the UK acts but I like old Lenny Bruce albums and Chris Rock is funny." Yet Miles Jupp, the versatile stand-up, sketch comic and presenter of children's TV show *Balamory*, admits he thinks *Frasier* is "absolutely the bar" for sitcoms. Some of his live humour is deliberately reminiscent of Kelsey Grammer or David Hyde Pierce's characters in the sitcom. Equally, Sam Kinison's influence on Jerry Sadowitz and Steven Wright's on Jimmy Carr are undeniable.

Direct influences are even harder to map on TV and film. British adoration of *The Simpsons* has prompted no copycat exercise, just as *Monty Python's Flying Circus*, much loved over there, was never cloned in America. No critically successful British sitcom has sprung from a US original, and though many sitcoms have travelled the other way, most don't pass the pilot stage. In film, Woody Allen and Mel Brooks are cherished but not aped, though you may hear Allen's influence in the stand-up of British Jewish comedians such as Adam Bloom.

What follows is a rundown of American acts that have, in the last thirty years, made the biggest splash across the pond in terms of stand-up, television and movies.

Woody Allen

1935–

Life turned on a dime in 1992 for Woody Allen when his affair with Soon-Yi Previn, the adopted teenage daughter of Allen's partner Mia Farrow (from a previous marriage with André Previn) was revealed. Allen's personal life was sensationally splashed across the media and his standing among critics, hitherto his staunchest supporters, has still not quite fully recovered.

The trade in cameos

Every year the West End is deluged by a surge of US movie stars, eager to tread the same boards as Gielgud and Olivier. When it comes to TV comedy, the Americans have remained uncharacteristically reticent. Johnny Depp famously appeared in the last episode of *The Fast Show*, as the dashing subject of the final "Suit You, Sir!" sketch, but that was an enjoyable vanity project for a man who is more European than American anyway.

Ricky Gervais has proved an effective ambassador for British comedy, winning American celebrity fans (including Samuel L. Jackson and Ben Stiller who appeared in *Extras*) and a slot as the first non-American to write *and* feature in an episode of *The Simpsons*. British actors who have fared better in American sitcoms are usually already well-established in movies, such as Michael York, who had a recurring role in *Curb Your Enthusiasm*, or Richard E. Grant, who popped up in *Frasier*. Either that or they are former Pythons. The show is so beloved Stateside that Michael Palin, Eric Idle and John Cleese could live on their guest appearances on shows of the calibre of *Cheers*, *Frasier*, *Saturday Night Live* and *The Simpsons*.

Yet Allen, a consummate wit, writer, filmmaker and formerly a stand-up, has a body of work that will stand the test of time – though much of his humour's appeal is nostalgic. Among his finest films are *Bananas* (1971), *Annie Hall* (1977), *Manhattan* (1979), *Hannah And Her Sisters* (1986), *Crimes And Misdemeanours* (1989), *A Midsummer Night's Sex Comedy* (1982) and *Shadows And Fog* (1992).

Allen began writing gags (and doing magic tricks) as a child. By age 16 he was writing (along with Mel Brooks, Carl Reiner and Neil Simon) for Sid Caesar, by 19 he was writing for *The Tonight Show* and, at 22, he won his first Emmy.

Allen was carving out a stand-up career in 1960s New York when he was spotted by a film producer and made his first movie *What's New Pussycat?* (1965). He didn't really have his own say on a film until he made his crime-documentary spoof *Take The Money And Run* (1969) in which a bank robbery is endangered because the bank teller can't read Allen's note. He moved up a gear with *Bananas*, his Latin American revolutionary send-up, and capitalized on its success with the funny Bogart homage *Play It Again Sam* (1972) and sci-fi caper *Sleeper* (1973). Allen's trademark New York, obsessive, neurotic onscreen character had emerged. Many quotes could sum up this persona but Allen's line that "Life is full of misery, loneliness and suffering – and it's all over much too soon" probably says it best.

This persona is so powerful it has obscured Allen's versatility. He's not all doom, gloom and wisecracks. In *Bananas* there's a delightful skit where a commentary runs over a scene in which Allen and Louise Lasser are making love, while one of the funniest scenes in *Play It Again Sam* involves him accidentally causing chaos with a hairdryer. For the full range of humour, you could do worse than read his short stories, *The Complete Prose* (Picador, 1998).

 The Woody Allen Collection Volume 1 (2004). This box set contains *Annie Hall*, *Manhattan*, *Sleeper*, *Bananas*, *Love And Death* and *Everything You Always Wanted To Know About Sex*. A great introduction to his canon.

 Standup Comic (1999). A fine CD compilation of Allen's legendary mid-1960s stand-up routines.

www.woodyallen.com is a good fan site.

Lenny Bruce

1925–2005

Within the comedy fraternity, few listen to Lenny Bruce's albums anymore. Yet his services as a taboo-breaker are felt by every comedian today, especially by Eddie Izzard who played him in the West End and called him "the Jesus Christ of stand-up comedy".

Born into a Jewish Long Island family, Bruce changed his name from Schneider in 1945 after three years in the US Navy. Though he had initially volunteered, Bruce was discharged after dressing in female clothes, an incident that may have inspired Klinger, the cross-dressing soldier in *M*A*S*H*.

Bruce started as a stand-up doing open spots at New York clubs, but after ditching standard fare for more abstract material and becoming closer to the club scene through marriage with stripper Honey Harlowe, he gained a reputation as an edgy comic, counting Hugh Hefner as an admirer.

In the run up to his legendary appearance at The Carnegie Hall in 1961, Bruce recorded many albums dealing with just about every controversial and contentious issue you can think of, all handled with lots of swearing. His growing notoriety led to a toned-down television appearance and to a backlash in the press, who labelled him a "vomic". Bruce hit back, saying that the really sick comics were contemporaries such as Jerry Lewis who used ethnic stereotypes to get cheap laughs.

Ironically, given San Francisco's liberal reputation, a concert there began Bruce's legal trials and tribulations, when he was arrested, in October 1961, for repeated use of the word "cocksucker". Bruce was often tried, seldom convicted, once invoking the First Amendment, but was sentenced in 1964 for obscenity after an act at Café Au Go

Lenny Bruce's comic heir

George Carlin (1937–) was regarded as carrying on Lenny Bruce's comic legacy. If Bruce was a rebel with attitude, Carlin was a rebel with jokes. Like Bruce, Carlin did military service (as an Air Force radar technician) and, also like Bruce, he was discharged, though no women's clothing was involved. While working as a DJ in Boston, he struck up a writing partnership with newsman Jack Burns that got him onto *The Tonight Show* (then hosted by Jack Paar) in 1962. Then he went solo, doing stand-up in coffee houses, creating such characters as Hippy Dippy Weatherman. His television appearances kept his comedy mainstream but as America became increasingly politically and socially aware, he changed his image, aligning himself with the bearded hippy community he had spoofed a few years before.

The apogee of Carlin's rebellion against his old career was his 1973 monologue on profanity, "Seven Words You Can Never Say On Television". Unlike some imitators, Carlin was too deft a wordsmith to be gratuitously profane, once asking: "If a pig loses its voice, is it disgruntled?" Despite the loss of his wife in 1997, and drug and heart problems, Carlin has prospered, boosted particularly by acting roles in both *Bill And Ted* movies, and his recordings are frequently referenced by British comics.

Go, in Greenwich Village, New York. The court voted to jail Bruce after reading a typed partial script of his performance including references to Jackie Kennedy trying to "save her ass" after her husband's assassination, sexual intimacy with a chicken and St Paul giving up "fucking" for Lent.

From then on, understandably, Bruce's material became obsessed by the law and all its mechanisms. His troubles exhausted and bankrupted him and he was found dead in his Hollywood Hill home in 1966 after overdosing on morphine.

Tony Allen, a pioneer of British alternative comedy, argues that Bruce's performance technique was his greatest contribution to comedy: "He chatted honestly and openly, confided conspiratorially, wisecracked asides, mused soulfully, shared very personal observations, pleaded world-weary bewilderment, groped earnestly to understand and laughed delightedly at his own conclusion. Listening to Lenny Bruce, you get the feeling there was nothing he couldn't express through stand-up comedy."

 Lenny Bruce Without Tears (1971). This mediocre documentary is still a good introduction to his life, with rare footage of him performing.

 The Lenny Bruce Performance Film (1965) offers a more complete gig, but by the time it was shot he was a broken man.

The Carnegie Hall Concert (1995). A great snapshot of his work, part stand-up routine and part critical assessment of American society.

Christopher Guest
1948–

That Christopher Guest is one of the few Americans to sound convincingly English in a movie should be no huge surprise given that his father was the English lord and diplomat Peter Haden-Guest. Christopher, understandably, chose to go single-barrelled when starting his acting career.

The incomparable Lenny Bruce

Spending much time in England, Guest fell for the charms of *Beyond The Fringe*, The Goons and Monty Python. With his insight into British humour, Guest struck gold in the late 1970s. While staying at the same hotel as a famous British rock band, he witnessed a ludicrous conversation about a "lost" bass guitar back at the airport that inspired his spoof masterpiece *This Is Spinal Tap* (1984), complete with his mockney character Nigel Tufnel, who believes he has synthesized Mozart and Bach (or "Mach" as he calls it) to produce his epic hit "Lick My Love Pump".

The effect of *This Is Spinal Tap* was immediate. Rock bands hated it, Iron Maiden walked out of the premiere believing it was parodying them, but eventually this hilarious, relentless exposé of rock cliché became staple viewing for rockers and comedians alike.

The mockumentary style, as director and co-writer Rob Reiner dubbed it (earlier examples, not using this term, include Allen's *Take The Money And Run*), would become key to British television comedy in the 1990s, influencing *The Office*.

Guest, meanwhile, created other mainly improvised mockumentaries including the pageant parody *Waiting For Guffman* (1996), dog show spoof *Best In Show* (2000), and folk send-up *A Mighty Wind* (2003). All these involved ubiquitous comedy actor Eugene Levy, while *A Mighty Wind* saw Guest work with *Spinal Tap* co-stars and co-writers Harry Shearer (best known now for playing multiple characters on *The Simpsons*) and Michael McKean (once known for sitcom *Laverne And Shirley*).

This Is Spinal Tap (1999). This great film has inspired many comedians, including The Comic Strip. Guest's *Best In Show*, *Waiting For Guffman* and *A Mighty Wind* are also available on DVD.

Rich Hall
1954–

Wiry, gravel-voiced Rich Hall rose from street performer to warm-up man for Talking Heads in the blink of an eye, an experience that left him tender but wiser: "I would have to walk out on stage in front of 3000 people shouting 'Psycho Killer' … After that, I was ready for anything."

Surviving that fiery baptism, Hall toured the US comedy circuit and became a regular on *Saturday Night Live*. In the 1990s he began to split his time between his native Montana and the UK with more time spent here as his Perrier Award-winning alter ego, jailbird country singer Otis Lee Crenshaw, author of such classics as "Do Anything You Want To The Girl (Just Don't Hurt Me)" became popular. Otis was a convenient vehicle for Hall to deliver his caustic stand-up set between numbers, often pontificating on every comic's favourite target George Bush.

Hall proved himself even more versatile than his fans suspected, writing *Self Help For The Bleak*, a parody of life-coaching books and his wry, innovative short story collection *Things Snowball*. He also has a hilarious routine about Tom Cruise's movie roles ("He was a racing driver, a good one, but then he had a crisis of confidence, until he met a beautiful girl who helped him become an even better racing driver") that ends with the star needing a Welsh girl to save him from a crisis of consonants in the board game Scrabble.

Otis Lee Crenshaw: Live (2001). Hall's dry creation is on superb form, as he runs through such comedy songs as "Rodeo Rider From The Shetland Islands".

www.offthekerb.co.uk/artists/a_artists_home.jsp?artist=rich_hall

Bill Hicks

1961–94

Even in death, the excellent Bill Hicks is contentious. While fans create websites dedicated to what he would have made of George W. Bush's administration, others shrug off his legacy because a certain kind of comedian is constantly being compared to him and because everyone – including Denis Leary – wanted to be him.

After spending his childhood crafting comedy routines with buddy Dwight Slade (who is still on the stand-up circuit) Hicks worked for a spell at LA's Comedy Store at 18, sometimes notching up stage time and showing skill as a performer. But he really found his comic identity when he returned to his native Texas where he became one of the Outlaw Comics, a group known for its rock'n'roll lifestyle and edgy approach to comedy, alongside the outspoken, hell-raising comedian Sam Kinison.

Hicks did not become the James Dean of stand-up until after his death, of pancreatic cancer, in 1994. Yet from 1990 onwards, he began to make his name and win fame. His performance at Montreal's Just For Laughs Festival garnered him a special on the HBO channel (and Channel 4 later), while his first album *Dangerous* received rave reviews. Britain soon discovered him, surpassing America with its passion for his humour.

Hicks's politically incorrect eulogies to smoking (routines that heavily influenced Leary), drink and drugs were much loved and were forceful even when he ditched such pleasures himself due to bad health. His candour about his love of pornography ("The Supreme Court says pornography is anything without artistic merit that causes sexual thoughts … Sounds like every commercial on television, doesn't it?") alienated some. But his

The Comedy Store LA

The Comedy Store, Los Angeles, inspired the London Comedy Store and provided the launch pad for America's greatest comedians. The LA Comedy Store was opened in 1972 by two comics, Rudy de Luca (who has appeared in many Mel Brooks films) and Sammy Shore (who used to open for Elvis). Shore's wife Mitzi, who suggested the club's name, took over running the Store when she and Sammy divorced in 1974. The club claims among its alumni: Sandra Bernhard, George Carlin, Jim Carrey, Whoopi Goldberg, Arsenio Hall, David Letterman, Michael Keaton, Jackie Mason, Eddie Murphy, Richard Pryor, Roseanne Barr, Garry Shandling and Robin Williams.

political beliefs also influenced his comedy, and his pot shots at the first Bush administration and the first Gulf War struck a chord. To give just one example: "You know we armed Iraq. I wondered about that too. You know, during the Persian Gulf war, those intelligence reports would come out: 'Iraq: incredible weapons – incredible weapons'. How do you know that? 'Uh, well … we looked at the receipts'."

If the duty of a comic is to show that the emperor is naked, Hicks, an exciting, brooding performer, could do that duty better than most. He richly deserves his place in comedy history.

 Sane Man (2005). Hicks at the height of his powers, filmed in Austin, Texas, in 1989, with the audience fully behind him.

Cynthia True's biography *American Scream* (Sidgwick & Jackson, 2002) is a lively, pacy introduction that gives an intimate insight into Hicks's short life.

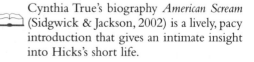 www.billhicks.com

The Just For Laughs Festival, Montreal:

Bill Hicks wasn't the only comedian to get his big break at Montreal. Every year, in the middle of July, the Quebec capital is swept, as the organizers cornily put it, by a "laughter virus" when the Just For Laughs Festival, or, if you will, the Juste Pour Rire Festival attracts comedians from around the world.

The festival began in 1983 as a four-day event comprising 16 Francophone performers catering for 5000 Quebecois spectators. It is now the biggest comedy event in the world, with a live audience of approximately two million people. Some 700 stand-ups, street performers and entertainers perform over ten days. The shows are usually split into different categories, the main divide being between those performed in English and those in French. Certain acts whose content is deemed *sympatico* are showcased together, such as QueerCom, which has previously showcased Graham Norton and Julian Clary. A particularly popular collection is BritCom. Montrealians relish what they call *l'humour brittanique* so Ben Elton, Eddie Izzard, Vic Reeves, Al Murray, Jimmy Carr and Omid Djalili have all performed here.

The Just For Laughs Festival has always tried to offer a global selection of the best comedy. So, the great comedic talents from North America have, to cite a few examples, been supplemented by comics from Australia (Brendon Burns, The Umbilical Brothers) Holland (Hans Klok), Russia (Sergei Pavlov) and South Africa (John Vlismas).

But, like the Edinburgh Festival and the Sundance Film Festival, Just For Laughs is facing increasing criticism, with many in the comedy industry seeing it as a corporate trade fair. When Matt Lucas and David Walliams performed at the festival in 1999, Lucas said it was "more for the trade than for the public", a view shared by many insiders, who feel Montreal is no longer a noble experiment in international live comedy, but a bloated cynical moneymaking exercise. Such criticism has done little to stem the festival's popularity.

Andy Kaufman

1949–84

He's been called an "anti-comedian'" for his reliance on happenings and for deliberately performing badly, but Andy Kaufman's legacy is sheer audacity, playfulness and a heightened sense of the fine line between fiction and reality – all weapons in any good comedian's arsenal.

In the early 1970s, after dropping out in true Greenwich Village style and tuning in again thanks to a college course in radio and TV production, Kaufman was discovered by Budd Friedmann, the founder of the original Improv Comedy Club in New York. Back then, Kaufman's act involved Foreign Man, a deliberately hopeless comic and impersonator, and a decent impersonation of his idol Elvis, which The King quite liked. He made his TV debut in 1974 on Dean Martin's *Comedy World* and, in 1975, started appearing on the new *Saturday Night Live*. Kaufman's most infamous TV appearance was on another sketch show, *Fridays* (1981), on which he abruptly went out of character and refused to say his lines, a stunt for which he later "apologised" as not enough cast members were in on the joke.

Among the unorthodox wheezes he devised for his live shows were reading *The Great Gatsby* and developing his ill-tempered lounge lizard crooner Tony Clifton, to wind up audiences and create a mystique – no one was totally sure if the two were one and the same (he was alternately played by Kaufman, his brother Michael and creative partner Bob Zmuda). Kaufman even secured Clifton a stint on *Taxi*, the sitcom he starred in as Latka (essentially his Foreign Man character), but Clifton was thrown off the set after a trademark fit of rage.

The Tony Clifton character, Kaufman's wrestling bouts with women and his staged spat with male wrestler Jerry Lawler didn't tell the whole story about Kaufman, who was admired for his habit of taking audiences out for milk and cookies after shows.

Kaufman's escapades ended with his unexpected death in 1984 from a rare lung cancer. He had been such a successful jester that many considered his death a stunt. In 1999 Jim Carrey skilfully immortalized Kaufman's antics in the movie *Man On The Moon*, introducing the Kaufman mystique to a new generation.

The Andy Kaufman Show (2000). This 1983 one-hour show was one of Kaufman's last appearances, as it was recorded just a year before his death. It features Foreign Man, lounge singer Tony Clifton, and Kaufman's Elvis impersonation. It is best watched in tandem with the biography *Lost In The Funhouse: The Life And Mind Of Andy Kaufman* (Fourth Estate, 2000) by Bill Zehme.

andykaufman.jvlnet.com is an informative fan site.

Sam Kinison

1953–92

When rock'n'roll comedian Sam Kinison was killed by a drunk driver, it was tragic but fitting. He had lived a high-octane drugs and drink lifestyle, even joking about how when you were driving under the influence it felt perfectly sane to crash the car just to get some sleep.

Kinison followed his father, a Pentecostal preacher, into the pulpit but when his sermons provoked his flock he became a comedian, retaining the fire-and-brimstone delivery, ranting and primal screaming that – along with his bandanas and smocks – became his trademark.

Kinison's rock'n'roll image was no put-on. He toured with a band and counted Mötley Crüe, Guns 'N' Roses and Ozzy Osbourne as friends (some appeared in the videos for his novelty records, the funniest being a fitting cover of The Troggs classic "Wild Thing").

Kinison belonged to a group of Houston comics known as the Outlaw Comics, bound together by hard-living and a determination to clear their path of anything that got in their way. While newer recruit Bill Hicks honed his satirical skills, Kinison was more scattergun. Hardly even-tempered, the rotund megamouth was even-handed, dishing out vitriol in every direction.

Take for example his ambiguous sympathy on famine: "I'm very moved by world hunger … Matter of fact, I have the answer … Stop sending these people food … Send them U-Hauls [removal trucks]. Send them a guy out there who says, 'Hey, we been driving out here every day with your food, for, like, the last thirty or forty years, and we were driving out here today across the desert, and it occurred to us that there wouldn't be world hunger, if you people would live where the food is! You live in a desert!'" Kinison's brazen, off-handed attitude to women was partly responsible for his being likened to infamously misogynistic shock comic Andrew "Dice" Clay. But Kinison fan and cartoon scriptwriter Mark Evanier points

Sam Kinison with trademark bandana

"I look for women I know are gonna bust me up good. Yeah, they all have the same line, they're so sweet – 'I'm not gonna hurt you like all the others. Really I'm not. I'm gonna introduce you to a whole new level of pain!'"

Breaking The Rules (2001). On this early recording, his rants aren't for the faint- or the fair-hearted but there is plenty here for your money with rare material as an extra.

www.samkinison.org

Steve Martin

1945–

Steve Martin – the bridge between Jerry Lewis and Jim Carrey – has lived out two lifetimes: one as a successful live performer and one as an international star of increasingly forgettable films. At one point, his reputation had sunk so low that when Dennis Pennis asked him: "Why aren't you funny anymore?" it seemed a perfectly appropriate question.

Martin's philosophy of comedy stemmed from his study of philosophy at California State University: "It changed what I think about everything … something about non-sequiturs appealed to me … you start to realize, 'Hey, there is no cause and effect! There is no logic! There is no anything!' Then all you have to do is twist everything hard – you twist the punchline, you twist the non-sequitur so hard away from the things that set it up, it's easy and thrilling."

out: "Kinison's rage, such as it was, was directed to the few, specific women he felt had wronged him … and only because he had loved them first." Certainly Kinison's act says more about the pain of idolization than wanton misogyny:

Martin's live act owed much to his gift for magic – the definitive twisting of logic. Tricks, banjo playing, juggling and balloon representations of venereal diseases would be thrown into his routine ad hoc. As his stand-up career developed, so did his writing career in television, especially after he got a job through a girlfriend on *The Smothers Brothers Comedy Hour* in 1967.

From the mid-1970s he started getting stand-up spots on television (he holds the record for the number of guest host appearances on *Saturday Night Live*). On the live circuit he opened for popular bands such as The Carpenters but by the end of the 1970s was topping bills at music venues. He then wrote and appeared in the Carl Reiner movie *The Jerk* (1979), an auspicious start put to good use when he starred in and wrote two more Reiner movies: the inventive *Dead Men Don't Wear Plaid* (1982), using footage of dead film stars, and *The Man With Two Brains* (1983).

Other notable comic high points of Martin's movie career include *Three Amigos* (with Chevy Chase and Martin Short, 1986) and *Planes, Trains, And Automobiles* (1987) with John Candy. Martin's "wild and crazy" shtick has influenced many British comics, especially Harry Hill and Vic Reeves.

 Saturday Night Live: The Best Of Steve Martin (1999). One of the few DVDs containing such classic Steve Martin stand-up and sketch routines as "The Coneheads" (made into a 1993 movie with Dan Aykroyd) and his zany King Tut persona.

www.stevemartin.com

Eddie Murphy
1961–

A skilled performer, outspoken – sometimes for the wrong reasons – with an infectious energy few can match, Eddie Murphy was too loose a cannon to truly inherit Richard Pryor's mantle. His early pot shots against homosexuals and AIDS sufferers led some, including Pryor, to think Murphy's act was just too mean. Murphy later apologized for his scathing attacks but never let up on his abusive style. Despite the reservations of his comic idol and liberal commentators, Murphy was incredibly successful in the 1980s.

Murphy began writing and performing routines involving celebrity mimics when he was 15. His breakthrough came at The Comic Strip, where co-owners Robert Wachs and Richard Tienken took on the task of managing him. Not that Murphy was green about promoting himself. Sheer persistence landed him a role on *Saturday Night Live* where, surviving a massive cast cull, he reigned supreme with Joe Piscopo in the early to mid-1980s. In 1983, he launched his successful live show *Delirious* and made his movie debut in the action/comedy *48 Hours* alongside Nick Nolte. *Trading Places* (1983), with Dan Aykroyd, and the smash *Beverly Hills Cop* (1984) soon followed.

Murphy's powers began to wane by the late 1980s, as his box-office allure began to disappear, and *Harlem Nights* (1989) was universally loathed, despised, even, by co-star Richard Pryor.

Despite a well-publicized incident when he was caught driving a 21-year-old transsexual prostitute, Murphy's career experienced a respectable renaissance in the 1990s with family comedies such as the remake of Jerry Lewis's *The Nutty Professor*. For most fans, though, he was better alongside Steve Martin in the Hollywood spoof *Bowfinger* (1999).

 Raw (2004). Only the 1987 gig *Raw* is available on DVD, but the superior *Delirious* can still be found secondhand on video. Both have lots of verve and dubious material. Murphy is at his best when using episodes from his own life, although the Mr T impressions and Michael Jackson-inspired material are good.

Emo Philips

1956–

Lanky, whiny and spooky, Emo Philips was lapped up by the British public in the mid-1980s. Sporting a medieval bob like that worn by Rowan Atkinson in *Blackadder*, Philips would deliver sinister, surprising non-sequiturs and one-liners about his dysfunctional family ("My mother was like a sister to me, only we didn't have sex quite so often") and his status as a social outcast ("I was with this girl … from the way she was responding to my skilful caresses, you would have sworn that she was conscious from the top of her head to the tag on her toes").

He started on the Chicago circuit in 1976 and, after getting a break on *Late Night With David Letterman* in 1984, took his superbly honed act onto British TV. "You Brits didn't have to suffer watching me learn my craft", Philips told *The Guardian*, "Americans were the guinea pigs, like the rabbits with bleeding eyes from the perfume sprays. You guys were the supermodels."

West End and Edinburgh runs followed. He even settled in London for a while with an English partner and toyed with writing a crime novel. Instead, he had an indirect success writing an independent movie called *Meet The Parents*, subsequently remade into the Robert De Niro/Ben Stiller hit of the same name. Philips carries an executive producer credit on the second film but didn't like the rewrite: "If *The Jew Of Malta* came after *The Merchant Of Venice*, that would be a good analogy."

Philips ditched the bobbed hairdo in 1997 and returned to Edinburgh in 2001, slick, silver-haired and plumper. Luckily the jokes remained the same: "My ex-wife, who shall remain nameless – if I'm ever left alone by her tomb with a sandblaster."

E=MO² (2005). In the sad absence of an Emo Philips DVD, this CD, recorded in the 1980s, is a great compensation. Goofy routines such as "I'm A Great Lover I Bet" and "College: The Best Six Weeks Of My Life" are beautifully delivered.

www.emophilips.com

Richard Pryor

1940–2005

The cliché that every comedian is using humour to hide the heartache was seldom truer than for Richard Pryor. To his fan Robin Williams, "Richard Pryor is an alchemist who can turn the deepest pain into the deepest comedy." Some agonies were inflicted upon him – like being raped by a teenager when he was just 6 years old – others were self-inflicted. While freebasing cocaine once, he famously doused himself in cognac and set himself alight. On top of that, two heart attacks, seven marriages and multiple sclerosis (diagnosed in 1986 when he was just 46) meant he was never short of inspiration for material. He may well have written his own epitaph when he said: "Be truthful and funny will come."

Pryor used these experiences on stage to become a vital performer, revered by comedians. David Letterman says: "To fully appreciate the power of Richard Pryor as a stand-up, you had to follow him at The Comedy Store. I did once, and I'm lucky to be alive."

Pryor's style originally mirrored Bill Cosby's but in 1969, during a Las Vegas show, he walked off stage asking what he was doing there. Finding his voice, he used comedy to air his social and racial grievances. Take this excerpt from his 1974 show *That Nigger's Crazy*, for example: "Police degrade you … it's often you wonder why a nigger don't go completely mad … You get your shit together, you work all week, right, then get dressed … go out, get clean, be drivin' with his old lady, goin' out to a club, and the police pull over … Now, what nigger feel like havin' fun after that? 'No, let's just go home, baby.' You go home and beat your kids and shit – you gonna take that shit out on somebody."

Pryor was credited with reclaiming the word "nigger" which he used liberally in his act. After a trip to Kenya in 1979 Pryor dropped the word from his set, prompting death threats from "fans", suffering, as ever, to make his point.

 Live In Concert (2004). As well as a host of decent extras, this DVD has an entire stand-up routine recorded live in 1979 and is the best live Pryor gig available. The routine about his heart attack and how it – literally – grabbed him is just one of the highlights.

 www.richardpryor.com

Richard Pryor, turning pain into comedy

Chris Rock

1965–

In the 1970s there was Pryor, in the 1980s Murphy, but in the 1990s Chris Rock was the black icon of comedy. Murphy was an idol for Rock, as Pryor had been for Murphy. All three stirred the pot, but Rock was especially outspoken in his observations of people from his own community, such as "niggas" who gave black people a bad name.

Though he had already appeared in movies, including *Beverly Hills Cop II* (1987), Rock didn't really catch the eye until he became a regular on *Saturday Night Live* in 1990, lampooning black political leaders and stars of pop and rap. The pop/rap skits spawned Rock's film *CB4* (1994).

For his stand-up, the benchmark was his Emmy-winning 1996 set *Bring The Pain*, addressing various racial issues, notably the African-American community's divided response to the trial of O.J. Simpson. Another part of the routine called "Niggas versus black people" remorselessly flayed those he characterized as "low-expectation havin' muthas". The use of the word "nigga" was controversial – Pryor had abandoned it over a decade before. Though he did not revisit this routine, Rock never apologized for it and the word has been used recently by American comedian, resident in Britain, Reginald D. Hunter.

Rock's routines, delivered in a gravelly, sharp, almost hoarse style, usually have a welcome edge. While most Americans agreed with his take on taxation ("they take money out your cheque each week and then they want some more money each April – what kind of gangster shit is that?") his suggestion, as host of the 2005 Oscars, that Jude Law was a second-rate Tom Cruise so upset

The Def Jam school

Beyond Rock, Murphy and Pryor lies a wealth of other American black comedic talent, relatively unknown in Britain. Many of these performers were showcased on the *Def Comedy Jam*, a 1990s TV series that brought a hip-hop sensibility to comic routines. The brainchild of Russell Simmons, co-founder of Def Jam, the record label of Run DMC and LL Cool J, *Def Comedy Jam* was a springboard for the careers of Martin Lawrence, Eddie Griffin, Cedric the Entertainer, Bernie Mac and Chris Tucker. All are now movie stars with impressive box-office clout, despite their predilection for starring in less-than-classic fare such as *Big Momma's House* (Lawrence and Cedric the Entertainer), *Scary Movie 3* (Griffin), and *Guess Who* (Mac).

Another *Def Comedy Jam* alumnus is Dave Chappelle. Best known in the UK through supporting roles in *The Nutty Professor* and *Con Air*, Chappelle's TV series, *Chappelle's Show*, is a mixture of stand-up and sketches that gives *Little Britain* a run for its money in the quotability stakes, with catch phrases familiar to every American student.

The creativity of these comics has done much to dispel the perception that black American comedians rely too heavily on "the difference between black people and white people". The mainly political repertoire of Wanda Sykes, a former collaborator of Rock's, has a universal appeal.

Spike Lee's film *The Original Kings Of Comedy* (2000), a documentary that eschewed Lee's usual sermonizing to showcase the charismatic stage performances of Bernie Mac, Cedric the Entertainer, Steve Harvey, and DL Hughley, was a crossover box-office success.

Sean Penn that the actor defended Law later in the show. Rock survived the Oscar fall-out to launch the acclaimed sitcom *Everybody Hates Chris* (Channel 5, 2006–) based on his experience going to a predominantly white school in Brooklyn.

 Bring The Pain (2002). This seminal set recorded live in 1996 is now available on DVD and video.

www.chrisrock.com

Rita Rudner
1956–

She is not as brash as Joan Rivers but Rita Rudner is not slow to dispense similar pearls of wisdom about life, love ("My mother buried three husbands and two of them were just napping") and the pursuit of material happiness: "Someday I want to be rich. Some people get so rich they lose all respect for humanity. That's how rich I want to be."

Rudner cites Jack Benny, George Burns and Woody Allen as inspirations. "Listening to Woody Allen, I realized you didn't have to be aggressive; my humour is more offbeat hysterical than it is raucous."

Before honing her stand-up act, Rudner was a Broadway dancer in hit musicals for ten years. A British comedy producer, Martin Bergman, spotted Rudner at the New York comedy club Catch A Rising Star in 1984, and guided her towards headline status. Her *annus mirabilis* was 1990. In that year, Bergman produced her BBC2 series, she won the American comedy award for best female stand-up, and she starred in her own HBO special *Born To Be Mild*. In 1991, she married Bergman. The two later scripted the ultimate luvvie movie *Peter's Friends*, directed by and starring Kenneth Branagh, with comedy mafia members Fry and Laurie in the cast.

The first female comedian to be initiated at the entertainment fraternity's Friars Club in New York, Rudner still performs stand-up, has written several successful humour books and a half-decent novel, *Tickled Pink*.

Rita Rudner (2000). This rare, but obtainable, video is a compilation of Rudner's six-episode BBC2 series from 1990 that mixed sitcom elements, observations on the trials of daily domestic life and deft surreal touches.

www.ritafunny.com

Doug Stanhope
1967–

Of the many American comics to play Britain, Doug Stanhope has probably been the most critically lauded; his very presence in Edinburgh seems to guarantee five-star reviews in *The Guardian*.

Any American comedian as blunt and as political as Stanhope will be measured against the likes of Bruce, Carlin, Pryor, Kinison and Hicks. He lives up to that tradition with an unorthodox, party-animal life (even though he has a long-term partner and a child) and a humour that pushes things to the edge, exploring abortion and sexual health in lurid detail. His routines twist logic to breaking point, as this rant about children shows:

"I have to pay for cable TV just to hear a comedian say 'fuck' – because of your kids. I have to struggle like a mongoloid with a safety lighter when I'm drunk – because of your kids. And at three in the morning, when I want to moon a sorority girl from a taxi cab – because I have issues going way back – I can't even do that, because the window will only go down halfway; to protect your kids."

Despite fronting some voyeuristic men's TV shows ("Nobody has more contempt for our viewers than I do", he said once) for money, the morally uninhibited comic remains a cult figure with attitude, bravely refusing to wear a badge honouring the NY Police Department after 9/11 because of their previous record of brutality.

 Deadbeat Hero (2004). Stanhope's assault on the senses leaves few stones unturned with his verdict on the NY police, the US army and twins joined at the hip.

www.dougstanhope.com (suitable for over 18s only)

Robin Williams

1951–

The undoubted charisma of Robin Williams was tested to breaking point in the movies, proving there are limits as to how far you can stretch a live stand-up persona. Too often, he seems constrained by Hollywood's idea of comedy, although the glorious exception, *Good Morning Vietnam*, gave him plenty of room to ad-lib.

Williams studied acting at the Juilliard School in New York City, whose alumni included his great friend Christopher Reeve, and amused himself by performing as a street mime, before trying his hand at stand-up in the early 1970s. His early influences included madcap comic Jonathan Winters. Egged on by a tutor, Williams headed west to hit the comedy clubs in and around San Francisco.

In LA, his big break was landing the role of the alien Mork in the smash hit TV series, *Mork And Mindy*, impressing producer Gary Marshall by sitting down head first ("I wanted an alien and he was the only alien to audition", said Marshall later). Williams was given free rein to show off his undoubted improv skills and soon attracted movie producers. While his movie career zigzagged, his stand-up was boosted by the exposure. One of the early highlights was playing Andy Kaufman's grandmother – a character that formed the basis for his 1993 movie role *Mrs. Doubtfire*.

Barry Levinson's *Good Morning Vietnam* (1987) cemented Williams as a box-office draw and the mid-1980s saw him at the peak of his stand-up powers. *Live At The Met* (1986) was a grand showcase for his talents, and routines such as likening childbirth to a scene from *Taxi Driver* and getting Reagan and Gorbachev to settle the Cold War in a bar were typically high-energy and have stood the ravages of time.

 Live On Broadway (2002). Copies of Robin Williams's *Live At The Met* (1986) are hard to find on video, but well worth hunting out. The more readily available *Live On Broadway* is a sound alternative, with Williams tackling subjects like the World Cup and the Winter Olympics with disarming gusto.

www.robin-williams.net is a useful fan site.

The Aristocrats

The most acclaimed comedy film to star Robin Williams since *Good Morning Vietnam* is a 2005 documentary called *The Aristocrats* – although Williams is merely one of many top comedians, showbiz veterans and Hollywood names to appear in this gem of a movie derived from a joke shared among industry insiders.

A man walks into a talent agency and says he has a brilliant new family act, complete with parents, son, daughter and dog. He then goes on to describe the most vile and depraved acts imaginable, including – but not limited to – incest, rape and murder. The stunned talent agent asks what the act is called, to which the man replies: "The Aristocrats".

This is the standard formula for a joke that has been told amongst comedians since vaudeville. Used variously as a back-stage warm-up act, a way for comics to compete against one another, and as the definitive shaggy dog story, with comics spending hours developing the gag in their own style, the joke was known amongst comedians, but deemed off limits for public consumption. And then one day two American comics decided to make a feature-length film about it.

In the movie, nearly a hundred comedians and comic actors analyse and retell the joke in their own styles. The repertoire of performers runs from the clean-cut Paul Reiser to shock comics Lewis Black and George Carlin and such respected Hollywood players as Carrie Fisher, Whoopi Goldberg and Hank Azaria. Other famous comics to contribute include Emo Philips, Chris Rock, Rita Rudner, Jon Stewart and Steven Wright and, representing Britain, Eddie Izzard, Eric Idle and Billy Connolly. The film even includes Phyllis Diller, an old hand in the comedy industry who was friends with Bob Hope, and is now nearly 90.

This diverse roster are all friends of the producer-director duo Penn Jillete and Paul Provenza. Jillete is the verbose half of the magic and comedy act Penn and Teller, who have amazed audiences for over twenty years with their gross-out tricks, which have included blood, chainsaws, guts and eighteen-wheel juggernauts. Provenza is a widely respected American stand-up, winning acclaim for his one-man show *The Incredible Man-Boy*.

Using handheld cameras, they produced a hilarious, candid and shocking low-budget film that reveals a great deal about the workings of the comic mind.

Steven Wright

1955–

Steven Wright is the master of deadpan and arguably the master gagsmith of all time. Certainly he's the most relentless. Never one to over-analyse his own craft, the conical-headed, wild-locked Wright claims: "I don't believe in politics. I barely believe in civilization. What I deal with is the stuff in the middle, the stuff that's between dust and the Big Bang."

His monotone delivery is exercised on matters of heightened logic with almost Zen results ("Everywhere is walking distance if you have the time"). Sometimes, he'll state an obvious logical flaw ("It doesn't matter what temperature a room is; it's always room temperature"), offering an absurdist twist ("I stayed up all night playing poker with Tarot cards. I got a full house and four people died.") or world-weary cynicism ("If you think nobody cares about you, try missing a couple of payments").

Steven Wright meets Lisa Simpson

Demetri Martin (1973–) has been described by Steve Jelbert in *The Independent* as resembling "Lisa Simpson doing stand-up". Bizarre as that sounds, the comparison is apt: this kooky Greek American New Yorker, a direct comedic descendant of Steven Wright, is cute and intellectually precocious.

While Wright grapples with the world's absurdities, Martin gently takes the world for an afternoon walk, and asks polite questions. His observations have bite ("Employee of the month is a good example of how somebody can be both a winner and a loser at the same time") but they can just be cute: "Whenever I investigate a smell, I find that the answer is always bad. It's never: 'What is that?' – sniff – 'Muffins!'"

Martin gave up a legal career for comedy, shocking his remaining family (his father, a Greek Orthodox priest named Dean Martin, had died a few years before) because he had not previously been "deliberately creative". The gamble helped end his marriage to his high school sweetheart but paid off professionally with live gigs leading to TV work and a 2003 Perrier Award. In 2005, Martin started a regular spot on the hugely popular *The Daily Show* with Jon Stewart and, a year later, sold his first movie concept to Hollywood.

Wright is so prolific – and so funny – that many copycat jokes have been circulated over the Internet and passed off as his, often to his embarrassment. Anyone writing a one-liner after 1983 must, in some way, have considered Wright. His most conspicuous comic descendants are Jimmy Carr and Demetri Martin.

Though Wright has come a long way from humble beginnings telling jokes at a Chinese restaurant in Boston, he has never cheapened his stage persona on film. Even his cameo in *Ghost*, often overlooked because of the movie's populist appeal, had gravitas. His other credits include Jim Jarmusch's *Coffee And Cigarettes* films (the original with Roberto Benigni, 1986, and the 2003 revamp) and the voice of the Radio DJ in *Reservoir Dogs*. In 1989, Wright won an Oscar for his short film *The Appointments Of Dennis Jennings*, the comic story of a man who kills his own psychiatrist, in which he starred opposite Rowan Atkinson.

A Steven Wright Special (1985). Available from his official website (below), this joyous hour made up entirely of Wright's weird and wonderful one-liners was recorded for an HBO special, which aired on BBC2 in 1989.

www.stevenwright.com

US comedy on TV

American TV comedy didn't make a serious impact on British television until *M*A*S*H* (BBC2, 1973–88) attracted a cult following. The first sitcom with a black comedy premise, set during the Korean War, *M*A*S*H* helped stretch sexual, behavioural and moral taboos, making political points about the futility of war as conflict raged in Vietnam. The show's gleeful gallows humour still influences comedy writers today.

Susan Harris made an even bigger splash with *Soap* (ITV, 1978–82), which became notorious with its hyperinflation of soap plotlines. The unlucky families, the Campbells and the Tates, came to all kinds of grief, with episodes that always lived up to the voiceover promising: "Confused? You will be after this week's episode of *Soap*". This was followed by the immortal *Cheers* and another Susan Harris hit, *The Golden Girls* (Channel 4, 1986–93), a *Sex In The City* for older women a decade ahead of its time. By the mid-1990s, with *Cheers*, *Frasier*, *Friends* and *Married With Children* all crossing the Atlantic, British TV was in the grip of the biggest American product invasion since Westerns rode off our small screens. The import/export business has ebbed and flowed since but American sitcoms have become part of Britain's cultural landscape.

Cheers: tightly scripted banter and peerless character dynamics were always the order of the day

Cheers

1983–93

Setting a sitcom in a bar seems like a no-brainer, but *Cheers* is probably the only truly great sitcom to exploit such a backdrop. The staff and regulars of Cheers bar in Boston kept the trivia and banter going for a staggering 270 episodes. The show was the second – and biggest – prime-time hit created by the *Taxi* team: Glen Charles, Les Charles and James Burrows.

Ted Danson, as ex-baseball star, former alcoholic, lothario and bar owner Sam Malone, was kept in his place by two shapely female nemeses: Shelley Long (as Diane Chambers) and Kirstie Alley (as Rebecca Howe). The rest of the staff were: Coach (Nicholas Colasanto, 1982–85), Sam's old baseball boss, replaced as the bar's most intellectually challenged figure by Woody

(Woody Harrelson) when Colesanto died, and Carla Tortelli (Rhea Perlman), the feisty waitress who dispensed more one-liners than drinks and was sweet on Sam. The most amusing customers were Norm, eternally thirsty and jobless; trivia-obsessed postman Cliff Claven; psychiatrist Frasier Crane and, later, his partner Lilith.

The rule among *Cheers* writers was "When in doubt, be funny" and this showed. The quality of the plots might have varied, especially near the end of its run, but the tightly scripted banter seldom flagged. The dynamics between the characters were almost peerless, giving the writers the chance to have sport with sex, intellectual snobbery, social class, feminism, stupidity and homosexuality.

Cheers spawned one notable spin-off, the classy, enduring *Frasier*. But the show's ensemble cast, the rapidity and quality of the one-liners, even the slogan for the bar "where everybody knows your name", all influenced *The Simpsons*. In Springfield, Homer, who often feels as if, to use Norm's eloquent phrase, "terrorists have taken over my stomach and are demanding beer", drinks at Moe's Tavern, the bar where nobody knows your name.

 All eleven seasons of *Cheers* are available on DVD.

Curb Your Enthusiasm

2004–

Even though it was not shot in the Big Apple, *Seinfeld* was a triumph of New York humour. Larry David's *Curb Your Enthusiasm* is unmistakeably LA. *Curb* has given us, in Larry David's on-screen persona, an icon of vanity, banality, superficiality and obsessive neurosis, a personification of a city – and an attitude.

While *Seinfeld* – which David co-created – was famously a show about nothing, *Curb* is much more darkly and savagely about nothing than its enormously popular predecessor – one episode revolves around a ripped shirt David inadvertently buys for his pal Ted Danson. The blurring of reality and fiction runs much deeper than in *Seinfeld* with a quasi-documentary style, in which many of the characters, especially the guest stars, play themselves. This isn't Larry David warts and all. At times, David's character is a projection of what he'd like to be were it not for the boundaries of social decency.

The scenes have clear guidelines but no actual lines, giving enormous scope to the actors and various guests stars (who have included Martin Scorsese, Rob Reiner, David Schwimmer, Mel Brooks and Ben Stiller). Jason Alexander and Julia Louis-Dreyfus from *Seinfeld* have appeared – and Jerry had a non-speaking cameo role – while Danson was David's friend and, in series three, partner in a restaurant until the rift of the ripped shirt.

Curb is essentially a comedy of manners reminiscent of Woody Allen's film comedies, with David resembling some of the roles played by Alan Alda. But David takes greater risks than Allen with our sympathy: his character can be so obsessive that, if he wasn't so funny, he would be tiresome. The show has divided critics. The majority, led publicly by Ricky Gervais, believe it is highly inventive but, for the minority, *Curb* is derivative and navel-gazing, accusations it would probably take in its stride.

 Series one to four (of five) have been released on DVD.

www.hbo.com/larrydavid

Frasier

1994–2005

No one expects much from a spin-off, especially if the mother series was as good as *Cheers*, but *Frasier* raised the bar again (and ran for 264 episodes). Frasier was more cerebral than *Cheers*. The writers prided themselves on squeezing in as many ten percent jokes (so called because only one tenth of the audience would get them) as possible, with gags about psychiatry, classical music and wine.

The art of sarcasm was pushed to new limits, usually between Frasier and his über-neurotic brother Niles (David Hyde Pierce) and often involving high art allegories such as:

The American concept of irony

Larry David: I have a tendency to nod to black people.

Jeff Greene: Wait … what reason would you have to…

Larry David: I don't know! I just find that I nod to them. More so than white … I never nod to white people.

Jeff Greene: I've never heard of, uh, "white liberal nodding guilt".

Larry David: Yeah. It's a way of kind of making contact. You know, like "I'm okay. I'm not one of the bad ones".

Curb Your Enthusiasm

Most Britons like to think Americans don't get irony. The assumption that Americans always take deadpan, ironic comments literally may cheer Britons but, as *Curb Your Enthusiasm* suggests, it isn't true.

The different transatlantic takes on irony were well illustrated by Ricky Gervais at the Golden Globes in 2004. Accepting a second award for *The Office*, Gervais thanked Jennifer Aniston and the audience for the "two bookends" he had received that night.

The average Brit understood the irony while many Americans saw Gervais' words as simply sarcastic. While both irony and sarcasm involve saying the opposite of what you mean to make a point, sarcasm specifically involves mocking or berating someone in this way. David Freedman, an American writer on

Friends, who now lives in the UK, says: "Americans do get irony, but to them there's a time and a place for it. Where you get into trouble is dropping irony into an everyday conversation in America. In Britain you hear it all the time."

Despite such a selective appreciation, *M*A*S*H*, *Seinfeld*, *The Larry Sanders Show*, *Curb Your Enthusiasm*, even *Friends* have all relied heavily on irony. Scripts for *The Simpsons* (Homer: "Kids, you tried your best and you failed miserably. The lesson is, never try.") sparkle with intelligent irony, as do the stand-up routines of Woody Allen and Billy Crystal.

A national dearth of irony hasn't stopped many Americans adoring such ironic British comedies as *Monty Python* and *The Office* (recently remade in the US) and welcoming such British comics as Eddie Izzard ("I grew up in Europe, where the history comes from").

Some critics suggested Americans lost their taste for irony after 9/11. A *Time* magazine writer in 2003 suggested that one of the few positive outcomes of the attacks could be the end of the "age of irony". But even 9/11 couldn't kill irony – not with George W. Bush as president. Last word on the subject goes to *Saturday Night Live*'s sketch character Bill Brasky, of whom it was said: "He hated Mexicans! And he was half Mexican! And he hated irony!"

Frasier: You know the expression "Living well is the best revenge"?

Niles: Wonderful expression. I just don't know how true it is, you don't see it turning up in a lot of opera plots. "Ludwig, maddened by the poisoning of his entire family, wreaked vengeance on Gunther in the third act by living well."

Frasier's return to Seattle to become re-acquainted with Niles and his father Martin – and the emergence of a wider family with Daphne, Martin's hired English care assistant, and Roz, producing Frasier's radio phone-in show – felt like a natural progression. The cast dynamic was soon so strong that, ironically, when *Cheers* characters came to visit, they looked completely out of place.

The Grammer school

The trick that made *Frasier* work was the creation of Niles, a younger brother who, as played by David Hyde Pierce, looked like a younger, slimmer Kelsey Grammer and was every bit as fussy, pedantic and pretentious as Grammer's character had been in *Cheers*. This allowed the writers to round out Frasier, making him more sympathetic, although, paradoxically, Niles got most of the best lines.

Nobody could order a cappuccino like Niles ("I'll have a double cappuccino, half-caf, non-fat milk, with enough foam to be aesthetically pleasing, but not so much it would leave a moustache") while, even as he prepared to furiously defend his wife's honour, he cried out: "I'm pumped, I'm psyched and I'm fairly certain that I've just swallowed an entire twist of lemon."

A veritable army of writers produced some beautifully crafted jokes and many, many quotable lines (e.g. "Her lips said 'No', but her eyes said 'Read my lips'."). Meanwhile, the almost constant farce played out by the characters was subtle when required and blunt as you like when the time was right. The show had occasionally lapsed into slick smarminess and was never as sure after Niles and Daphne got hitched, but in the sitcom world it really doesn't get better than this.

Seasons one to six and eleven, the final season, are available on DVD, and the others will undoubtedly follow shortly.

www.frasieronline.co.uk

Friends
1995–2004

They were self-obsessed, irritating and mostly so gorgeous (even Chandler, the "ugly" one, hardly had a face that would stop a clock) they were bound to provoke mockery. But the characters of *Friends* were also funny, enduring and probably worth every penny of the six-figure fees the actors behind them later commanded. Created by Marta Kauffman and David Crane who had already scored a hit with *Dream On* (1990), *Friends* was the first and last word in twenty-something sitcom and a cultural phenomenon in the UK where urban twenty-somethings even held parties where guests dressed as their favourite Friend.

Collectively, Ross, Rachel, Monica, Chandler, Phoebe and Joey were cute, geeky, sexy, vain, competitive, neurotic, sarcastic, insecure, ditzy, spiritual, dense and big-hearted. The hub of the action was Central Perk, the café they had virtually colonized, unrealistically occupying the same seats for what seemed like an eternity. The show's endurance was partly down to the range of storylines offered by the combination of any two characters. The strongest dynamics were between Joey and Chandler as boy buddies and Ross and Rachel as on-off-on-off lovers, though Chandler and Monica were the surprise package later on. Phoebe would float in and out, generally being altogether kooky but somehow getting the best lines after Chandler.

Even if you lacked empathy for any of the characters it was impossible not to admire the quality of the writing and the actors' timing. British comedian David Baddiel has rightly waxed lyrical over David Schwimmer's ability

Friends: the last word in twenty-something comedy both sides of the Atlantic, starring (left to right) Lisa Kudrow, Matthew Perry, David Schwimmer, Matt Le Blanc, Jennifer Aniston and Courtney Cox

to convey comic indignation with one word. Courteney Cox was brilliantly cast as control freak Monica. In real life, she once escorted a friend to the dentist and ended up telling the dentist how to do her friend's teeth. And Joey's stupidity produced some endearing moments: "You don't own a TV? What's all your furniture pointed at?"

All ten series are widely available separately on DVD, and as a complete 30-disc box set.

www2.warnerbros.com/friendstv/index.html

It's Garry Shandling's Show/The Larry Sanders Show

1987–90 and 1993–99

When Garry Shandling stopped writing for other sitcoms and wrote his own he created two shows that broke "the fourth wall" in very different ways. The premise of *It's Garry Shandling's Show*, written with *Saturday Night Live* writer Alan Zweibel, was that the characters knew they were in a sitcom and referred to plots and events in the show, often directing their comments to viewers. Shandling's character was not unlike his stand-up persona, an anxious, defensive candidate for a nervous breakdown with some great one-

Trading places

The quirkiness of the transatlantic trade in sitcoms is summed up by the fact that the British sitcom *Coupling*, which deliberately aped *Friends*, was sold back to the US so it could be remade there to replace the sitcom it was imitating.

It's easy to imagine the allure of *The Office* (which has been remade in Europe too). It's harder to understand why America bought *Dad's Army* (not having had their own Home Guard) or *Absolutely Fabulous* (acquired, then canned because the American public couldn't accept the idea that Jennifer Saunders' character was a bad mother – they didn't mind the drugs and booze references though) or *Fawlty Towers*, acquired, then shelved because network executives wanted to cut one character – the guy who ran the hotel.

In return, British TV has remade only a handful of US sitcoms, usually with mixed fortunes. ITV's professionally done, deadly dull *The Upper Hand* (starring Joe McGann) sprung from *Who's The Boss?* (starring Tony

Danza) and attracted reasonable audiences, while adaptations of *The Golden Girls*, *Mad About You*, *Married … With Children*, *That 70s Show* (*Brighton Belles*, *Loved By You*, *Married For Life*, *Days Like These*) quickly sank.

Don Taffner Jr, the American executive producer of *As Time Goes By* and *My Family*, says: "The most successful shows in the US (therefore the most likely to be formatted) make it to the air in the UK in some form. Any time these shows have been formatted (*Brighton Belles* and *Married For Life* come to mind) the audience preferred the American shows. And, especially for younger viewers, there is an attraction to all things American."

Adapting the product isn't easy, says Taffner: "*That 70s Show* was such a disaster for ITV because it did not make the required cultural changes. If there is any secret to format production, it's knowing what to keep from the original show (to prevent change for change's sake) while making needed cultural changes."

liners. Discussing a romantic disappointment, he asks: "What do fish say when they break up? There's plenty more chicks on the beach?"

The Larry Sanders Show saw Shandling as a talk show host (he had guest-hosted *The Tonight Show*) and the line between fact and fiction was blurred as Sanders' guests included such actual celebrities as Warren Beatty, Billy Crystal, Roseanne, Elvis Costello and even David Letterman and Jay Leno.

The comedy was edgier, darker – anticipating the LA humour of *Curb Your Enthusiasm* – and Shandling's character was more assertive, if needy, and suffered from bouts of paranoia. Aside from Sanders the principal characters were his producer Artie (Hollywood veteran Rip Torn),

who kept Larry sweet by fair means or foul, and his stooge, the dense and materialistic Hank (the prolific Jeffrey Tambor).

The Larry Sanders Show inspired a decent, slightly inferior, British remake, *Bob Martin* (ITV, 2000), set on a game show and starring Michael Barrymore and Keith Allen.

 Seasons one and two (of six) of *The Larry Sanders Show* have been released on DVD.

www.sonypictures.com/tv/shows
/thelarrysandersshow/tvindex.html

Roseanne

1989–97

The closest Roseanne Barr came to professional training was to live in a mountain retreat for artists in Colorado. By the time she started performing at the end of the 1970s she was married with four children. She knew from her upbringing in a working-class Jewish family that she was funny, a view shared by the customers at the café where she worked in Colorado. They encouraged her to start her career in Denver's comedy clubs and soon, with help from fellow comedians Sam Kinison and Louie Anderson, she was playing LA's Comedy Store and appearing on *The Tonight Show*.

Roseanne Barr's robust perspective on everyday working-class life and her feminist slant proved to have universal appeal, though, at first, her act had a predominantly lesbian following. Her quips had a certain brutal force ("My husband and I didn't sign a pre-nuptial agreement, we signed a mutual suicide pact") and she soon attracted TV interest.

Roseanne the sitcom started in 1988, quickly overtaking the hugely popular *The Cosby Show* in the ratings. Both shows centred on the family hearth but there the similarity ended. *Roseanne* was much more about poor finances, unruly kids, problems about sex, contraception and drugs, not cosy yet not bleak. Crucially, in a sitcom universe increasingly dominated by middle-class characters, *Roseanne* was a blue-collar comedy. The behind-the-scenes tales from the show entered showbiz legend. One writer left saying he was going to put an ad in *Variety* for a writing job somewhere quieter – like Beirut. To which Roseanne replied: "Yeah, well, they won't think you're funny there either."

The show was equally popular in Britain, where Jo Brand had succeeded with a reasonably similar, albeit tamer, act on the comedy circuit. In February 2006, Roseanne Barr appeared at The Leicester Comedy Festival with an eagerly anticipated stand-up monologue but, sadly, failed to impress.

Roseanne series one to four (of nine) have so far been released on DVD.

www.roseanneworld.com

Saturday Night Live

1975–

Saturday Night Live, in the breathless prose of British television writer Mark Lewisohn, "single-handedly revolutionized sketch and stand-up comedy on American TV, establishing a strong foundation for intelligent, adult humour". Although *Monty Python's Flying Circus* inspired the programme's creator Lorne Michaels, there is no enduring British equivalent of this sketch show, just, with the Ben Elton-hosted *Friday Night Live/Saturday Live*, a short-lived imitator.

Unusually for such a groundbreaking show, *Saturday Night Live* (or *Saturday Night* as it was briefly known when it came on air in 1975) has stuck to a tried and tested formula, lasting ninety minutes, relying on a resident cast, guest host and musical guest, and keeping to a fairly fixed running order mixing gags, routines, spoof commercials, sketches, celebrity impressions, film or TV parodies and music.

When Michaels quit *Rowan And Martin's Laugh-In*, which he felt had become pedestrian, to launch *SNL*, his move could hardly have been better timed. A whole new generation of comic talent was emerging, typified by performers like Andy Kaufman and some exciting improv troupes. Two especially notable troupes were The Second City In Chicago (which nurtured such talent as James and John Belushi, Shelley Long, Bill Murray, Harold Ramis and George Wendt) and Toronto (Dan Aykroyd, John Candy, Eugene Levy, Mike Myers, Harold Ramis and Ryan Stiles).

The roll call of those who have appeared on *SNL* – either as guest presenters or as troupe performers – is a who's who of American comedy. The show's most famous alumni include Steve Martin, John Goodman, Alec Baldwin, Chevy Chase, Tom Hanks, Danny DeVito, Bill Murray, Adam Sandler, Mike Myers, Eddie Murphy, Kevin Kline, Sam Kinison, Jim Carrey, Jon Stewart, Christopher Guest, Will Ferrell, Andy Kaufman, Rich Hall, Steven Wright, Ben Stiller and Chris Rock. The British contingent included – as presenters or guests – Eric Idle, Michael Palin, Peter Cook, Dudley Moore, Morwenna Banks, Tim Curry, Miranda Richardson and Alan Cumming. Sadly, *SNL* has been aired extremely erratically in the UK, by ITV in 1982 and BBC2 ten years later.

The show was usually broadcast live although Richard Pryor, Sam Kinison and Andrew "Dice" Clay were transmitted with a seven-second delay. The show's more controversial moments include a 1994 sketch where Alec Baldwin played a paedophile scoutmaster and Sinead O'Connor's appearance in 1992, when she ripped up a picture of Pope John Paul II after performing Bob Marley's "War" and shouted: "Fight the real enemy!" The stage set has often been destroyed, notably by LA punk band FEAR playing on the 1981 Halloween edition – at John Belushi's invitation – whose crack team of slam dancers trashed the stage.

A wide variety of *Saturday Night Live* DVDs are available, from a complete ten-disc collector's set to best-of compilations specifically focusing on Adam Sandler, Chris Rock, Eddie Murphy, Jerry Seinfeld, Steve Martin and many more.

www.nbc.com/Saturday_Night_Live

Seinfeld
1993–2001

Jerry Seinfeld is the epitome of the "Have you ever noticed?" school of observational humour. Luckily his observations are acute and his one-liners first class. As a stand-up, he can spin the world so you see it in a different light and wonder why pharmacists must be two feet higher than anyone else, why astronauts drove on the moon and whether illiterate people get the full effect of alphabet soup.

Such pearls of wisdom would introduce each *Seinfeld* show. Alan Simpson, who co-wrote *Hancock's Half Hour*, says the cliché that the show is about nothing is misleading. "They were very good at developing three plotlines throughout a show, most British sitcoms only have one, and they had the nerve to drop in subjects like abortion. There was a darkness about *Seinfeld* I liked, which stemmed from the fact that the characters are quite nasty underneath."

For Simpson, casting was crucial. "Because they're always looking for the best gag, each actor only gets a line to develop, which means the actors have to be superb." Seinfeld had the easiest job, essentially playing himself, a peripheral character whose stand-up routine glued the show together. As Jerry's old school friend George, Jason Alexander excelled with a more aggressive, less sympathetic, neurotic and unreliable variation on Woody Allen's movie character, while Michael Richards' exaggerated physical comedy perfectly suited Kramer, the wildly optimistic fruitcake, and Julia Louis-Dreyfus was a perfect foil as Elaine, Seinfeld's old flame.

For most of the show's duration, fellow stand-up Larry David was co-creator and writer. David was an obvious inspiration for George, a character who now looks like a rough draft for David's misanthropic alter ego in *Curb Your Enthusiasm*. By the time *Seinfeld* ended, the stock situations and phrases had become part of America's national consciousness. Certainly no one who watched the "Master Of Domain" episode, in which the four engaged in a contest to see who could abstain from masturbating for the longest time, will ever forget it.

 Seinfeld seasons one to six (of nine) are available on DVD.

 Jerry Seinfeld Live On Broadway: I'm Telling You For The Last Time (1999). In this live show, Seinfeld mulled amusingly on such subjects as Florida, doctors and silver medallists. A collector's item.

www.sonypictures.com/tv/shows/seinfeld/tvindex for the TV show.

Sex In The City
1999–2004

Sex In The City did more for chick wit than any show since *The Golden Girls*. The show, derived from Candace Bushnell's *New York Observer* column, celebrated hedonistic freedom, female solidarity and penis size – an obsession which some critics felt had more to do with the show's gay writers than the sitcom's characters.

Carrie (Sarah Jessica Parker) represented the perfect woman, an irresistible mix of wit, savvy and beauty. Charlotte (Kristin Davis) was a blue-blooded conservative easily shocked by the others, especially Samantha (Kim Cattrall), whose carnal adventures prompted complaints about the show's morality and who lived by the mantra: "Women are for friendships, men are for fucking." Finally there was Miranda (Cynthia Nixon), direct, practical and down-to-earth but quick-witted and almost a double-act with Carrie. Well-weighted checks and balances between the members of this all-girl group helped the banter flow easily.

Although love, sex and fashion were at the show's heart, the sitcom may be best understood as a pure celebration of womanhood, with or without men, a celebration made truly memorable by the remarkable chemistry between the actresses. For some male viewers, watching *Sex In The City* was almost like watching a female focus group to understand women. The show was never short of observations about the war between the sexes. The promiscuous Samantha would hypocritically note: "Men cheat for the same reason dogs lick their balls: because they can" while, as a columnist, Carrie could muse on female foibles: "While women are certainly no strangers to faking it – we've faked our hair colour, cup size, hell, we've even faked fur. Are we faking more then orgasms? Are we faking entire relationships? Is it better to fake it than to be alone?"

 All six series of *Sex In The City* are available individually or as a complete box set.

 www.hbo.com/city

Just an allusion

A large part – possibly even 35 percent – of the fun in watching *The Simpsons* is spotting the allusions. Among the artists, theories, events and inventors alluded to are E.M. Forster's theory of the novel, Alexander Graham Bell (Mr Burns always answers the phone "hoy-hoy", the words Bell recommended we use when he invented the telephone), artist Jasper Johns (there's a line about him stealing light-bulbs: much of his early work was based on light-bulbs), the slavery controversy (Grandpa says once, "It'll be a cold day in hell before I recognize Missour-ah!": abolitionists refused to recognize Missouri as a slave state) and Gabriel Garcia Marquez (Lisa is seen reading a book called *Love In The Time Of Colouring Books*, an obvious pun on the novelist's bestseller *Love In The Time Of Cholera*). There are many, many, more, but we don't want to spoil it for you.

The Simpsons

1996–

The Simpsons started life as short animations by Matt Groening between sketches on *The Tracey Ullman Show*. Their insertion baffled some viewers and puzzled BBC2 who, in a remarkable act of pop-cultural vandalism, cut them out of the show. But as trailers in American cinemas, the animations were such a hit that Groening, with veteran sitcom writer/producer James L. Brooks and *Taxi* writer/producer Sam Simon, developed them into a series that capitalized on the animation boom triggered by *Who Framed Roger Rabbit?* (1988).

The greatest testimony to the depth and insight of *The Simpsons* was that the show felt more real than most sitcoms. With clever asides, and a level of background detail that repaid reviewing, *The Simpsons* took a swipe at almost every political, social or cultural standpoint. Central to the show was beer-swilling, doughnut munching Homer Simpson, the lazy, loveable dolt, husband of the improbably big-haired Marge (voiced by *Rhoda* star Julie Kavner) and father of street-wise, mischievous son Bart, precocious brainiac daughter Lisa and mute baby Maggie.

With jokes skilfully calculated to please adults and kids, *The Simpsons* soon acquired a huge celebrity following with the likes of Elizabeth Taylor, George Harrison, Mickey Rooney, Rupert Murdoch and Stephen Hawking all appearing as themselves. The shows soon had the honour of being lambasted by President George Bush Snr, who once lamented, "We need a nation closer to *The Waltons* than *The Simpsons*." To which Bart replied: "Hey, we're just like *The Waltons*, we're waiting for the end of the Depression too."

Although there are claims that the show is not the force it was, one of Groening's shrewder strokes is to use animation to create a cast any sitcom producer would die for. If the family need a rest, there is no shortage of supporting characters – from rogue industrialists and cheesy TV presenters to doughnut-obsessed police chiefs – ready, willing and able to take the strain of being funny.

Seasons one to eight (of seventeen) are available on DVD.

www.thesimpsons.com

Taxi
1980–85

The Paramount-sponsored creative family behind *Taxi* have a remarkable legacy. They assembled on *The Mary Tyler Moore Show* and went on to produce a string of subsequent hits, including *Taxi*, *Cheers* and *Frasier*.

Taxi's simple but enjoyable premise was inspired by an article in *New York* magazine about the kind of people who became taxi drivers. *Taxi* is now synonymous with Danny DeVito, as the Sunshine Cab Company's mean-spirited boss Louie De Palma. Originally, DeVito's role was incidental to the main focus, Judd Hirsch's character Alex Reiger, a divorced, world-weary man ("I'm not really a cab driver. I'm just waiting for something better to come along, you know, like death") resigned to going the distance only as a cabbie, and not in his relationships. Alex had a fling with divorcee Elaine (Marilu Henner) and they formed the show's de facto couple. The other employees were ex-boxer Tony Banta (Tony Danza), still dreaming of a shot at the big time, resting actor Bobby Wheeler (Jeff Conaway), Latka (Andy Kaufman's Foreign Man character) and the marvellously absent-minded Reverend Jim (Christopher Lloyd bringing humanity and depth to what could have been a caricature in lesser hands).

Taxi is sometimes dismissed as merely an ancestral bridge between the *Mary Tyler Moore Show* and *Cheers*. But the scripts, and the quality of the ensemble acting, made this one of the few shows judged not to have jumped the shark – i.e. lost the plot – by online TV enthusiasts. The exchanges between Alex Rieger and Reverend Jim could be simply priceless. For example:

Judd Hirsch's world-weary taxi driver, Alex Reiger, and Danny DeVito's mean-spirited boss, Louie De Palma, in ensemble sitcom *Taxi*

Alex Rieger: Jim, when I said you were a flake, I meant you'd done some weird things.
Reverend Jim: Name one.
Alex Rieger: You lived in a condemned building for five years.
Reverend Jim: You're confusing flakiness with style!

 Seasons one to three (of five) are available on DVD.

 jimsmarios.tripod.com is a good fan site.

Which Americans make British comics laugh?

Chris Addison: "Demetri Martin and Mitch Hedburg – ridiculously brilliant jokes, trimmed so they're all muscle and no fat. And Harland Williams, who's actually Canadian. Daftness and stupidity has to be done well and as a stand-up almost nobody does it better than Harland Williams."

Dave Gorman: "Janeane Garofalo is very different to the normal run-of-the-mill, snappy, sassy kind of comic. Todd Barry is great in a modern-day-slightly-creepy-Woody-Allen way. One of the most amazing things I've seen live was Steve Martin doing a short routine about his singing testicles. He didn't speak a word but every detail was spot on and he just oozed class."

Richard Herring: "Larry David because *Curb Your Enthusiasm* is the greatest comedy TV show ever. The team behind *Spinal Tap* who influenced my entire generation of comedians more than anyone could imagine. Woody Allen because I would like to be him – apart from the bit about marrying your own daughter."

Russell Howard: "The extraordinary Mitch Hedberg. I have only heard CDs but they capture his live comedy brilliantly. His stuff is just a series of sublime one-liners."

Robin Ince: "Bill Murray – the best at laid-back and nonchalant wisecracking and now mining a brilliant seam of pathos. Phil Silvers – the best wise-ass conman. Garry Shandling – because he gave Rip Torn a chance to show that he was the best swearer in the world: "Fuck Hank, last time I saw him he was puking and weeping in the toilet." Larry David – because *Curb Your Enthusiasm* is the most painful farce in the world."

Arthur Smith: "George Carlin for his originality and Richard Jeni because he once caused me to fall over laughing. Once, in a club in San Francisco, I fell in love with a comic called Bernadette Luckette. Would it have been better if I had spoken to her?"

Will Smith: "Obviously Oliver Hardy was just the greatest. Will Ferrell is the greatest comic actor in the world right now. The commitment and ferocity he brings to a performance mark him out as great. I could watch the *Saturday Night Live* sketch "Angry Boss" every day and it would still make me cry laughing. Stand-up wise, Eddie Murphy's *Delirious*, apart from the disgraceful, ignorant AIDS jokes, is a tour de force. I love what I've heard of Chris Rock."

Laura Solon: "Always liked Eddie Murphy and Steve Martin – I grew up watching them in films. I am a very late convert to Larry David's *Curb Your Enthusiasm*. Jane Kaczmarek – who plays Lois in *Malcolm In The Middle* – is a very talented comic actress."

Jim Tavare: "In Britain we love persona comedy – Lee Evans, Frankie Howerd, Tommy Cooper. In the US, it's a lot more about what you say. Steven Wright and Jackie Mason are miles sharper than their British equivalents."

Waen Shepherd: "*Police Squad* was hilarious. As a student, I really liked Bill Hicks, for all the usual reasons. Steve Martin was an influence – I think it's the left-field thing again, plus the manic energy – *The Jerk* is possibly one of the greatest comic films of all time, along with *This Is Spinal Tap*. As I've grown older, I've got a lot fonder of Woody Allen. The sense of the personal he puts into his work can't be beaten. *Curb Your Enthusiasm* is a truly inspired show that really makes me feel very, very happy."

The talk show experience

The American talk show has given us "Here's Johnny" (the Johnny Carson catchphrase that served Jack Nicholson so well in *The Shining*), some great questions (Jay Leno to Hugh Grant after *that* limo ride: "What were you thinking of?") and the sight of Peter O'Toole offering Heineken to a camel.

The role the talk show has played in promoting US comedy cannot be overestimated. The holy trinity of Johnny Carson, David Letterman and Jay Leno launched careers, whereas their imitators in the UK – chiefly Bob Monkhouse and Des O'Connor – were more successful at introducing American acts like Joan Rivers, Steven Wright and Rita Rudner to British audiences than at nurturing British talent.

On US talk shows, the satirical tradition runs deeper than a few hastily constructed topical gags delivered by the host. The latest show in this vein is *The Daily Show* with Jon Stewart (on More4 in the UK), a strange, yet often compelling, mix of Chris Morris's *The Day Today*, Michael Moore's *TV Nation* and *Parkinson*.

The most influential host – in comedic terms – is David Letterman (1947–) who has given many comedians their TV debuts, brought the talk show into the *Saturday Night Live* era and inspired a host of British imitators from Jonathan Ross to Noel Edmonds and Danny Baker.

Letterman started out as a sarcastic regional TV weatherman before moving to LA in the mid-1970s and doing stand-up. He soon became a regular guest on Johnny Carson's *The Tonight Show* and then, thanks to Carson's support, won his own NBC show, first the short-lived *David Letterman Show* (1980) and then *Late Night With David Letterman* (1982–93) directly after *The Tonight Show*. In 1993, after failing to inherit Carson's old slot, he switched to CBS for *Late Show With Letterman*.

Letterman was the perfect late-night talk show host for a generation not reared on Carson, with regular comic set-pieces such as "Stupid Pet Tricks", an unpredictable attitude to guests (his duel with a ranting, swearing Madonna was dubbed "a battle of wits with an unarmed woman" by Robin Williams) and the off-chance that something truly daft will happen. In 1995, when Letterman's show came to London, a very merry Peter O'Toole rode onto the set on a camel (his first appearance on the back of such a beast since *Lawrence Of Arabia*), dismounted and proceeded to give the camel a beer.

Geography Lessons:
comedy around Britain

Cult comedy club Up The Creek
in Greenwich, southeast London

Geography Lessons:
comedy around Britain

Comedy just wouldn't be comedy without local roots. And that is why, in this chapter, we take you on a tour of British comedy from Cornwall to the Scottish Highlands, visiting local comedic landmarks, clubs and festivals.

Comedy is prey to the same homogenizing forces that have made Starbucks globally ubiquitous but humour doesn't travel so easily or predictably as cappuccino. In the past, slang, regional vocabulary, accents and local knowledge have often limited a comic's appeal, explaining why such acts as George Formby and Tommy Trinder never quite transcended the north/south divide. Yet a character as localized as Alf Garnett, the charismatic Cockney bigot in the sitcom *Till Death Us*

Do Part, was successfully re-created in America, Germany and Israel, suggesting that comedy that touches, however lightly, on universal truths can be exported around the world.

A comic's roots, cherished or spurned, are crucial to their humour. The small screen has made it easier for contemporary acts – notably Johnny Vegas, Peter Kay and Ben Elton – to achieve national recognition while retaining a regional identity. Since the 1980s, a more adventurous approach to sitcoms has meant that shows such as *The Royle Family* have had a much more authentic local flavour than most of their predecessors. Yet TV has smoothed the path for other acts – Frank Skinner, once thought of as a Brummie comic, being a good example – to achieve fame and fortune in London and, if you like, become "capitalized".

Every few years, a report will surface in the media – often as a prelude to the launch of a comedy festival – suggesting that a certain place (often London or Lancashire) is the funniest in the UK. In November 2005, *The Guardian*'s Charles Nevin disproved his own theory that certain parts of the country were inherently funnier than others. If there was a geographical theme to British comedy, it was that, as Linda Smith told him: "A lot of comics come from the edge of nowhere." Smith often argued with other comics over whose home town was the most boring. How comics react to that boredom may be a profound early influence. Some, notably Vic and Bob, took refuge in surrealist flights of fancy. Others, like Victoria Wood, created their own cast of local characters. And some, like Mark Lamarr, just left.

What follows is a gazetteer of British comedy, dawdling occasionally to mention local heroes and iconic locations while detailing the main comedy clubs, a few more offbeat venues and the best comedy festivals – not all of which are in Edinburgh.

East Anglia

In comedic terms, East Anglia seems to exist entirely as a butt for tractor jokes. It doesn't help that one of the region's most enduring comic images is that of Alan Partridge failing to maintain an ounce of dignity in the hinterland between London and Norwich.

Stephen Fry is the biggest figure heading up East Anglia's comic heritage, having been brought up in Booton, Norfolk, but Charlie Higson runs him a very close second. Higson studied at Norwich's University of East Anglia (he met Paul Whitehouse there) and was involved with the successful post-punk band The Higsons who, between 1980 and 1986, recorded several Radio 1 sessions for John Peel. Yet the region's most durable comic icon is probably Walmington-on-Sea: *Dad's Army*'s fictional town was actually Thetford in Norfolk.

When *The Guardian* was "investigating" comedy's local roots, comedian Helen Lederer did say: "East Anglia? My hardest gig ever (no one laughed) was just outside Cambridge. Could it be due to the large areas of flat land? Are they funny in Holland?" The Dutch have produced at least one internationally acclaimed comedy act, so maybe Lederer was just unlucky.

The Red Card Comedy Club

21 Doman Road, Norwich NR1 3AW. Tickets 01603 219034 www.redcardcomedyclub.com

Ever popular, The Red Card is Norwich's biggest comedy club, and puts on shows roughly once a month at Norwich City Football Club.

The Forum

2 Millennium Plain, Bethel Street, Norwich NR2 1TF. Tickets 01603 727950 www.theforumnorwich.co.uk/

The Comedy Store circuit pays monthly visits to Norwich's Forum Building.

The Fat Cat Comedy Club

The Corn Exchange, Bury St Edmunds. Tickets 01284 754252 www.fatcatcomedyclub.com

The Fat Cat in Bury St Edmunds flourishes with monthly comedy nights.

London

In 1909, the writer G.K. Chesterton insisted: "It is surely sufficiently obvious that all the best humour that exists in our language is Cockney humour." London has inspired the humour of Chaucer, Dryden and Dickens … and, later, Jim Davidson, Ben Elton and Lee Hurst.

The Cockney stereotype – as smooth-talking wideboys whose heart is usually in the right place even if their ethics don't always stand close scrutiny – has been celebrated and satirized in such sitcoms as *Only Fools And Horses* and *Till Death Us Do Part* and casts a long shadow over London's humour.

The city's tradition of motor-mouthed comics – represented today by Ben Elton and Lee Hurst – goes back to music hall days and was personified by Max Miller (even though the self-styled "Cheeky Chappie" was from Brighton). But there's more to London's comedy than fast-talking, soft-hearted, diamond geezers. It was, after all, at The Comedy Store in Soho in May 1979 that the alternative comedy revolution got seriously underway.

The city's comedy scene has been enriched by a myriad of races and beliefs. The Jewish sense of humour hasn't marked London's comedy as decisively as, say, it has New York's. Still, the success of Matt Lucas, Sacha Baron Cohen and David Baddiel suggests Britons might be laughing less frequently without the Jewish influence.

The comedy of Lucas and Julian Clary, who spent his early years on the city's southwestern fringes, is a reminder that London has a strong camp comic heritage. The king of camp – though Frankie Howerd might have contested the title – was Kenneth Williams, who was born near Euston station and lived alone in a small, obsessively tidy flat in Marylebone, next door to his mother Lou. Lucas has admitted: "I loved all the camp comics of my childhood – John Inman, Frankie Howerd and Kenneth Williams."

In London, the theatres, broadcasting studios, TV companies and drama schools have helped make the city almost as central to British comedy

The London comedy A to Z

Balham

John Sullivan grew up here.

Belsize Park

Graham Chapman lived here, in a block where Frank Skinner now lives. Michael Palin is a neighbour.

Bermondsey

Arthur Smith was born here in 1954 but soon moved to Balham.

Bethnal Green

Lee Hurst lives here and runs his comedy club here.

Bloomsbury

Catherine Tate was born here – not that she's bovvered – as was Dick Emery, a huge influence on Matt Lucas.

Catford

Ben Elton was born here in 1959.

Clapham

Paul Kaye, still best known as Dennis Pennis, was born here in 1965.

Chelsea

The Mighty Boosh's Noel Fielding was born here in 1973.

Ealing

Sid James lived in Gunnersbury Avenue, convenient for trips to Ealing Studios.

Elstree

Sacha Baron Cohen was born here in 1971 – not, as many have assumed, in Staines. Cohen, Matt Lucas and David Baddiel all went, at different times, to the Haberdashers' Aske's public school in Elstree.

Eltham

Bob Hope was born here in 1902 and has a theatre named after him.

Finsbury Park

Gina Yashere was born here, though she grew up in Bethnal Green.

Hampstead

Stephen Fry was born here in 1957 but soon left for East Anglia.

Hounslow

Carry On star Charles Hawtrey was born here in 1914.

Lewisham

Spike Milligan was born in Poona, India, but grew up in Lewisham, while *Spaced*'s Jessica Stevenson was born in Lewisham but raised in Brighton.

Marylebone

Kenneth Williams spent most of his life here and Norman Wisdom was born here in 1915.

Parsons Green

Paul Merton was born here in 1957 – as Paul Martin – and moved across the river to Merton, adopting the borough's name as his stage surname.

Stanmore

Matt Lucas was born in this part of Jubilee Line country in 1974.

Teddington

Julian Clary was born here in 1959 but divided his childhood between here, Surbiton and Ealing.

as Hollywood is to US showbiz. For the entertainer Sid James, the ultimate diamond geezer who was actually born in Johannesburg, a ticket on a ship to London in 1946 was his passport to success. The city is still a magnet for acts. Down from the Midlands, Frank Skinner met his partner David Baddiel in Camden Jongleurs during the 1990 World Cup.

The proximity of a cultural-industrial base has, over the years, helped many comics get their first break. Spike Milligan's interest in showbiz was fuelled when he won a Bing Crosby crooning competition at the Lewisham Hippodrome. Frankie Howerd, who grew up in Woolwich, made his first live appearance at a London working men's club in 1921, when he was just four, and learned his trade as a live comedian in the city's music halls.

London was the capital of British music hall – the city still hosts a couple of fine examples today, notably the Hackney Empire and The Grand in Clapham – and still has a dynamic live comedy scene. In the 1960s, Peter Cook launched The Establishment, as much a social club as a venue for professional wits (though Lenny Bruce did play there). The club didn't last long., but Cook had had the right idea and, in 1979, the launch of The Comedy Store revived live comedy in the city and signalled a new era. Peter Richardson's club The Comic Strip, launched a year later, honed the talents of Rik Mayall, Adrian Edmondson, Nigel Planer, Jennifer Saunders, Dawn French and Robbie Coltrane, who would all follow Richardson – and The Comic Strip – onto Channel 4.

On the London circuit, though stand-up is no longer a club exclusively for white men, black comics can find it harder to break through. John Simmit has launched the Upfront comedy night at the Albany Empire in Deptford to help remedy this, and acts like Gina Yashere, who grew up in a Nigerian immigrant family in Bethnal Green and has often gigged in British National Party-supporting areas of east London, have helped break down barriers.

Large, easy to scout, and right on the broadcasting industry's doorstep, London has featured in countless sitcoms from *Steptoe And Son* (set in Shepherd's Bush) to *Spaced* (set in Tufnell Park). In many series, London is just a convenient backdrop but, in a few great sitcoms, the city has almost become a character in its own right. It is impossible to imagine *Desmond's* being set anywhere but the Afro-Caribbean area of Peckham. The same locale – in particular the Nelson Mandela estate – gave *Only Fools And Horses* a nicely con-

What's so funny about Balham?

For such an obscure part of south London, Balham has a rich comic heritage. The utter insignificance of the place was satirized in the Frank Muir/Dennis Norden sketch *Balham Gateway To The South*, a fake travelogue recorded by Peter Sellers in the 1950s. Twenty years later, John Sullivan was sitting in a Wimpy bar in Balham when he noticed some blokes outside desperately trying to sell copies of *Soviet Weekly*. Amused, Sullivan used the memory to create *Citizen Smith*, a sitcom about a wannabe revolutionary catalyst called Wolfie Smith, who shouts "Power to the people!" a lot. Balham didn't really get the credit it deserved for inspiring this classic 1970s sitcom, as Wolfie led the Tooting Popular Front and posed, fist raised, in front of Tooting Bec tube station. Another Smith – the alternative comedian Arthur Smith – now styles himself the Mayor of Balham, often making his claim in song.

Balham – still the "gateway to the South"

crete sense of place. The show was never as funny when it visited exotic foreign parts in a desperate, unnecessary, bid for Christmas viewers.

Equally, Bloomsbury is intrinsically right as the backdrop for Dylan Moran's miserablist bookstore owner in *Black Books* and it's not just alliteration that makes the idea of *Bottom* flatmates Eddie and Richie as "Hammersmith hardmen" so mysteriously appropriate. Sean Lock's witty underrated sitcom *15 Storeys High* drew much of its downbeat ambience from exploring the bizarre lives of the residents of a tower block in Kennington.

East London's working-class culture is superbly, affectionately and occasionally unflatteringly caught by Johnny Speight's *Till Death Us Do Part* (BBC1 1965–75), set in Wapping. Garnett would, you suspect, have disapproved of the media's colonization of nearby Shoreditch as

violently as Chris Morris did in his shortlived satire *Nathan Barley* (Channel 4, 2005).

At the other end of the social scale, the borough of Westminster has been the setting for three classy Whitehall sitcoms – *Yes, Minister/Yes, Prime Minister*, *The New Statesman* and *The Thick Of It*, which Alan Yentob calls "the bastard son of *Yes Minister*".

British programme makers have often shied away from the obvious London landmarks. But the Tower of London featured in the *Friends* episodes devoted to Ross's ill-fated wedding to Emily (*Cold Feet* star Helen Baxendale). In London, love blossomed for Monica and Chandler, while lust blossomed for Joey, whose repeated cries of "London, baby" even irritated Chandler.

Banana Cabaret

The Bedford Arms, 77 Bedford Hill, Balham, London SW12 9HD. Tickets 020 8673 1756 www.bananacabaret.co.uk

This long-established amphitheatre-style club has hosted almost every stand-up. The club is held in the theatre behind The Bedford pub.

Canal Café

Delamere Terrace, Little Venice, London W2 6ND. Tickets 020 7289 6056 www.canalcafetheatre.com

This leading comedy fringe venue hosts several shows a week, including the cult in-house show *NewsRevue*, a fast-paced topical show of sketches and songs, updated weekly, which helped start the careers of Josie Lawrence, Bill Bailey and the *League Of Gentlemen* team.

Chuckle Club

London School Of Economics Bar, Houghton Street, London WC2. Tickets 020 7476 1672 www.chuckleclub.com

Now in its twentieth year, the Chuckle Club was described by *The Observer* as "London's friendliest comedy club" and offers student prices every Saturday night with a strong selection of circuit performers. Proceedings usually start with a rendition of the "Chuckle Club Song" and a round of *Minnie The Moocher* with the audience compelled to join in by regular compere Eugene Cheese. There are three main comics and two or three open spots, often from new acts. Al Murray, Alistair MacGowan and Junior Simpson all cut their teeth on open spots here.

The Comedy Café

66/68 Rivington Street, London EC2A 3AY. Tickets 020 7739 5706 www.comedycafe.co.uk

The bright spacious Comedy Café is in the heart of hip Shoreditch. The Café became one of the top clubs on the London circuit in the 1990s. Tickets can cost £15 at weekends but Wednesday's new act night is free.

The Comedy Café is run by revered promoter and comic Noel Faulkner, of whom Ardal O'Hanlon says: "Noel is probably the finest comic I've ever seen." Faulkner is a lifelong Tourettes Syndrome sufferer but only identified his condition in his late thirties, soon after harnessing it for his comedy act. His eclectic career path has included the Merchant Navy, acting, dancing and escapology. Faulkner's interest in

comedy was stimulated when he went to comedy clubs with Robin Williams, while living, for twenty years, on a houseboat in San Francisco Bay. Faulkner no longer does stand-up but has played Edinburgh with a show based on his amazing life story.

The Comedy Store

1a Oxendon Street, London SW1 4EE. Tickets 0870 154 4040 www.thecomedystore.co.uk

The Comedy Store is Britain's most influential comedy institution. Opening in 1979 above a Soho strip club, this comedy night was originally held in the cramped Gargoyle Club, with comics changing in a broom cupboard. The Store moved in 1982 to Leicester Square and in 1993 to Oxendon Street.

Among the groups to form under the club's auspices were the Comedy Store Players in 1985. The group was originally inspired by Mike Myers (of *Austin Powers* fame) and Kit Hollerbach, who taught Neil Mullarkey, Dave Cohen and Paul Merton the games they had played in North America (many of which were originally games for deprived children

The opening line-up

The original running order for the first ever Comedy Store gig on May 19, 1979 at Dean Street was: Lee Cornes, David English, Tom Ticknell, Bill Beckett, Micky Mills, Alexei Sayle, Paul Goodman, Bob Peyton, Arnold Brown, Bob Flag, Phil Munnoch, Simon McBurney and Sandi, Brian Beck, Jimmy and Clive, Ed Shirman, Nina Fineburgh, Jon Jon Keefe, Harry Dickman and Eric Hoyer. Sayle and Peyton compered.

The Jongleurs story

Britain's biggest chain of comedy clubs was the brainchild of a young drama teacher, Maria Kempinska, who opened her first club in 1983 in an old roller-skating rink in south London, with a £300 overdraft. From such modest beginnings, Jongleurs quickly became one of Britain's top club chains.

The initial venue in Battersea still runs today. Like The Comedy Store, it has staged many then-unknown comics over the years – including Jack Dee, Paul Merton and Frank Skinner – who have later made their names.

In 1993 Kempinska and her husband John Davy opened a new club in Camden Lock. The network has continued to expand: there are now seventeen Jongleurs nationwide. Kempinska and Davy have now sold their stake in the company to Regent Inns, who plan to expand the chain further in the next few years.

Disliked by some critics for what has been described as a "chicken in the basket, stag do" approach to comedy, Jongleurs is hugely profitable.

in Chicago in the 1950s). The Players grew in popularity, developing the show *Whose Line Is It Anyway?* (Channel 4, 1988–98).

Another long-running improv night to emerge from the London Comedy store is The Cutting Edge, partly founded by Mark Thomas and Kevin Day, in which comics make jokes on the spot about recent events, as suggested by the audience.

Tickets vary from £10 to £15. The Comedy Store is still the most prestigious place to play in Britain. The *Guardian* comedy writer William Cook memorably dubbed it "comedy's unofficial National Theatre" – a fitting sound bite with an unfortunate acronym.

Downstairs At The King's Head
2 Crouch End Hill, London, N8 8AA. Tickets 020 8340 1028 www.downstairsatthekingshead.com

In this basement bar below a pub in a north London suburb, alternative comedy's original spirit endures. Downstairs At The King's Head is known for its friendly, intimate atmosphere. Founded in 1981 by Peter Grahame and Huw Thomas, the club has hosted names that have

long outgrown venues of this size, such as Rich Hall, Lee Mack and Ed Byrne. Ticket prices are, by London standards, low.

The Hen And Chickens
109 St Paul's Road, Islington N1 2NA. Tickets 020 7704 2001 www.henandchickens.com

The Hen And Chickens, by Highbury Corner roundabout, is one of London's most famous fringe theatres, offering a range of comedy nights, including stand-up, sketches and comedy dramas. The grand Victorian interior, with its traditional auditorium and candle lighting, creates an intimate atmosphere, making it a no-frills alternative to bigger London venues. The theatre was used by Eddie Izzard to try out new material in 2004.

Lee Hurst's Backyard
231 Cambridge Heath Road, E2 0EL. Tickets 020 7739 3122 www.leehurst.com

Situated in Bethnal Green, the heart of the East End, Lee Hurst's Backyard is a popular venue, purpose-built by the onetime star of BBC1 sports quiz *They Think It's All Over*. Hurst opened its doors in 1998; a former builder, he personally laid the club's floor. The comedy is pretty uncensored. Most big names have played here at one time or another, and Hurst himself regularly comperes.

Lowdown At The Albany

240 Great Portland Street, W1W 5QU. Tickets 020 7387 5706 www.lowdownatthealbany.com

Beneath the Albany pub resides a cellarful of noise and wit laid on by a series of monthly comedy nights from Robin Ince's Book Club, a cerebral attempt to move stand-up away from stag dos and stale booze. Ince reads from the biography of a mainstream celebrity (Sid Little's

The Backyard's Lee Hurst

has come in for a ribbing in the past), obscure indie cover records are played and acts range from stand-up to character comedy and sketch groups.

Up The Creek

302 Creek Road, Greenwich SE10 9SW. Tickets 0208 858 4581 www.up-the-creek.com

Up The Creek owes its cult reputation largely to Malcolm Hardee, who drowned in 2005, trying to row to his house barge. Hardee opened London's notoriously tough Tunnel Club at the southern end of the Blackwall Tunnel in 1984, compering, performing and leading the heckling. As a punter, you never knew if he was going to use his penis to urinate on you or to imitate Charles de Gaulle's nose. When The Tunnel closed, Hardee decamped in 1991 to Up The Creek, a

A pain in the backside

Chris Lynam recalls the gig where he burned his butt:

"When I was with *The Greatest Show On Legs* (Malcolm Hardee and Martin Soan's nude balloon act) the finale was Martin lighting the fountain clenched between my buttocks. At the Albany Empire once, there was an almighty explosion as the bloody thing backfired, sending me running with a loud ringing in my ears and a louder tingling in my arsehole. The thing had buggered me. I shot into the dressing room like a bullet out of a gun, and emptied a bucket full of ice for keeping drinks cool into the basin and sunk my stinging sizzling buttocks into its coolness. The smell of burnt butt filled the air. Malcolm walked into the dressing room, and in his wry sardonic understated way says: 'Fancy a curry Chris?'"

slightly better behaved venue in Greenwich. The club (which now has venues in Croydon and Maidstone) is going strong and has a splendid mural depicting Hardee surrounded by a dozen of his most famous peers, in an irreverent re-creation of *The Last Supper*.

London Comedy Festival
www.londoncomedyfestival.com

The festival occupies around 600 venues across the capital, with 250 events and over 1000 performers. London's biggest-ever celebration of humour aims to cover all comedic disciplines from stand-up to film, literature and art.

The Midlands

The Midlands has been the target of some memorable comic send-ups, such as the Harry Enfield character "I am considerably richer than you", Timothy Spall's despondent electrician Barry in *Auf Wiedersehen Pet* and, best of all, Kevin Turvey, Rik Mayall's wide-eyed berk of an investigative reporter from Redditch. But the Midlands has never been short of home-grown wit. Birmingham, Britain's second city, dominates public perception of this region's comedy thanks, largely, to Jasper Carrott, Lenny Henry and Frank Skinner.

Carrott (1945–) grew up in Birmingham's Acocks Green suburb and started a Solihull folk club called The Boggery when he was 16. He played folk songs and compered but, noticing his banter got more reaction than his songs, soon focused on comedy. Another Solihull lad, Stewart Lee, formed a comic double act with Richard Herring when the two met at Oxford University.

Just outside Birmingham, Lenny Henry (1958–) was born Lenworth Hinton in Dudley. His family had emigrated from Jamaica in the 1950s. His formative comedy years were spent in working men's clubs where he was unique – a young black man impersonating white characters such as Frank Spencer from *Some Mothers Do 'Ave 'Em* – and often told racist gags, realizing the error of his ways after appearing in the sitcom *The Fosters* (ITV, 1976–77).

Rik Mayall spent most of his childhood in Droitwich, Worcestershire. His first great character, Kevin Turvey, created for the sketch show *A Kick Up The Eighties*, was, he said, "just an accent, a mood, from the southwest Midlands". Frank Skinner (1957–) was born (as Christopher Graham Collins) in the Worcestershire town of Oldbury and was expelled from sixth form after being caught selling cut-price school meal vouchers to pupils.

Professional comics become harder to find as you head east across the Midlands. Python Graham Chapman was born in Leicester in 1941 during an air raid, but the east Midlands' undoubted capital of mirth is Nottingham: Steve Coogan collaborator Henry Normal, satirist John Bird, stand-up Jo Caulfield and comic actor Richard Beckinsale were all born there.

Birmingham Glee Club

The Arcadian, Birmingham, West Midlands B5 4TD. Tickets 0870 241 5093 www.glee.co.uk

Winning Chortle's Midlands Club Of The Year award in 2004, Glee established the first comedy night to become a big success outside London. Glee was created by a former City analyst Mark Tughan for whom building a comedy club was a lifelong dream. "We are first and foremost about comedy, but our audience is intelligent, we've never had that bear pit mentality", he says. Glee showcases big names and breaks many new acts. Every September, the club contributes a newcomers' night to the Birmingham Comedy Festival. Tickets for Glee can cost up to £15 but there are discounts and concessions.

Just The Tonic

Cabaret, 22 Fletcher Gate, Nottingham NG1 2FZ. Tickets 0115 912 9000 www.justthetonic.com

Just The Tonic has been running at the 240-capacity Cabaret Club for eleven years. The night aims to provide an edgy comedy alternative, showcasing acts with spark and originality. Ticket prices – even when a stand-up like Ed Byrne is playing – are very reasonable. There is a sister Just The Tonic club in Derby.

Promoter and compere Darren Martin also holds a weekly Wednesday night at Madame Jo Jo's in London's Soho. The club won Chortle's Midlands Club Of The Year award in 2002 and 2005. Memorable comedy nights here include Ross Noble's famous audience hair-cutting competition and Johnny Vegas's "pass the wheelie bin" night.

Leicester Comedy Festival

February www.comedy-festival.co.uk

The Leicester Comedy Festival has grown from a student project to Britain's biggest stand-alone comedy event, incorporating 180 events in 50 venues, and pulling in big names like Mark Lamarr, Jo Brand and The Mighty Boosh.

The Northeast

The Likely Lads, the classic comedy of class and culture set in Newcastle (co-written by local boy Ian Le Frenais), dominates the nation's image of northeastern comedy. From Terry and Bob, it's not too fanciful to draw a line of comically mismatched duos – one sensible, the other more anarchic – through Vic and Bob to Ant and Dec. There is a surrealist strain to northeastern comedy – exemplified by Vic and Bob, Mark Gatiss, co-founder of the League of Gentlemen, and Ross Noble. For Noble, who was born in Cramlington in 1976, such humour was a natural reaction to growing up in a town that was "the ultimate in dullness". He says: "There was nothing to do so I used my imagination a lot."

One of the League of Gentlemen's strokes of comic genius was to call the bizarre town in their show Royston Vasey – the real name of Roy "Chubby" Brown, Middlesbrough's answer to Bernard Manning.

A comic universe away from Chubby, but also born in Middlesbrough, was Bob Mortimer (1959–). After studying law, he moved to London where he met Vic Reeves (who, at the time, was impersonating Bryan Ferry, another northeastern cultural icon in exile) and established the Vic and Bob partnership. Reeves, born James Roderick Moir in Leeds in 1959, grew up in Darlington where he formed the Fashionable Five, a group of friends who would follow bands on stage and perform pranks.

Mark Gatiss became a connoisseur of weirdness growing up in Sedgefield, Durham. He lived opposite an Edwardian psychiatric hospital where his father sometimes worked as an engineer. "When I was little, we'd watch films with the patients. I remember being more concerned with frightening shapes in the shadows than whatever was onscreen. People routinely got out of their seats and shuffled towards you, like in *Dawn Of The Dead*", he recalls.

Rowan Atkinson (1955–) was born in Consett. His father owned a farm there. Atkinson attended Durham Choristers School and St Bees, then studied electrical engineering at Newcastle University before moving on to Oxford University and fame.

The Hyena Café

Leazes Lane, Newcastle Upon Tyne NE1 4PF. Tickets 0191 232 6030 www.thehyena.com

This purpose-built new venue in Newcastle's city centre often has the best showcase of acts in the northeast. The crowd is normally enthusiastic – as tickets are reasonably expensive they may want to get their money's worth – and acts like Mark Thomas, Ross Noble and Johnny Vegas have passed through. Hyena runs a monthly amateur sketch show called *Soup* and comedy workshops.

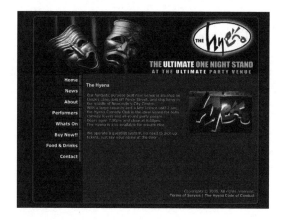

The Northwest

The northwest's famous cutting, sardonic wit has shaped the region's local culture, its influence exemplified both by the northwest's musicians (especially The Beatles and Morrissey) and by the plethora of local comedians the area has produced over the years.

Lancashire

Before alternative comedy, the ultimate accolade for a comedian was to become a national treasure. Lancashire has given Britain at least three such treasures. George Formby (1904–61), the master of the ukulele and innuendo, was born in Wigan. Eric Morecambe (1926–84) took his stage name from the Lancastrian seaside town in which he was born. Les Dawson (1931–93) lived at Lytham St Annes, which was, he said, "so posh, when we eat cod and chips we wear a yachting cap".

The caustic Jenny Eclair (1960–) also grew up in Lytham St Annes, although she was born in Kuala Lumpur. Born Jenny Hargreaves, she started calling herself Eclair while pretending to be French at a Blackpool nightclub.

Mike Harding (1941–), the self-styled "Rochdale Cowboy", emerged in the 1970s with a distinctive blend of music and comedy. Harding's stand-up shows were shown on the BBC in the late 1970s and early 1980s and he may hold the record for the world's longest televised joke: he devoted a whole thirty-minute episode to a gag about a budgie.

Liverpool

Second city in the northwest is not a title Liverpool readily accepts so it is no great shock that Kevin Fearon, owner of the city's successful Rawhide club, claims: "No other city can draw on such a heritage and has a reputation for comedy like Liverpool."

The city's contribution to comedy includes music hall legend Arthur Askey, Jimmy Tarbuck, Kenny Everett (who, as Maurice Cole, trained for the priesthood in Crosby) and the great Ken Dodd, born on the city's outskirts in Knotty Ash. Yet the most influential comedy to emerge from Liverpool may have been Richard Lester's Beatles movie, *A Hard Day's Night*. Like Tarbuck, John Lennon went to Dovedale school. Ringo Starr grew up in Dingle, the city's rundown Protestant area featured in *Bread*, the Carla Lane sitcom in which Paul McCartney made an unprecedented cameo.

Co-written by Lane and Myra Taylor, *The Liver Birds* was the city's feminine answer to *The Likely Lads*, charting the comic adventures of two young women sharing a flat on Huskisson Street near the city centre. The series' title originated from the name given to the two sculpted birds that adorn the Royal Liver Building at Pier Head.

Though born in Blackpool, Ricky Tomlinson lived in Liverpool for years and began his stand-up career playing banjo and telling jokes as Hobo Rick in the city's gangster-filled drinking clubs. Politically outspoken, Tomlinson had been deeply involved with local trade unions (after a stint in the National Front) and was imprisoned on a contested charge of political conspiracy for two years in 1972. Finding it hard to get work back in the building trade, Tomlinson turned to comedy.

Another politically minded Liverpudlian comic is Alexei Sayle who, though semi-officially known as the city's leading alternative comedian, recently had to apologize for remarks about Liverpudlians being prone to sentimental "oh we're the greatest people, you'll never walk alone shite". Maybe it's just as well that Sayle lives in Bloomsbury now. Meanwhile, Michael Joseph Pennington, better known as Johnny Vegas, hails from St Helens, on Merseyside.

The Laughter House

Baby Blue, Edward Pavilion, Albert Dock, Liverpool L3 4AF
The Sports Café, Sir Thomas Street, Liverpool L1 6BW
Tickets 0870 20 266 339 www.laughterhouse.com

The Laughter House was originally based in Liverpool's Slaughterhouse venue (formerly an abattoir) but has now spread across two venues. Baby Blue in the city's Albert Dock has Friday and Saturday night shows, while it's Fridays only at the Sports Café on Sir Thomas Street. The 10-year-old club has hosted the likes of Donna McPhail, Junior Simpson and former drug smuggler turned raconteur Howard Marks.

Rawhide Comedy Club

Royal Court Theatre, 1 Roe Street, Liverpool L1 1HL. Tickets 0870 787 1866 www.royalcourttheatre.co.uk

The most respected comedy name in Liverpool, Rawhide is the place to catch the biggest acts passing through the city. Moving this year to its fifth home in the Victorian setting of The Royal Court, Rawhide has grown from modest beginnings in 1995 in the foyer of the Everyman Theatre. Typically you should expect to pay between £5 and £13.50 at weekends, though special events may be priced differently.

The club has a boisterous reputation. Famously, when Mark Lamarr performed at the nearby Neptune Theatre, one heckler announced: "This is crap, I'm off to Rawhide", and left, leading Lamarr to make the impromptu decision to follow, taking the entire audience along with him.

Liverpool Comedy Festival

June–July www.liverpoolcomedyfestival.co.uk

Liverpool holds an annual comedy festival, which in 2005 offered over a hundred shows across forty venues. Headline acts included Jimmy Carr, Daniel Kitson, Dylan Moran, Johnny Vegas, Peter Kay, Paul Merton and Liverpudlian circuit favourites Simon Bligh and Anvil Springsteen.

Manchester

The historical birthplace of the industrial revolution, Manchester has always had an active comedy scene. The pre-alternative era of comedy in Manchester and beyond was the subject of Trevor Griffiths' acclaimed play *Comedians*, in which stand-ups betray their teacher's social-democratic ideals of comedy to win a judge's approval in a northern club. Griffiths was born in the city's Ancoats area in 1935 and set the play there. A politically charged drama, *Comedians* anticipated the new alternative comedy that made traditional working men's club comics such as Bernard Manning look obsolete.

Obsolete or not, Bernard Manning's World Famous Embassy Club – only really famous in the UK – is still open in Rochdale Road, in Harpurhey, the less salubrious part of north Manchester. Manning still hates alternative comedy: "It's all the fuckin' dog and the fuckin' cat and the fuckin' car, long drawn-out stories like they're talking to themselves." Manning is, however, said to be fond of Peter Kay, possibly because he thinks Kay has drawn on the Embassy Club for his *Phoenix Nights* series.

Many notable comedy stars have been born or launched their careers in Manchester. Les Dawson is from the Collyhurst district. Ronnie Barker (1929–2005) joined the Manchester Repertory Company as an assistant stage manager in his twenties, while Eric Sykes (1923–) was born in Oldham. Stand-up Chris Addison, whose *Civilization* show was one of the hits of Edinburgh in 2004, was born in Didsbury and admits he based his comedy on local DJ James H. Reeve who ran a phone-in show in the 1980s on Manchester radio. Fiona Allen, of *Smack The Pony* fame, was born in Bury, where Victoria Wood, born in Prestwich, went to school. Heading further east, Peter Kay grew up in Bolton where *Phoenix Nights* co-stars Dave Spikey and Patrick McGuinness hail from.

Manchester University was a seedbed of alternative comedy. Alumni Ben Elton, Rik Mayall and Adrian Edmonson were among the first televised alternative comedians who did not go to Oxford or Cambridge.

Even before the 1990s economic boom began to repair the ravages of two decades of industrial and economic decline, Manchester was basking in a musical renaissance, spawning such classic bands as The Smiths, New Order and "Madchester" bands such as the Happy Mondays. The history of these bands and the notorious Factory record label they signed for was documented in Michael Winterbottom's comedy film *24 Hour Party People* (2002), which featured some half-decent acting from some significant contemporary British comedians, notably Rob Brydon, Dave Gorman, Peter Kay and Steve Coogan.

Coogan's portrayal of Tony Wilson, the head of Factory, was described by New Order bassist Peter Hook as "the second biggest twat in Manchester playing the biggest twat in Manchester". Probably the most famous contemporary Manchester comic, Coogan (1965–) was born in Middleton, north Manchester, into a large Irish family. He first gained recognition as Alan Partridge on *The Day Today*. Other Coogan characters include his drunken Mancunian wag Paul Calf. Coogan later starred in the film comedy *The Parole Officer* (2001) which was set in Manchester.

Paul Calf's capacity for ineptitude is equalled only by Frank Gallagher, the central character of the successful Manchester comedy drama *Shameless* (Channel 4, 2004–), created and produced by Paul Abbott, who grew up in nearby Burnley and based much of the raucous series on his own upbringing.

Manchester's greatest sitcom is *The Royle Family*. Starring Ricky Tomlinson and Caroline Aherne, this affectionate, rounded satire of family life in the working-class northwest was co-written by Caroline Aherne (who, though born in London, grew up in Withenshaw) and fellow Mancunian Craig Cash. Cash co-wrote and starred in another amusing affectionate take on Mancunian life, *Early Doors* (BBC2, 2003). Set in The Grapes, a small pub in Manchester, the series offered well-timed gags underpinned with real emotional poignancy.

The Frog And Bucket

102 Oldham Street, Manchester M4 1LJ. Tickets 0161 236 9805 www.frogandbucket.com

The Frog And Bucket started life in a small Yates's pub in Manchester city centre in 1993. Rough and ready, it was originally known as

The Little Frog until it bought out the pub in 1996. It has since welcomed the likes of Dave Gorman, Caroline Aherne and Johnny Vegas, and provided a stage for some of Peter Kay's early stand-up. Manager David Perkins remembers Kay's performances: "When he compered, acts couldn't follow him. He was just too funny."

Big-name acts still lend support, and Vegas compered The Frog's new act competition for the Manchester Comedy Festival in 2003. Steve Coogan tried out new comedy characters on the same night, as well as airing old favourites Paul and Pauline Calf. Tickets can cost from nothing (Monday nights are free) to £12 on Saturday.

XS Malarkey

Bar XS, Wilmslow Road, Fallowfield, Manchester M14 6SS
Tickets 0161 257 2403 www.xsmalarkey.com

XS Malarkey is perhaps the most underground comedy club in the UK, and has won the Chortle website's Club Of The Year award four years in a row. The night, which champions stand-up's grassroots, is run on a not-for-profit basis. Tickets can't be booked and the club runs on a first come, first served basis with a capacity of just 200.

Starting eight years ago in Scruffy Murphys, the club has for the last four years been located at Bar XS, in a converted railway station in Fallowfield, the heart of Manchester's student area. The club is open every Tuesday and for occasional one-off shows. Compere and club organizer Toby Hadoke says the night gives people the chance to see a quality of stand-up no longer found on TV.

The Comedy Store Manchester

3 and 4 Deansgate Locks, Whitworth St., Manchester M1 5LH. Tickets 0870 593 2932 www.thecomedystore.co.uk

This sister club to the London Comedy Store works in a similar way, offering premium circuit acts and big names, and a capacity of 500. The original Comedy Store players – such as Paul Merton and Greg Proops – often visit.

Manchester Comedy Festival

September–October www.manchestercomedyfestival.com

Venues across the city host top acts and comperes such as Paul Merton. Jimmy Carr is a big fan: "A lot of towns have comedy festivals and it feels like it's just a bunch of gigs, but this is quite a cool thing."

Scotland

"Ten years ago there wasn't much of a comedy scene in Scotland", says Scottish comedian Sandy Nelson, part of Glasgow's cult improv act Dance Monkeyboys Dance. While London paid higher prices and pulled in bigger names, live comedy in Scotland – outside of the Edinburgh Fringe Festival – languished. But today, with the impressive rise of the Stand clubs in Glasgow and Edinburgh, live comedy is a significant business in Scotland. Jongleurs in Glasgow has over 27,000 names on its mailing list and the Stand clubs sell out over 70 percent of their shows.

Scottish broadcasting has proved central to the country's comedy boom, nurturing new talent and developing its own programmes, most notably the legendary sketch show *Absolutely* (Channel 4, 1989–93) and the unusual sitcom *Rab C. Nesbitt* (BBC2, 1989–99).

Absolutely was nominated for a Golden Rose of Montreux. In a mainly Scottish cast, two of the principal actors – Morwenna Banks and Jack Docherty – would get their own TV series. Docherty hosted a Channel 5 chat show in 1997, while Banks had a self-titled programme on Channel 5 and enjoyed some American success, appearing on *Saturday Night Live* and HBO's sitcom *Dream On*.

Scotland's most characterful sitcom, *Rab C. Nesbitt* began life as a sketch on the BBC Scotland comedy show *Naked Video* (BBC2, 1986–91). Set in Govan, the show followed Rab as he got drunk, chased women, got drunk again and got arrested – all in a strong Glaswegian dialect that made the show impenetrable for many. Like many a cantankerous, skiving drunkard, Rab fancied himself as a "street philosopher". The series reflected, some viewers complained, the most damaging stereotypes of Glaswegian and Scottish working-class life. But despite setting what one critic called "a new gutter standard for British television", the show was enduringly popular. Gregor Fisher (1953–), who played Rab, was born in Glasgow and had seen enough real-life Rabs to give his characterization vulnerability and depth.

Billy Connolly (1942–) used Scottish working-class life to inspire his comedy. Born in Glasgow, to Irish immigrant parents, he was brought up in the city's Anderston and, later, Partick districts. The Big Yin, as he became known in Scotland, soon gave up welding in the shipyards to become a folk singer and a comedian. In one of his best-known comedy skits, "The Crucifixion", he likens Christ's Last Supper to a drunken night out in Glasgow.

Glasgow is also the birthplace of the laconic alternative comedy pioneer Arnold Brown (1936–) and writer/producer/director Armando Iannucci (1964–), while Jerry Sadowitz (1961–) was born into a Jewish family in New Jersey, but raised in Glasgow after his parents' divorce.

John Sessions (1953–) was born in Largs, North Ayrshire, and is best known for his brilliance on improvisation shows like *Whose Line Is It Anyway?*

Glasgow Stand

333 Woodlands Road, Glasgow G3 6NG Tickets 0870 600 6055

Edinburgh Stand

5 York Place, Edinburgh EH1 3EB Tickets 0131 558 7272
www.thestand.co.uk

The Stand was the brainchild of comedian Jane Mackay and Tommy Shepherd, a former Labour party official. Living in London in the 1980s, they saw comedy clubs sprout up all over the English capital. Moving to Edinburgh in the early 1990s they were amazed to discover that the city which hosted The Fringe Festival did not have a dedicated comedy venue of its own.

Established in 1995, the original Stand still runs in Edinburgh. A second club was opened in Glasgow in 2000. While the Edinburgh club has attracted an international audience, the Glasgow club welcomes a more local crowd. For Shepherd, locality is key: "We programme our acts so the club is always of the city. We always have Scottish MCs and lots of Glaswegian acts, presenting them on bills alongside the best comedians in Britain."

The Stand clubs promise five acts on most bills, and attract big names and lesser-known comedians alike. The club also offers beginners' spots, comedy workshops and open mike nights. Prices vary from £1 to £10.

Edinburgh

Every August, Edinburgh becomes Britain's comic capital as the host of the world's biggest comedy festival. That isn't the city's only contribution to British comedy – Rory Bremner (1961–) and Ronnie Corbett (1930–) were both born there – but the Edinburgh Fringe Festival has made the Scottish capital a pivotal force in British comedy.

The Edinburgh Fringe Festival (www.edfringe.com) is actually an umbrella term for a group of independently organized festivals running simultaneously, showcasing books, films, theatre, music and comedy. The most vibrant, by some distance, is comedy which now sells over a million tickets every year.

The Edinburgh International Festival was launched in 1947, as a lofty post-war initiative designed to help Europe reunite through culture. The event soon attracted more performers than it could handle and eight companies (six Scottish, two English) decided to ignore the competitive entry process, turning up uninvited to fend for themselves and, in the process, inventing what we now call the Fringe.

A notable by-product of the Fringe is the Perrier Award, created in 1981 as the Oscars of live comedy, which has rewarded such diverse talent as Frank Skinner, Lee Evans and The League Of Gentlemen.

The Fringe fills Edinburgh, calling on over 250 venues, even filling churches, converted flats and bank vaults. In the late 1980s, three venues emerged as the main showcases for comedy talent, The Assembly Rooms, The Gilded Balloon and The Pleasance. These have been joined, in recent years, by The Underbelly.

The Fringe also has dozens of free shows, showcase performances on the Royal Mile every day and a massive free outdoor event, Fringe Sunday (on the second Sunday of the festival).

The Assembly Rooms

George Street Assembly Rooms, 54 George St., Edinburgh EH2 2LR

Assembly Hall, Mound Place, Edinburgh EH1 2LU

St George's West, 58 Shandwick Place, Edinburgh EH2 4RT

Queen's Hall, Clerk Street, Edinburgh EH8 9JG

Tickets 0131 226 2428/624 2442 www.assemblyrooms.com

The Assembly, one of the Festival big hitters, offers top Fringe acts including comedy, theatre and music. There are four venues, fitted only for the festival, at George Street, Assembly Hall, St George's West and Queen's Hall. The Assembly bars are a good place to luvvy-watch, attracting many famous faces. The members–only Club Bar at the George Street Assembly Rooms sometimes opens its doors to the public with various membership schemes.

Pleasance Courtyard

60 The Pleasance, Edinburgh EH8 9TJ. Tickets 0131 556 6550 www.pleasance.co.uk

The Pleasance, Edinburgh, opened its two main theatres for the 1985 festival in the eastern end of Edinburgh's old town. Twenty years later, this highly respected venue offers eighteen theatre spaces ranging in capacity from 50 to 740 across

two locations – the Pleasance Courtyard and the Pleasance Dome. New companies and performers are placed alongside more established comics and the theatre acts. In 2005, 240,000 people passed through its doors either to see comedy – in a typical day, 160 shows are running – or to use one of its ten bars.

Underbelly

46 Cowgate, Edinburgh, EH1 1EG

Baby Belly

The Caves, Niddry Street South (off Cowgate), Edinburgh EH1 1EG

Tickets 0870 745 3083 www.theunderbelly.co.uk

Underbelly opened in 2000 as a small performance venue used by long-running Fringe company Double Edge Drama. Inspired by another acclaimed Scottish company, Grid Iron, who performed in the vaults below Edinburgh's Central Library, the club took their comedy shows underground.

The comedy of bananas

Stand-up Mark Maier recalls his first festival:

"My introduction to the Edinburgh Festival was via the street. Standing on a crate, I would eat bananas to the tune of "Chanson D'Amour", timed so that a banana would be chomped on each ratatatat of the song. Aficionados of the Manhattan Transfer classic will know the song has six ratatatats ergo six bananas. Three shows a day, six bananas a show, by the end of August 1987 I had consumed 393 bananas (this includes rehearsal bananas). I waddled away from Edinburgh with twenty eight pounds and forty four pence. Or more precisely, two stone and forty four pence."

Underbelly's atmospheric setting in the former bank vaults under George IV Bridge has become a must-see Fringe attraction. In 2005 the company added the Caves on Niddry Street to its list of spaces, now known as Baby Belly.

The Gilded Balloon

25 Greenside Place, Edinburgh EH1 3AA. Tickets 0131 668 1633 www.gildedballoon.co.uk

The Gilded Balloon, established in 1986, is a large, renowned festival venue now operating seven venues with over seventy shows per day.

In 1989 the Balloon devised *So You Think You're Funny?*, a competition to uncover new comic talent whose past winners include Rhona Cameron, Dylan Moran and Peter Kay.

The venue's home and largest performance space for sixteen years was in the heart of the Cowgate area. The Studio, where it all began, was a festival favourite along with its Gilded Saloon bar that opened all year round. In December 2002, a huge fire in the heart of Edinburgh's Old Town destroyed the Studio and other buildings. The company focused on its second major venue, Teviot Row House, teaming up with Underbelly to publicize shows, and eventually recovered.

The Gilded Balloon is also famous for its popular late-night show *Late 'N' Live* that kicks off at 1am and has welcomed comics and impromptu guests like Frank Skinner, Jo Brand and Lenny Henry over the years.

The Southeast

If you accept Linda Smith's theory that a lot of comedians come from the edge of nowhere, the southeast – having more deeply marginal towns than most parts of Britain – should have produced more than its fair share of comic talent. And so it has. Smith herself hails from Erith, in Kent. The other comic talent to hail from the southeast's marginal towns includes David Walliams (Reigate), Peter Sellers (Southsea), Jo Brand (Hastings), Jimmy Carr (Slough), Junior Simpson (Luton), Jeremy Hardy (Aldershot), Harry Hill (Woking) and Simon Munnery (Watford). Jack Dee, born near Orpington, was brought up in Winchester. Writers to hail from the region's equally inconsequential places include Dick Clement (Westcliff-on-Sea), David Nobbs (Petts Wood), Simon Nye (Burgess Hill) and David Renwick (Luton).

Some great sitcoms have made imaginative use of the southeast's banality. *The Office* (2001) wouldn't be as funny if the paper merchants weren't set in Slough, the sprawling new town John Betjeman hoped "friendly bombs" would destroy. The town only appears in the opening sequence, which shows the bus station and industrial estate, but it is the perfect setting for such a mockumentary. Ricky Gervais (1961–) was actually born in Reading, well placed to capture the ambience of the M4 corridor. *The Office*'s setting was the latest in a glorious tradition of insignificant sitcom locales which stretched back via Walmington-on-Sea (*Dad's Army*) to East Cheam (*Hancock's Half Hour*).

The coast has proved a reasonably fertile breeding ground for comedians. Apart from Eddie Izzard (who grew up in Bexhill-on-Sea), Peter Sellers (1925–80) was born to a family of entertainers in Southsea, Tony Hancock (1924–68) grew up in Bournemouth where his mother and stepfather ran a small hotel, and *Spaced*'s Jessica Stevenson was raised in Brighton.

Komedia Brighton

44 Gardner Street, Brighton BN1 1UN Tickets 01273 647100 www.komedia.co.uk

This award-winning venue was forced to expand in 1998, moving into a former Tesco supermarket in Gardner Street where it rapidly became the south's premier live performance venue.

Komedia started in 1994, converting a Grade II-listed former billiard hall in Brighton's Kemp Town area into a theatre and cabaret bar. It staged then burgeoning acts such as Graham Norton, Al Murray, Omid Djalili and The League Of Gentlemen. The company promotes new work and runs several venues on the Edinburgh Fringe. Ticket prices are pretty reasonable, especially for the southeast.

Brighton Paramount Comedy Festival

www.brightoncomedyfestival.com

The inaugural Brighton Paramount Comedy Festival was launched in 2005. Organizers hope with time it will become England's answer to the Edinburgh Fringe. The festival's mix of old and new talent included the likes of Daniel Kitson, Jimmy Carr and Peter Kay.

Wales

The English joke that the Welsh have no sense of humour. But English stereotypes of miserable, moody Welshmen don't explain how the principality came to produce some of the comic talent behind The Goons, *Monty Python's Flying Circus*, *The Fast Show*, French and Saunders and *Marion And Geoff*. Welsh humour is – as Welsh interviewees told Polish researchers on a British

Undergraduate humour

The universities of Oxford and Cambridge have nurtured some of Britain's finest wits and hugely influenced the development of sketch comedy and satire since the 1960s.

Founded around 1209, the University of Cambridge has probably never been as culturally influential as in the last fifty years, as many of its alumni moved into film and broadcasting. Cambridge University's Footlights drama society has produced some of Britain's best-known comedians including Douglas Adams, Clive Anderson, Peter Cook, Stephen Fry, Clive James, Simon Jones (who was actually born in Oxford), Rory McGrath, Bill Oddie, Tony Slattery, Morwenna Banks and Sandi Toksvig.

Oxford University traces its roots back to the eleventh century and, in the last half-century, has produced such wits and comics as Alan Bennett, Dudley Moore, Rowan Atkinson, Griff Rhys Jones, Hugh Grant, Richard Herring and Stewart Lee.

Monty Python was a true Oxbridge merger, created in the late 1960s by Graham Chapman, John Cleese, Terry Gilliam, Eric Idle, Terry Jones and Michael Palin. The team had got to know each other gradually, first meeting through university – Chapman, Cleese and Idle were at Cambridge together, while Jones and Palin were at Oxford – with Gilliam joining the troupe later. The success of *Beyond The Fringe* (with Cook, Bennett and Moore all playing a part) and *Python* established Oxbridge humour as a mini-genre, renowned for its satirical bent, intellectual allusions and a certain comic anarchy. Although some later comics have regarded Oxbridge humour as culturally elitist, the universities continue to nurture comic talent.

For comedy nights in the two university towns check out:

Oxford:
The Bullingdon Arms (01865 244516)
The Oxford Free Beer Show at The Cellar (01865 244761)

Cambridge:
The Bath House Pub (01223 350969)
The Junction (01223 511511)

Council project – dry, sardonic, sarcastic, so self-deprecating as to be almost masochistic, addicted to wordplay and driven by certain recurring motifs: rugby, social pretensions and the arrogance of the English. Nicky Thompson, a stand-up from Cardiff, says: "We are Celts, we love to talk, we are a nation of great storytellers and weavers of magic."

Swansea was the setting for the comic movie *Twin Town* (1997) which launched the career of Welsh comic actor Rhys Ifans, latter better known as Hugh Grant's unhygienic flatmate in *Notting Hill*. This dark take on regional life after two decades of industrial decline highlighted the social divisions in a city that Dylan Thomas once dubbed the "graveyard of ambition". One-time *Comic Strip* star Keith Allen, who plays a magic-mushroom-eating farmer in the movie, was born in nearby Llanelli.

The Goon Show's Harry Secombe (1921–2001) was born in a hillside-terraced house in Swansea's St Thomas area. Rob Brydon (1965–) was also born in Swansea, though he moved to Baglan, near Port Talbot. His cuckolded cabbie character Keith Barret was introduced on the BBC Wales radio show *Rave*.

Among the comics born in and around Cardiff are Griff Rhys Jones (1953–), though his family soon moved to Sussex, and *The Fast*

Show's Paul Whitehouse (1959–), who was born in Stanleytown in the Rhondda Valley.

Legendary comedian and magician, Tommy Cooper (1921–84) was born in Caerphilly. The fact that he moved to Exeter when he was three hasn't stopped Caerphilly planning to honour him with a huge bronze statue. Hywel Bennett (1944–), who starred as laconic, lazy graduate Shelley in the eponymous sitcom, is from the coaltown of Ammanford.

The most iconic Welsh comedian is Max Boyce (1945–), from Glynneath in southwest Wales. His *We All Had Doctors' Papers* became the first comedy album to top the UK charts in 1975. Boyce is an acknowledged inspiration for Carmarthen-born stand-up Rhod Gilbert (1969–), whose habit of telling surreal stories

about rural life suggests there's something in the idea that the Welsh are born storytellers. In northwest Wales, Dawn French (1957–) was born in Holyhead while former Python Terry Jones (1942–) is proud of his Welshness, though he left Colwyn Bay when he was five.

Cardiff Glee Club

Mermaid Quay, Cardiff Bay CF19 5BZ Tickets 0870 241 5093 www.glee.co.uk

Voted Chortle's Club Of The Year for Wales and the West in 2003, 2005 and 2006, the Cardiff Glee Club in the recently redeveloped Cardiff Bay area has hosted the cream of British stand-up. Tickets can cost up to £15, though there are discounts with concessions and online booking.

The West Country

The West may not have a sharply defined comic identity but it has been home to such different comedians as Peter Cook (born in Torquay), John Cleese (Weston Super Mare), Mark Lamarr (Swindon), Charlie Higson (Frome) and the greatest British comedy actor of the last century, Cary Grant (Bristol).

Bristol

Though *The Young Ones* was set in north London, their student house was in Bristol, at 1 Coddrington Road, Bishopston, while The Kebab And Calculator (their local pub, seen in the epi-

sode *Boring*) is actually The Cock O' The North in Henleaze, one of only two round pubs in Britain.

Fresh-faced new stand-up Russell Howard, Perrier nominee Mark Watson, John Bird and Justin Lee Collins (famous for his catch phrase, "I love it", delivered in a thick Bristolian accent) were all born in Bristol. Other promising young stand-ups from here include Jon Richardson, James Dowdeswell and Mark Oliver, while Lee Evans was born in nearby Avonmouth. His father Dave Evans was a popular entertainer in working men's clubs whose constant touring meant Evans regularly changed schools, always feeling like the "new kid" nobody knew.

Bristol University has a remarkable comic pedigree. Chris Morris studied Zoology there, while other alumni include *Spaced*'s Simon Pegg and Nick Frost, Marcus Brigstocke, Danny Robbins (creator of the music/comedy crossover character DJ Danny) and *Little Britain*'s Matt Lucas and David Walliams.

Jesters Comedy Club

142 Cheltenham Road, Bristol BS6 5RL. Tickets 0117 909 6655 www.jesterscomedyclub.co.uk

Jesters is Bristol's biggest comedy club. Every Friday and Saturday night promises four good-quality circuit acts with the occasional bigger name. Student Comedy Night runs every Wednesday through term time and the first Sunday of every month showcases gay comedy. Previous guests include Four Poofs And A Piano, Dan Antopolski and Ian Cognito, who lives nearby on a canal boat. Prices vary from £5 to £12.

Slapstick January

www.slapstick.org.uk

Bristol hosted its first tribute to silent slapstick in January 2005, compered by long-time slapstick fan Paul Merton. Organized by local silent film buffs, the festival airs a host of rarely seen gems from such silent greats as Buster Keaton and Harold Lloyd.

Bath, Somerset and Swindon

Bill Bailey (1964–) and Julia Davis (1966–) were both born in Bath, with Davis joining a local the-atre group and then forming an improv troupe with Rob Brydon. Richard Herring (1967–), raised in Cheddar in Somerset, says: "When we did *Lee And Herring*, we used to make jokes about Somerset being backward, so we did get some mileage out of it." His partner Stewart Lee claims his grandfather nearly ran a hotdog stand near Cheddar Gorge but became ill: "If we had moved, Rich and me would have gone to the same school."

Mark Lamarr has less humorous memories of his home town, Swindon. He left for London as soon as he could saying: "It's a very, very narrow-minded and bitter little town. I don't want to be all London, London, aren't I brilliant for living here, but in a sense, I do think you end up where you deserve or where you want to be. People who live in Swindon probably haven't got that much enthusiasm for life generally."

Devon and Cornwall

Torquay is home to two of British come-dy's greatest legends: Peter Cook, who was born in Bronshill Road, and Basil Fawlty. John Cleese's immortal creation was based on a real Torquay hotelier who distinguished himself by telling Terry Gilliam his table manners were too American and throwing Eric Idle's briefcase into the street in case it had a bomb in it. The first character based on that hotelier appeared in an episode of ITV's Sunday evening sitcom *Doctor At Large* in 1973. After the episode had been shot, producer Humphrey Barclay told Cleese: "You could probably build a series around that char-acter." Elsewhere in Devon, Peter Richardson, the genius behind *The Comic Strip*, hails from Newton Abbott.

The famously lewd comic Jethro (1948–) was born in the small village of St Buryan, West Cornwall. The son of a farmer, with a distinct Cornish accent, he is a local legend. Though she had to go to Scotland to get her break, Morwenna Banks (1964–) was born in the Cornish coastal village of Flushing.

Yorkshire and Derbyshire

With the exception of Frankie Howerd (born in York in 1917, though he soon moved to London), the east side of the Pennines is probably more famous for comic characters than stand-up comedians. The most popular sitcom set here is *Last Of The Summer Wine* which has made the charming Peak District town of Holmfirth a tourist magnet. The north Derbyshire town of Hadfield has provided the backdrop for *The League Of Gentlemen*, a hybrid sitcom/sketch show. Given the bizarre events in the show's fictional northern village, it's hard to imagine Hadfield experiencing a similar tourist boom.

In the last twenty years, the region has inspired several movie comedies that have offered a grittier, socially conscious, working-class alternative to the London-centric, English Heritage view of Britain presented by such Richard Curtis movies as *Four Weddings And A Funeral*.

The urban decay of Bradford's Buttershaw estate was the setting for Alan Clarke's 1986 movie *Rita, Sue And Bob Too*, a story of a married man's illicit affair with two teenage babysitters. *Brassed Off* (1996), set in the Yorkshire town of Grimley, is Michael Frayn's dark comedy about the troubles faced by a Yorkshire colliery brass band after their pit closes. The same mix of comedy and social statement drives *The Full Monty* (1997), the Oscar-winning comedy drama musical about six unemployed British steel workers in Sheffield who form a male striptease act.

The Northern Irish scene

In 2006 the BBC announced a host of new comedies for radio and television for its Northern Ireland viewers, proof that Jimmy Cricket and Frank Carson are not the be-all and end-all of comic talent north of the Irish border. The comedy scene in Belfast got a kick-start in the early 1990s when Patrick Kielty helped set up its first comedy club, The Empire. Other comics who have subsequently crossed over in club and TV terms include Michael Smiley (*Spaced*, *15 Storeys High*) and Colin Murphy (*People Like Us*). Smiley and Murphy still contribute to home-grown comedy productions.

Northern Ireland's recent history presents an obvious problem for live comedians but Derry stand-up Daniel McCrossan says it's hard to avoid the subject. "You see so many comedians here using the troubles because it's personal, we've experienced it." Ignoring it – unless a comic has a surreal or physical style that legitimizes that choice – would shackle a comic and, to an audience that has endured the same events, feel distinctly odd.

Local hero Michael Palin says *The Full Monty* has changed the city's image: "I was a teenager living in Sheffield, an uncompromising industrial city without a hint of glamour, until recently, when the demise of its industry became the subject of *The Full Monty*."

A native of Sheffield, Palin (1943–) made his first dramatic appearance at Birkdale Preparatory School as Martha Cratchit, in a school production of Dickens' *A Christmas Carol*, suitable preparation, you might think, for some of his later Python roles.

Sheffield's greatest gift to alternative comedy is probably the comic actor Graham Fellows (1959–), now better known as the "versatile singer/organist" John Shuttleworth. In his fictional biography, Shuttleworth was a security guard for a sweet factory in Rotherham.

Alan Bennett (1934–) was born slightly further up the M1 in Leeds though, like Palin, he got his first real taste of the comedy business at Oxford. Bennett met Dudley Moore, Jonathan Miller and Peter Cook at Oxford University, achieving instant fame with the influential satirical revue *Beyond The Fringe*. Bennett is now best known for his *Talking Heads* monologues, his TV adaptations and his hilarious memoirs.

Leeds is also the birthplace of Julian Barratt, half of The Mighty Boosh. Ade Edmondson, grew up in nearby Bradford. The Perrier-Award-winning comic Daniel Kitson is from Denby Dale, famed more for its pottery than for its comedy.

Hull has been home to Maureen Lipman, Boothby Graffoe and Reece Shearsmith, famous as Papa Lazarou in *The League Of Gentlemen*. The League – also Mark Gatiss, Steve Pemberton and co-writer Jeremy Dyson – met as drama students at Bretton Hall in Wakefield, West Yorkshire, and discovered a shared taste for the nasty classics of British sci-fi and horror cinema.

The Last Laugh

The Lescar Hotel, 303 Sharrow Vale Road, Sheffield S11 8ZF. Tickets 0114 267 9787

The Roundhouse, Ponds Forge Sports Centre, Sheffield S1 2PZ. Tickets 0114 223 3505

www.lastlaugh.biz/content and www.sheffieldcomedy.com

The Last Laugh Comedy Club was started over a decade ago by former comic Oliver Double (who now lectures on stand-up comedy) and friends. The club is now compered by local comedian Toby Foster (Les in *Phoenix Nights*). Dara O'Briain, Daniel Kitson and Will Hodgson have played here, and there are Edinburgh previews every summer and an annual festival in October.

Thursday evening is held at The Lescar, Yorkshire's longest-running comedy club, where Foster still comperes most weeks. On the weekend, shows are at the Roundhouse with four comedians every week, a late bar until 1am and, inevitably, higher ticket prices.

The HiFi Club

2 Central Road, Leeds LS1 6DE. Tickets 0113 242 7353
www.thehificlub.co.uk

Originally The Central School Of Ballroom Dancing in the 1950s, this venue was famous for its northern soul and disco nights in the 1960s and 70s. After a makeover, the club reopened as the HiFi in 2000. Primarily a music venue, the HiFi hosts Friday and Saturday comedy sessions, drawing in big names like Richard Herring. Tickets normally cost £10 or less. On Saturday nights, audience members are invited to stay on for the Boogaloo club that runs until 3am.

City Varieties Music Hall

Swan Street, Leeds LS1 6LW. Tickets 0845 644 1881 www.cityvarieties.co.uk

The City Varieties Theatre in Leeds has been a popular entertainment venue since the eighteenth century, first in a pub called the White Swan and then, from 1865, at the City Palace Of Varieties.

Famous performers from the past to have played here include Houdini, Bud Flanagan and Charlie Chaplin but the theatre is best known as the setting for BBC1's music hall show, *The Good Old Days*. The theatre has hosted such notable current comedians as Sue Perkins and Ross Noble.

Grin Up North – The Sheffield Comedy Festival

www.sheffieldcomedyfestival.com

The first ever Grin Up North, the Sheffield Comedy Festival, was launched in 2005. Running over two weeks, the festival showcases new talent as well as drawing in the big names.

A Comedy Store: the information

Having a laugh: front-row seats at Roy "Chubby" Brown's
comedy show in 1995

A Comedy Store:
the information

If you're hooked on humour and want to find out more, worry not. This chapter points you to books, websites and other resources that will deepen your knowledge and your laughter lines.

Despite an explosion in the number of comedy-goers, comedy nights and budding comedians, sources of information on live comedy are not as plentiful as one might imagine. Books, websites, DVDs and CDs relating to the acts profiled in this guide are listed under their entries in The Icons (for British acts) and Atlantic Crossings (for US acts), while web addresses for comedy clubs are under their entries in Geography Lessons. What you will find below are specific suggestions for books and websites that will help you garner more information about comedy or simply entertain you.

Books

Non-fiction

There are tons of comedy books, but only a few seminal titles talk about the history and craft of comedy. Here are the best.

Attitude: Wanna Make Something Of It?
Tony Allen (Gothic Images Publications, 2002)

More a collection of thoughts and moments than a conventional biography, Tony Allen's book is a good first-hand account, by one of the founders of alternative comedy, of the movements that changed British comedy history.

The Comedy Store
William Cook (Little Brown, 2001)

The Comedy Store is explored in great depth with a look at many of the people who have worked and played there, including Eddie Izzard, Mark Lamarr, Lee Hurst, Bill Bailey and John Hegley. If you like this, John Connor's *Comics* (Macmillan, 2002) does something similar for The Assembly Rooms in Edinburgh and Stephen Dixon and Andre Falvey's *The Gift Of The Gag* (Blackstaff, 1999) covers the vibrant Irish comedy scene in the 1990s.

Comic Insights: The Art Of Stand Up Comedy
Franklyn Ajaye (Silman-James Press, 2002)

Seinfeld, Roseanne, Chris Rock, Garry Shandling and Ellen DeGeneres are among the American comedians who are interviewed in this book. The tricks of the trade – US-style – are discovered through chats with club owners and agents.

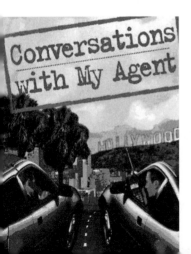

Conversations With My Agent
Rob Long (Faber and Faber, 1996)

Half of this is true, says *Cheers* writer Rob Long. The conversations with his agent – and between writers – are very funny but Long's insight into the sitcom business and his dark tales from therein, such as the day one half of a comedy duo beat the other half almost to death with a lamp, are worth the cover price.

Didn't You Kill My Mother-In-Law?
Roger Wilmut and Peter Rosengard (Methuen, 1989)

Picking up after *From Fringe To Flying Circus*, this traces the story of stand-up comedy from the beginning of The Comedy Store. It charts the careers of the main protagonists, such as Ben Elton, Rik Mayall and French And Saunders, but the extracts from Alexei Sayle's first stand-up routines are the real highlight.

From Fringe To Flying Circus
Roger Wilmut (Methuen, 1980)

This authoritative study deals, as the title suggests, with the period going from *Beyond The Fringe* to *Monty Python's Flying Circus* in some detail, taking in shows like *That Was The Week That Was* and reclaiming forgotten series like *The Complete And Utter History Of Britain* from oblivion.

Funny Way To Be A Hero
John Fisher (Paladin, 1976)

A vivid, heartfelt portrait of British comedy from the music hall to the post-war variety circuit, John Fisher's history predates the time frame covered by this book but it is worth reading for its own sake and because alternative comedy, as it has developed, has become increasingly willing to acknowledge this legacy.

Ha Bloody Ha: Comedians Talking
William Cook (Fourth Estate, 1994)

An informative post-alternative snapshot of the comedy scene, with profiles and memories from such figures as Eddie Izzard, Reeves and Mortimer, Newman And Baddiel, and Lee And Herring.

The Naked Jape
Jimmy Carr and Lucy Greeves
(Penguin, 2006)

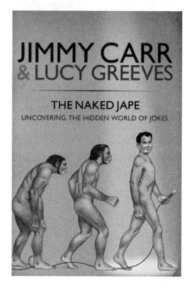

An entertaining, insightful investigation of the jokes business from comedian Jimmy Carr and comedy-venue manager and comedy writer Lucy Greeves. It is well worth reading for the theories expounded and for the hundreds of jokes.

Radio Comedy, 1938–68: A Guide To 30 Years Of Wonderful Wireless
Andy Foster and Steve Furst (Virgin, 1996)

A guide to radio comedy's glory days featuring transmission details and commentaries on series including *The Goon Show*, *Hancock's Half Hour* and *Round The Horne*.

The Radio Times Guide To TV Comedy
Mark Lewisohn (BBC Books, 2003)

The definitive guide to British television comedy, in all its forms. Everything that made us laugh or merely wince is listed, with profiles of the bigger stars and everything you need to know about the programmes themselves.

The Rough Guide To Comedy Movies
Bob McCabe (Rough Guides, 2005)

Profiling the major comedy films, directors and stars of the twentieth century, *The Rough Guide To Comedy Movies* is an invaluable companion to this book.

Sit-Down Comedy
Malcolm Hardee and John Fleming
(eds) (Ebury Press, 2003)

A quirky collection of nineteen stories from stand-up comedians, including Tim Vine's tales of nuclear toothbrushes and Simon Munnery's take on Sherlock Holmes. Also featured are Stewart Lee, Jenny Eclair, Ed Byrne Dominic Holland, Arthur Smith and Boothby Graffoe.

Stand-Up!: On Being A Comedian
Dr Oliver Double (Methuen, 1997)

Getting The Joke: The Inner Workings Of Stand Up Comedy
Dr Oliver Double (Methuen, 2005)

Both of these books by the former comedian, now comedy lecturer Oliver Double blend comedy history and trends with matters of style and delivery. Taken together or separately, each book gives a broad knowledge of stand-up, without undermining the mystique of the art form or falling into over-analysis.

Sunshine On Putty
Ben Thompson (Harper Perennial, 2004)

If you can get past the cheesy sub-headings, this is a very entertaining read about the main players in 1990s comedy. It's very much of the opinion that Vic and Bob ruled the world but nods at the other major influences, such as Steve Coogan and Chris Morris.

Writing Television Sitcoms
Evan S. Smith (G.P. Putnam's Sons, 1999)

A very thorough guide to the sitcom writing process. Though geared for the American market, the book offers many invaluable, transferable pearls of advice.

Writing Sitcoms
John Byrne and Marcus Powell (A&C Black, 2003)

A brief, down-to-earth guide to the art of sitcom writing, which is very accessible for the absolute beginner and comes complete with script samples.

Fiction

So many comedians now write novels, the joke is that when future comics are born they'll find a letter from a publisher awaiting them. But five stand out: Ben Elton's *Popcorn* (Black Swan), Stephen Fry's *The Liar* (Arrow), David Baddiel's *Whatever Love Means* (Abacus), Alexei Sayle's *Overtaken* (Sceptre) and Robert Newman's *The Fountain At The Centre Of The World* (Verso). The comedy craft has not inspired many professional literary gents. Jonathan Franzen's "Two's Company", published in *New Yorker* magazine in 2005, is a nicely observed short story. Here are two of the best from a small bunch of comedy-inspired novels.

Funnymen
Ted Heller (Abacus, 2004)

A fictional oral biography about a crooner and a comedian who are Dean Martin and Jerry Lewis by any other name, this is not quite up there with his dad Joseph's *Catch-22* but it's a dazzling comic achievement.

The book of the show

Most TV tie-in books are either factual guides for anoraks or crass exploitation exercises. Occasionally, a tie-in will enhance the stature of the show it comes from, and work in its own right. One of the first books to achieve this was *The Brand New Monty Python Book* (1974). Written by the Python team and featuring horoscopes, rat recipes and illustrations aplenty by Terry Gilliam, this cult favourite has been through several reprints.

The comic possibilities of a tie-in book have always appealed strongly to British comedy's more surreal elements. Vic Reeves and Bob Mortimer's *Shooting Stars* book (1996) features off-kilter profiles of the show's players and characters, a game you can play at home and a CD of indistinguishable indecipherable pop hits performed by Reeves in pub-singer style. The League of Gentlemen had fun making their book, *A Local Book For Local People* (2000), which comes complete with maps and tour guides of Royston Vasey, all bound in a flesh-like cover.

The Killing Joke
Anthony Horowitz (Orion, 2005)

A bizarre, frantic novel in which the hero sets out on a hilarious quest to trace the source of a sick joke. Anthony Horowitz's denouement is as duff as a fluffed punchline but the rest of the novel is fast-paced and genuinely funny with an intriguing premise.

Websites

General

Many websites cover listings for comedy clubs, programme details and so forth, while some carry links to press articles. If you're interested in a reasonably well-established comedian, en.wikipedia.org is a good place to start, while Paramount Comedy Channel has a decent directory of UK live acts, plus reviews and interviews, on www.comedyisparamount.com/comedy/comedians.

Chortle
www.chortle.co.uk

The most informative UK comedy site, gathering listings (about 2500 shows on the system at any one time), profiles, interviews, news features and MP3 downloads in one place. The site enjoys 11,000 visitors a day and runs its own well-respected Comedy Awards and a student competition. With links, news items and web articles, Chortle is comedy's equivalent to The Drudge Report.

BBC Comedy Guide
www.bbc.co.uk/comedy/guide

At the heart of this terribly useful site is an electronic version of Mark Lewisohn's *The Radio Times Guide To TV Comedy* (see above), but it also features clips and links to other BBC Comedy

The site manager

Chortle was started in February 2000 and is still operated by its founder Steve Bennett. His interest in comedy was sparked by going to Ha Bloody Ha in Ealing, where, as a local newspaper journalist, he often judged new acts.

Chortle started as an exercise for Bennett to learn the HTML language websites are created in: "I chose comedy for my website experiment because no one else was doing it. If I did a music or film site, I couldn't hope to compete with NME or IMDB – and I could see a comedy site being useful. Magazines only have the space to print a list of names, which wouldn't mean anything to most people. With the Internet, you could link those names to reviews and descriptions, so people would know what to expect of a night out. I always think it's odd that people go out for a night of comedy without knowing who's

on. You wouldn't go out for a night of music without knowing the band, or at least that they played the kind of music you liked."

resources. Comedy Connections (from the TV series of the same name illustrating the family trees of British sitcoms and comedy shows) is an archive that enables you to find out when, for example, *The Thick Of It*'s Chris Langham made his small-screen debut (on Spike Milligan's *Q* series). There are also background notes on comedy shows on Radio 4 and Radio 7. For current programmes, a blog and general comedy news try www.bbc.co.uk/comedy.

Comedycv
www.comedycv.com

Though not every profile on this site is detailed enough, it does embrace everyone from established comedians to newcomers, with useful press quotes, lists of awards and sizeable press photo shots.

Laugh
www.laugh.com

A well-stocked American site where MP3s, CDs, videos and DVDs can be bought for an array of US comics ranging from Adam Sandler to Victor Borge. You can find rarities here – such as Bob Hope and Jack Benny's radio shows – alongside recordings of the latest comics on the circuit.

Laughingstock
www.laughingstock.co.uk

The online store for the independent comedy record label Laughing Stock, established in 1991 by Colin Collino, Mike O'Brien and Pete Brown. You can buy audio releases from the likes of Jo Brand, Greg Proops, Eddie Izzard, Sean Hughes and Bill Hicks, and videos from the likes of Whoopi Goldberg, Hicks, Garry Shandling and Rob Newman. One useful tip: acts are alphabetized by their first name.

Laughlab
www.laughlab.co.uk

The website set up by the University of Hertfordshire to find the world's funniest joke. Once you've read that you can also discover such dubious trivia as the ideal length for a joke (103 words, it says here) and whether your frontal lobe affects the kind of joke you like.

Sitcom
www.sitcom.co.uk

This guide to British sitcoms is reasonably comprehensive – it has over 800 sitcoms in its index – and is a useful resource for potential sitcom writers, with a good area devoted to the craft, complete with tips, courses and reviews of relevant books.

Cult heroes

The Internet is cluttered with terrible sites devoted to comedians. Here are a few decent ones devoted to particular comics.

Peter Cook
stabbers.truth.posiweb.net/stabbers

This lavish site – named The Establishment after the London club Peter Cook founded – not only challenges all those clichés about the taller half of Cook and Moore being an abject failure, but also offers hours of fun, recalling this alcoholic wit's many triumphs. The site is maintained by the Peter Cook Appreciation Society and is packed with detail, even chronicling *Consequences*, his bizarre treble-album rock/drama collaboration with Godley And Crème.

DIY comedy

Youtube.com and ifilm.com represent the logical conclusion of the legacy of *Candid Camera*, *You've Been Framed*, *It'll Be Alright On The Night* and Dom Joly's *Takeover TV*, allowing the general public to be a star of the show in a less demeaning way than the freak show that is *Big Brother*. Budding directors are encouraged to send in films they have made – be it by camera phone or video cam – of weird and wonderful moments such as the Tetris music played on piano or those ubiquitous pets doing the funniest things. Alongside these epics are videos of heated celebrity press conferences, funny TV moments and a chance to watch all those Japanese commercials the big stars don't want you to see. With the twin lures of potentially being talent-spotted and watching Ewan MacGregor advertise coffee, everyone's a winner. Well, except Ewan.

Jack Handy

snl.jt.org/deep/index.phtml?i=1

Jack Handy's surreal one-liners and stories became a cult feature on America's *Saturday Night Live*. The best are archived here, including his immortal observation: "It takes a big man to cry but it takes a bigger man to laugh at that man."

Chic Murray

members.fortunecity.com/gillonj/chicmurray

A collection of one-liners by the Scottish comedian Chic Murray (1919–85) who, though only dimly heard of in England, was much loved in Scotland and by his peers who voted him 38th best comedian in Channel 4's 2005 poll.

Leonard Rossiter

www.leonardrossiter.com

Lovingly detailed site devoted to a great British comic actor. Among the more intriguing material is the story of his powerful performance as a Hitler figure in Bertolt Brecht's *The Resistible Rise Of Arturo Ui*. It was, he said, one of two roles that truly satisfied him, the other being Rigsby.

Mort Sahl

www.mortsahl.com

American satirist who has offended everybody since the 1960s. This official site is a useful introduction to the range of his humour, with gags about cosmetics, politicians, Yuppies, liberals, Jews and Mel Gibson.

Music

Not content with making the world laugh, some comedians want to teach the world to sing. Although Billy Connolly's take on Tammy Wynette's "D.I.V.O.R.C.E.", retold as a story about a man with an ill-tempered dog, was a UK number one in 1975, he wasn't the first British comic to make money parodying popular music.

In 1959, *Goon Show* star Peter Sellers reached number three in the album charts with *The Best Of Sellers*, a collection of songs and skits produced by George Martin. The best track was "I'm So Ashamed", a sublime sob by a 9-year-old pop star fretting he's past it. Martin's work with Sellers impressed the Beatles (John Lennon was a big fan of the comic actor) and, in the mid-1960s, Sellers

recorded two Beatles hits: "A Hard Day's Night" in the style of a ham Shakespearean actor and "She Loves You" in the style of Dr Strangelove.

In 1975, the year Connolly topped the charts, Jasper Carrott almost sold a million with "Funky Moped/The Magic Roundabout", the latter gaining notoriety because Dylan told Dougal to "piss off", with Carrott noting "and so Dougal did – all over Florence". In 1978, Graham Fellows reached number four with the punk lament "Jilted John". Alexei Sayle had a hit in the early 1980s with the used-car anthem "'Ullo John, Got A New Motor?", though his "Albanian World Cup Song" was funnier. Frank Skinner's singing ambitions are painfully obvious on his chat shows and he has

Five of the best

Comedy records have a long, often excruciating, history – Cliff and The Young Ones, Charlie Drake, Rolf Harris. But these five are worth a listen.

"Entirely A Matter For You"
Peter Cook (Virgin)

This parody of the judge's summing up in the 1977 trial, for attempted murder, of disgraced Liberal leader Jeremy Thorpe was improvised for the Amnesty International fundraiser The Secret Policeman's Ball and is best remembered for the phrase "self-confessed player of the pink oboe". Cook's improv was released on the 12" single "Here Comes The Judge".

"She Loves You"
Peter Sellers as Dr Strangelove (EMI)

The Beatles meet the Nuremberg Rally – it's odder than it sounds. Simply unforgettable.

"'Ullo John, Got A New Motor?"
Alexei Sayle (Island)

This earned Sayle a chauffeur-driven ride in a limo from the BBC to Warwick just so he could plug his single on *Top Of The Pops*.

"Doin' Up The House"
Harry Enfield as Loadsamoney (Mercury)

This got Loadsamoney on to *Top Of The Pops* and included the immortal lyric "bosh bosh, joom joom wallop dosh".

"(Is This The Way To) Amarillo?"
Peter Kay and Tony Christie (ProTV)

Tony Christie's cabaret classic verged on self-parody even before Peter Kay made a funny, charming video to promote its re-release.

twice topped the charts with different versions of the England football anthem "Three Lions" with David Baddiel. Steve Coogan's sinister crooner Tony Ferrino wasn't that funny but his 1996 single "Bigamy At Christmas", with the fine couplet "Think of the man who has two wives/He's in a pickle when Christmas arrives", was a classic.

Picture credits

The Publishers have made every effort to identify correctly the rights holders and/or production companies in respect of images featured in this book. If despite these efforts any attribution is missing or incorrect, the Publishers will correct any errors or omissions once they have been brought to their attention in a subsequent reprint.

Cover Credits

Ricky Gervais at the Make Trade Fair live concert, 2004 © Corbis.

Illustrations

Avalon PR: (42), (62), (78), (86), (88), (100); courtesy Richard Bucknall Management (50); BFI Stills: (117) Humphrey Barclay Productions/Channel 4, (114) Assembly Film and Television/Channel 4, (120) Hat Trick Productions/Channel 4/RTE, (126) Hartswood Films/BBC, (130) Yorkshire TV/ITV, (132) BBC, (135) LWT/Paramount/ITV, (140) Channel 4, (145) BBC, (149) BBC (152) Television/Spitting Image Productions/ITV, (155) Talk Back Productions/Channel 4, (200) Charles/Burrows/Charles Productions/Paramount Television, (204) Warner Bros Television/Bright/Kaufmann/Crane Productions/NBC, (211) John-Charles-Walters Productions/Paramount Television/ABC; CIBSE: (222) courtesy Chartered Institution of Building Services Engineers; Comedy Store Management (52); Corbis: (4) © Hulton-Deutsch Collection/CORBIS, (6) © S.I.N./CORBIS, (8) © S.I.N./CORBIS, (10) © S.I.N./CORBIS, (15) © Lisa O'Connor/ZUMA/Corbis, (16) © Nicolas Asfouri/Corbis Sygma, (19) © McPherson Colin/Corbis Sygma, (164) © Bettmann/CORBIS (169) © Rune Hellestad/Corbis (170) © S.I.N./CORBIS (173) Corbis © Rune Hellestad/Corbis; John Fleming, www.malcolmhardee.co.uk (57); courtesy Noel Gay (71); courtesy Andy Hollingworth (28); Tracy Hopkins (215); courtesy Lee Hurst's Backyard Comedy Club (225); courtesy International Artistes Ltd (37); courtesy Karushi Management Ltd (106); Geraint Lewis (31), (35), (40), (55), (59), (67), (77), (83), (90), (96), (102); Real Talent (92); Rex Features: (47), (109), (187), (192), (195), (245) all © Rex Features Ltd; (98) courtesy Arthur Smith; Tim Vine (104). Special thanks to Daniel Bee, Steve Bennett, Colin Dench, John Fleming, Richard Howard, Victoria Lepper, Dan Lloyd, Kirsty Lloyd Jones, Lee Martin, Rob Sandy, Arthur Smith, Paul Sullivan, Susan Williams, Jessica Williamson, Richard Wiseman and Tim Vine.

Index

Page references to comedians discussed in the Icons chapter and comedy shows discussed in the Canon chapter are indicated in **bold**.

INDEX

INDEX

INDEX

M

INDEX

INDEX

X

Y

Z

Rough Guides presents...

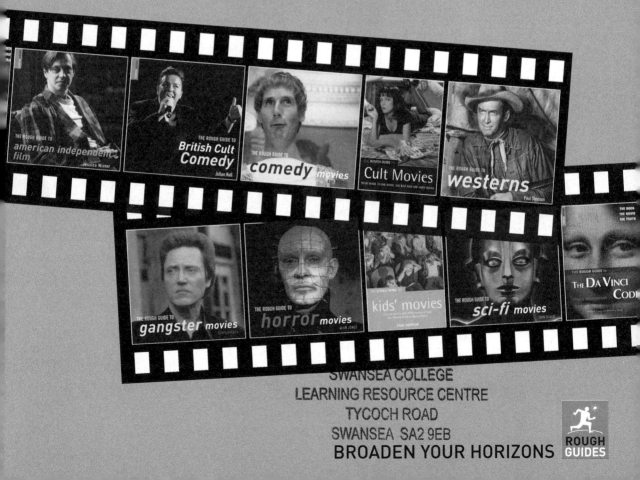

SWANSEA COLLEGE
LEARNING RESOURCE CENTRE
TYCOCH ROAD
SWANSEA SA2 9EB
BROADEN YOUR HORIZONS

ROUGH
GUIDES

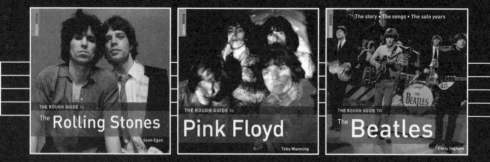